Racial and Ethnic Diversity in the Performing Arts Workforce

Racial and Ethnic Diversity in the Performing Arts Workforce examines the systemic and institutional barriers and individual biases that continue to perpetuate a predominately White nonprofit performing arts workforce in the United States. Workforce diversity, for the purposes of this book, is defined as racial and ethnic diversity among workforce participants and stakeholders in the performing arts, including employees, artists, board members, funders, donors, educators, audience, and community members. The research explicitly uncovers the sociological and psychological reasons for inequitable workforce policies and practices within the historically White nonprofit performing arts sector, and it provides examples of the ways in which transformative leaders, sharing a multiplicity of cultural backgrounds, can collaboratively and collectively create and produce a culturally plural community-centered workforce in the performing arts.

Tobie S. Stein, Ph.D. is a sociologist and Professor Emerita, Department of Theater, Brooklyn College, The City University of New York.

Routledge Research in the Creative and Cultural Industries
Series Editor: Ruth Rentschler

This series brings together book-length original research in cultural and creative industries from a range of perspectives. Charting developments in contemporary cultural and creative industries thinking around the world, the series aims to shape the research agenda to reflect the expanding significance of the creative sector in a globalised world.

Published titles in this series include:

Racial and Ethnic Diversity in the Performing Arts Workforce

Tobie S. Stein

Routledge
Taylor & Francis Group

NEW YORK AND LONDON

First published 2020
by Routledge
605 Third Avenue, New York, NY 10017

and by Routledge
2 Park Square, Milton Park, Abingdon, Oxon, OX14 4RN

First issued in paperback 2021

Routledge is an imprint of the Taylor & Francis Group, an informa business

Publisher's Note
The publisher has gone to great lengths to ensure the quality of this reprint but points out that some imperfections in the original copies may be apparent.

Library of Congress Cataloging-in-Publication Data
A catalog record for this book has been requested

ISBN 13: 978-1-03-208638-5 (pbk)
ISBN 13: 978-1-138-18845-7 (hbk)

Typeset in Sabon
by Apex CoVantage, LLC

I dedicate this book to my parents, Elaine and Bernie Stein, who shared their passion for the performing arts and social justice with me.

Contents

Foreword

Antonio C. Cuyler, Ph.D.

In the year 2045,[1] when the United States shifts from a White majority society to a People of Color majority society, as reported by the U.S. Census Bureau, how far will the performing arts have come with dismantling the pervasive White Supremacy that has served as the primary principle for its existence? I oscillate between despair and hope when contemplating this question. The path to the liberation of People of Color and White people flows like a river through the highest of hopes and the deepest depths of despair.

Nevertheless, when I focus on that which makes me hopeful about the state of racial and ethnic access, diversity, equity, and inclusion (ADEI) in the performing arts, *Racial and Ethnic Diversity in the Performing Arts Workforce*, gives me hope. Conceptualized and led by a White ally identified scholar who has a proven record of demonstrating remarkable cultural sensitivity to the plight of People of Color in the performing arts in her research, the book articulates the complexity of White cognition, fragility, and privilege as well as, moreover, its pervasive and ubiquitous impact on the evolution of the performing arts, and People of Color in U.S. society. In *Racial and Ethnic Diversity in the Performing Arts Workforce*, it feels as though, for the first time, a purposefully gathered collective of scholars has masterfully centered the voices of racially marginalized and oppressed peoples in the performing arts by sharing their perspectives across the gamut, from artist and arts manager to audience member. In addition, the emergence of a focus on racial equity in arts conferences across the country in Boston, Los Angeles, Minneapolis, and Nashville heartens me. Still, two observations plunge me into an abyss of despair when contemplating the state of ADEI for People of Color in the performing arts.

First, the transformation I envision for the performing arts depends on White people acknowledging and dismantling their privilege, not to the point of causing debilitating White guilt, or a White savior complex, but truly grappling with the violence that White privilege continuously inflicts upon People of Color in U.S. society. Most White people's inability to reckon with their privilege has further entrenched the systems put into place to maintain their dominance. However, this reckoning must not happen due to the critical and emotional labor of People of Color. White people should not ask People of Color to bear the cultural taxation of helping them to become less racist. After all, if anything, People of Color can share their lived perspectives on how Whiteness has impacted their lives. However, White allies who continuously work to understand the burden of their Whiteness on the performing arts and society should do the work of helping other White people become less racist.

In the second observation, I reflect on the question: How does one incentivize humans, in this case White people, discontinuing the use of unearned privilege that they have always had? Similar to a child whose parents have never told him no, on the day that he can longer behave with impunity he will most definitely kick and scream in a temper tantrum. This will inevitably become the case in the performing arts, too. Indeed, asking White people to dismantle their privilege has real economic implications. For example, this might appear as less White actors and actresses auditioning for roles that might go to actors and actresses of Color. Or White arts managers stepping aside in applying for internships and jobs to give more opportunities to People of Color. While I acknowledge at the highest level these actions are absolutely necessary, at the same time I wonder how realistic is it that White people will adopt these practices?

Where affirmative action, as a formidable policy for racial and ethnic ADEI could have demanded these behaviors, the policy failed largely due to its undermining by White people who disparage it as giving unqualified People of Color unearned opportunities. The juxtaposition here of unearned privilege with unearned opportunities is glaringly ironic to say the least while too many White people refuse to do something meaningful about their role in the multitude of disparities created by their privilege.

Alas, I wonder what impact *Racial and Ethnic Diversity in the Performing Arts Workforce* will make in the performing arts. It feels wrong to project my hopes for seismic anarchistic transformation on this book. At the least, I hope that *Racial and Ethnic Diversity in the Performing Arts Workforce* inspires performing arts organizations to institutionalize racial and ethnic ADEI in the same ways that they have institutionalized budgeting, fundraising, marketing, and programming. Taking this essential step could significantly move the industry towards parity with museums, who have made tremendous funding strides in initiating critical change. If these organizations do not take this revolutionary step towards the liberation of People of Color and White people, the performing arts will have squandered an opportunity to initiate a much desired and needed transformation.

Note

1. William H. Frey, "The US Will Become 'Minority White' in 2045, Census Projects," (March 14, 2018), www.brookings.edu.

Acknowledgments

It is with deep gratitude that I thank the individuals who have contributed to this work.[1] I want to thank David Varley at Routledge for giving me the opportunity to write this book. Thank you to Mary Del Plato at Routledge who guided me through the writing process. I am eternally grateful to the 70 gifted respondents who shared and trusted their time, expertise, perspectives, histories, and legacies with me. Thank you to my author-contributors: Antonio C. Cuyler, Emma Halpern, Brea M. Heidelberg, and Abid Hussain. Thank you to Antonio C. Cuyler, Brea M. Heidelberg, Emma Halpern, and Amy Hughes for reading and advising me on the manuscript. Thank you to my research assistants: L. Catherine Stewart, David Irving, Michael Raine, Megan Bandelt, and Marni Raab. Thank you to my students. I appreciate the important contributions of the following people who also guided me and lent their expertise to the project: Ganesh Pawan Kumar Agoor, Bushra Akbar, Ofronama Biu, Fred Blackwell, Kerry Boettcher, Kelly Brown, Gia S. Casteel-Brown, Joan Myers Brown, Santiba Campbell, Megan Cassidy, Danielle Ceribo, Elena Chang, Rodney Christopher, Randy Cohen, Conscious Style Guide, Kelvin Dinkins, Jr., Woody Doane Jr., Teresa Eyring, Maureen Fox, August Gabriel, Richard Grossberg, Todd Haimes, Peter Haldis, Brian E. Herrera, Adam Horowitz, Perry G. Horse, Theresa Ruth Howard, Stefanie A. Jones, Graciela Kahn, Julienne Hanzelka Kim, Mark R. Kramer, Stacy Lavin, Stefanie Lazer, Russell Lehrer, Robert L. Lynch, Joseph Matthews, III, Bronwyn Mauldin, David P. McKay, Nick Mecikalski, Pamela Mendels, Sara Morgulis, Brisa Areli Muñoz, Chelsea Newhouse, Grace Chiang Nicolette, Rebecca L. Noricks, Rebecca Novick, Kimberly Nwamanna, Dave O'Brien, Evren Odcikin, Stephen Patrick, Laura Penn, Craig T. Peterson, Bill Rauch, Sarah Rebell, Eileen Rivera, Martine Kei Green-Rogers, Jesse Rosen, Roger C. Schonfeld, Madeline Schrock, Kimberly Ayers Shariff, Holly Sidford, Johnnia Stigall, Stephanie Burrell Storms, Mitch Swain, Paul Tetreault, Denise Saunders Thompson,

Russell Thornton, Viviana Vargas (Yura Sapi), Dan Venning, Patrick Willingham, Hansi Lo Wang, Tim Wilson, and Susan Whitmore.

Note

1. While I have strived to acknowledge and include everyone who played a part in the creation of this book, please know it was not my intention to inadvertently overlook anyone who played an important role.

Preface

Leadership positions, particularly in the larger organizations, are not very diverse and the majority of those positions are still held predominantly by White males.

White respondent, Workforce Diversity study

Racial and Ethnic Diversity in the Performing Arts Workforce examines the systemic and institutional barriers and individual biases that continue to perpetuate a predominately White nonprofit performing arts workforce in the United States. Workforce diversity, for the purposes of this book, is defined as **racial and ethnic diversity** among workforce participants and stakeholders in the performing arts, including employees, artists, board members, funders, educators, donors, audience, and community members. The research explicitly uncovers the sociological and psychological reasons for inequitable workforce policies and practices within the historically White nonprofit performing arts sector, and it provides examples of the ways in which transformative leaders, sharing a multiplicity of cultural backgrounds, can collaboratively and collectively create and produce a culturally plural community-centered workforce in the performing arts.

Based on my first-hand empirical knowledge of historical injustice in the predominately White performing arts workforce and my own efforts to eliminate structural access barriers within the mutually reinforcing historically White performing arts and higher educational ecosystem, I am compelled to write a book in which the social construction of race and its historical, social, psychological, economic, and legal impact continues to play a starring role in perpetuating a White-dominated inequitable performing arts field. My Workforce Diversity study respondents, who are predominately People of Color (POC), drive the social justice research I have conducted and the social justice conversation throughout the book. My respondents along with my author-contributors, Antonio C. Cuyler, Emma Halpern, Brea M. Heidelberg, and Abid Hussain, are the authentic champions for social justice, social action, and social change.

In achieving transformative leadership in the performing arts, I believe that POC along with White antiracist allies across the intersecting and mutually reinforcing performing arts, educational, and philanthropic industries must collectively dismantle persisting and systemic undemocratic barriers and collaboratively create a racially and ethnically accessible, diverse, equitable, and inclusive (ADEI) workforce in the performing arts.[1]

Why does this research matter? In one of my college classes, I asked my students, who are predominately White, to read an article that I wrote on the same subject matter for *The Journal of Arts Management, Law and Society* more than twenty years ago entitled: "Creating Opportunities for People of Color in Performing Arts Management." I asked my students to share their impressions after reading the article. One young White woman raised her hand and politely said, "The article is dated." Was she right? In 1996, four years before I published my article, an Independent Sector study revealed that "only 8.8 percent of the arts and cultural workforce were Black, and 6.5 percent of the workforce were of Hispanic origin (there was no data reported on any other racial or ethnic group)."[2] Today, the racial and ethnic demographic profile of the performing arts workforce is strikingly similar, with the majority of artists, arts managers, employees, and board members identifying as White non-Hispanic.[3] Twenty years ago, I recommended that both performing arts programs in higher education and the performing arts workforce closely examine their intersecting opportunity structures that together perpetuate a homogeneous, primarily White performing arts workforce. I argued for scrutinizing higher education's credentialing of the field, probing the extent to which higher education and workforce recruitment and internship opportunities are linked and preserved through homogeneous White-dominated networks, and investigating the degree to which POC, who are admitted into selective higher education programs and hired as employees, are mentored and supported by the White-dominated hierarchy of higher education and the performing arts workforce.

As a sociologist, who identifies as White, and as the director of the M.F.A. program in performing arts management at Brooklyn College for over twenty years, I asked these same questions of my own work as a scholar, educator, and mentor to my students from a multiplicity of cultural backgrounds. What structural barriers were preventing students of Color from attending Brooklyn College? How conscious was I of the extent to which my own implicit bias played a role in perpetuating these institutional barriers? Interrogating my own racialized socialization and implicit bias, and developing greater race consciousness were essential to creating a culturally plural ADEI-centered master's degree program. Along with the support of my alumni, educational and professional colleagues, and philanthropists who champion a racially and ethnically diverse workforce, I embraced efforts to diversify my own majority-White, homogeneous professional networks. I raised grant money to support students and future leaders of Color in the performing arts. I mentored and placed my students of Color in internships and jobs. And finally, upon spending an intensive week working with culturally diverse faculty from the National Center for Institutional Diversity at the University of Michigan,[4] I began the process of acknowledging and transforming my Eurocentric arts management college curriculum.

Throughout my tenure at Brooklyn College, my students of Color shared stories of struggle, courage, and triumph with regard to succeeding at the intersection of a White-dominated performing arts and educational ecosystem in which their perspectives were not always respected and heard. Not everyone in the intersecting educational and performing arts sectors are inclusive and welcoming. Not every college class or professional staff meeting is culturally responsive and restorative to students and employees from underrepresented communities in the performing arts. Many students and employees of Color find significant access barriers and implicit bias throughout their career paths. So, despite the fact that I wrote a journal article twenty years ago, which today may appear "dated" to some, many POC continue to experience a field where White privilege overshadows race awareness, equity, and social justice.

Methodology

Racial and Ethnic Diversity in the Performing Arts Workforce is based on empirical research, in which a convenience sample[5] of 46 Workforce Diversity study respondents, 34 of which are People of Color, share their worldviews, histories, and legacies of the ways in which race has impacted their own career paths as well as the performing arts field itself. Although the Workforce Diversity study respondents frame and lead the conversation in this book, quantitative and qualitative studies from a broad array of academic disciplines support the Workforce Diversity study respondents' experiences and perspectives, informing and substantiating the ways in which U.S. society uses the racial hierarchy to inform workforce decisions. In addition to the poignant stories of oppression and struggle, Workforce Diversity study respondents also provide social justice solutions grounded in resistance, resilience, and transformative leadership and social change.

The Workforce Diversity Study Respondents

I designed a college class to explore racial and ethnic diversity in the performing arts workforce. Thirty-one workforce participants and stakeholders in the performing arts, primarily from New York, were invited to participate, either as a featured guest or as a member of a two- to three-person panel. Of the 31 guests/respondents, 21 were POC. Each student was responsible for conducting a two-hour in-depth recorded interview with one Workforce Diversity study respondent in class, using a six-page survey instrument I designed to collect data for the book. Students, who largely self-identified as White, were instructed on how to conduct an interview. The students not participating in the interview were asked to be silent participant observers, with the understanding that listening to the 31 Workforce Diversity study respondents would collectively inform and affirm their own social justice practices, as well as challenge their socialization, the construction of their social identities, and existing implicit bias. The students signed an agreement that ensured that the responses of every Workforce Diversity study respondent were to remain confidential, not to be discussed outside of the classroom. If the interview was not completed, one of my five research assistants followed up in person and finished the interview with the Workforce Diversity study respondent or panel of Workforce Diversity study respondents. Each Workforce Diversity study respondent also signed a letter of consent, with the understanding that if I wanted to use specific quotations in my published work, I would ask for written permission, as well as protect the confidentiality and anonymity of their name and organizational identity throughout the book.

In addition to the 31 class Workforce Diversity study respondents, the majority of whom also participated in follow-up field interviews, 39 additional Workforce Diversity study field respondents were interviewed by my research assistants with the same survey instrument. If the Workforce Diversity study field respondent was local, a face-to-face interview was conducted;[6] if the Workforce Diversity study field respondent resided outside of New York, the research assistant conducted the field interview via Skype or by phone. Of the 39 Workforce Diversity study field respondents, 26 were POC. The Workforce Diversity study field respondents were also told that they would receive a release form, granting me permission to use their quotations, while protecting the confidentiality and anonymity of their names and organizational identities.

Of the 70 Workforce Diversity study respondents interviewed in the classroom and in the field; 46 are represented in this book. Seventy-four percent of the Workforce Diversity study respondents (34) are POC and 26% (12) identify as White. As this is a sociological study on race and ethnicity in the performing arts, I asked my Workforce Diversity study respondents for written permission to share their stories, as well as permission to recognize them in the ways in which they racially and ethnically self-identified throughout their interviews.

The Survey Instrument

The over seventy-question survey instrument was divided into three sections: Workforce Diversity Definitions and Concepts; Workforce Diversity Respondents' Career and Education Paths; and Organizational

Diversity. The first section asked the Workforce Diversity study respondents to self-identify with regard to their race and/or ethnic heritage. Additional questions in this section focused on definitions and discussions around the state of racial and ethnic diversity in U.S. nonprofit performing arts organizations; White privilege and its effect on the recruitment process in historically White performing arts organizations; the cultural stereotypes that prevent ALAANA (African, Latinx, Asian, Arab, and Native American) members from being hired and selected as employees and board members in historically White performing arts organizations; and what it means to be the "the only POC" in a predominately White performing arts organization.[7]

The Workforce Diversity Respondents' Career and Education Paths section asked the Workforce Diversity study respondents to describe the extent to which the performing arts and its various educational and career opportunities were made visible throughout childhood and young adulthood; the importance of seeing yourself or people like you in classes, on stage, and in organizational settings; and the extent to which educational and career opportunities are linked. In addition, Workforce Diversity study respondents were asked to share their experiences regarding opportunities that are perceived to be accessible and restricted based on race and ethnic heritage, and the role that unconscious bias may play in the recruiting and casting processes in predominately White performing arts organizations. Survey questions also asked the Workforce Diversity study respondents to contemplate the degree to which personal networks help an artist or a manager gain educational and employment opportunities; the mentor's role in helping his or her protégé gain access to education and employment; as well as the degree to which the Workforce Diversity study respondent was made to feel welcome, was made to feel as though his or her contributions mattered, and was included in the design of programs and decision-making processes in a historically White performing arts organization.

In the final section, Organizational Diversity, the Workforce Diversity study respondents were asked questions concerning the extent to which racial and ethnic diversity is considered a core value within their organization; the types of programs that encourage a racially and ethnically diverse group of employees, audience, and community members; the extent to which recruitment practices are dedicated to fostering a racially and ethnically diverse applicant pool; the degree to which their organization was engaging in equitable ALAANA community-centered partnerships; the role of multicultural competency training in creating a culturally plural ADEI-centered workplace environment; and the degree to which there are programs in place to mentor, promote, and retain employees of Color.

Language Matters

As *Racial and Ethnic Diversity in the Performing Arts Workforce* is a study on race and social justice in the performing arts, it is important to appreciate the race and ethnic heritage of the 46 respondents. With advice from the American Psychological Association (APA) and permission from all of my Workforce Diversity study respondents as to how each self-identifies, I have intentionally capitalized the race and ethnicity of my Workforce Diversity study respondents, as well as the social identities POC and artists and managers of Color throughout the study, unless the scholar or study cited has specifically used lowercase spellings.

Throughout the book, I eliminate the hyphen often used to separate the dual heritage of individuals who identify as African American and Asian American. In my analysis, I use the racial identifiers White to describe organizational members who are predominately of European heritage,[8] and Black and African American as social identifiers of members of the African Diaspora. I recognize that while there are scholars and practitioners that use the racial identifiers White and Caucasian interchangeably, and Black and African American interchangeably, I honor both White and Black respondents' decisions to self-identify in the way that matters to them.

Workforce Diversity study respondents and scholars throughout the book use the social identities Asian American as well as Asian and Pacific Islander (API) to represent "ancestry traced to the origins of the countries, states, jurisdictions and/or the diasporic communities of these geographic regions."[9]

I, along with scholars and Workforce Diversity study respondents, use the social descriptors Native and Native American, Indigenous, American Indian, Native Hawaiian and Alaska Native as well as specific tribal affiliations to name individuals whose "parentage, clan relationships, kinship patterns, descendant status, [and] tribal name [are] validated by the individual's tribal government."[10]

In addition, I have intentionally included the social identity Latinx as a gender neutral descriptor to identify individuals who self-identify as having Latin American heritage. For purposes of this book, Workforce Diversity study respondents and scholars use Latinx, as well as the social identifiers Latino(s), Latina(s), and Hispanic to describe people of Latin American and Spanish descent.

I emphasize that the broad social descriptors Latinx, African American, Asian American, Native American, and White are reductive and do not adequately represent the multiplicity of cultural and ethnic traditions represented within these categories. In many cases, Workforce Diversity study respondents, practitioners, and scholars intentionally use cultural, ethnic, religious, and tribal affiliations to describe their own social identities, as well as the rich variety of social identities that reside within their communities.

Additionally, while I recognize that both the socially inclusive terms ALAANA members and POC do not fully recognize all underrepresented and marginalized communities, I have chosen to use these terms interchangeably to signify performing arts and community members who are often ostracized in U.S. society. Furthermore, Florida State University scholar Antonio C. Cuyler believes that

> it is challenging to find an appropriate 'catch all' term that remains sensitive to the perspectives of People of Color, especially given the differences in our group experiences. ALAANA attempts to be cultur-ally sensitive to those who object to the term People of Color. At the same time, the term People of Color tries to unite all racially disen-franchised people around their common experiences of racism, even when it plays out differently for each group. Perhaps we've stumbled upon an existential fault line here in that racism has worked bril-liantly in keeping us apart around naming.[11]

Several Workforce Diversity study respondents and scholars use the term Culturally Specific Organization to define ALAANA-led perform-ing arts organizations that explicitly serve communities of Color. With permission from my respondents, I intentionally capitalize Culturally Specific Organizations to emphasize their significance, prominence, and critical contributions to the performing arts workforce.

In capitalizing People of Color, artists of Color, communities of Color, and Workforce Diversity study respondents of Color my intention is to bring dignity to individuals who are often marginalized as well as emphasize through capitalization the Primarily White Organizations (PWOs)[12] that historically have excluded employees, board members, organizations, and communities of Color. I intentionally do not use the term nonwhite,[13] as I recognize that this social identity places the social construction of Whiteness at the center of the descriptor, denigrating the many communities oppressed in a White-dominated society.

In capitalizing the White social identity of both my Workforce Diver-sity study respondents and the predominately White performing arts pro-fession, my intention is to make visible what is often invisible: White privilege and its destructive influence on the field. Workforce Diversity study respondents who identify as White or Caucasian candidly share their own journeys in fighting their own racialized socialization and their efforts to transform their implicit bias and establish a racial and eth-nic ADEI-centered workforce ecosystem practiced in collaboration with their colleagues and communities of Color.

Study Limitations

The convenience sample, based on in-depth interviews with 46 Work-force Diversity study respondents, limits my ability to generalize my find-ings. However, the 46 Workforce Diversity study respondents and their experiences drive my analysis, supported by quantitative and qualitative data on race and ethnicity in the U.S.

I also am acutely aware that although my research is driven and framed by my culturally diverse Workforce Diversity study respondents and supported by multiethnic scholars within multiple academic disciplines, I recognize fully that my own socialization and White privilege impact my worldview. It is with extreme gratitude and appreciation that I acknowledge scholars Antonio C. Cuyler and Brea M. Heidelberg for providing me with necessary and critical feedback on the manuscript. It is with their support and guidance that I present this subject matter with a heightened degree of humility, race consciousness, and regard. In addition, contributor Emma Halpern, who self-identifies as a White arts journalist and theater practitioner, received critical feedback from historians of Color during several reiterations of Chapter 2: "Race and Performance: A Brief History."

Finally, I acknowledge that while race and ethnicity are the salient social identities analyzed in this book, further critical research and analysis is required on systemic workforce discrimination based upon social identities that intersect with race and ethnicity, including but not limited to gender identity, sexual orientation, age, disability status, and socioeconomic status.

Chapter Summaries

Racial and Ethnic Diversity in the Performing Arts Workforce consists of six chapters.

Chapter 1, "Racial and Ethnic Diversity in the Performing Arts Workforce" introduces and defines the terms access, diversity, equity, and inclusion in the context of creating a racial and ethnic ADEI-centered performing arts workforce where multiple community-based perspectives drive the sector's leadership and relevance. When the entire performing arts workforce becomes racially and ethnically diverse, there will be recognition that intersectional social identities (race and ethnicity, socioeconomic status, gender identity, age, disability status, sexual orientation, religion, etc.) are community connectors. When racial and ethnic workforce diversity becomes a core value, cultural pluralism will replace systemic racism throughout the entire performing arts workforce and ecosystem. Unfortunately, the nonprofit historically White performing arts sector still has a lot of work to do in realizing a racially and ethnically ADEI-centered workforce. U.S. national and regional data prove time and time again that cultural pluralism is not a collective core value in this country's predominately White performing arts workforce. The workforce doesn't reflect the racial and ethnic diversity of the U.S. and many major metropolitan areas. Performing arts disciplines are not racially and ethnically representative and performing arts audiences, board members, and grantmaking institutions, which are also predominately White, appear to perpetuate the lack of racial and ethnic access, diversity, equity, and inclusion in the historically White performing arts workforce. In addition, the majority of White wealthy individual donors and primarily White philanthropic institutions are likely to contribute to performing arts workforce inequities through an unbalanced distribution of donations and grants, where White performing arts organizations are favored over ALAANA-led performing arts organizations. Racial and ethnic workforce inequity is rooted in this country's history of systemic inequity and injustice and its impact on all cultural institutions.

Chapter 2, "Race and Performance: A Brief History," written by Emma Halpern, discusses the history of White-dominated discriminatory practices in the U.S. performing arts sector that continue to perpetuate a primarily White exclusionary workforce. The chapter also highlights some of the many significant contributions that ALAANA individuals and organizations, and social justice proponents both POC and White, have played in the field's history.

In Chapter 3, "Race, Identity, and Social Relations," social scientists reveal that racial and ethnic identities are formed in childhood, as young as three years of age. Throughout our lives, we are bombarded with implicit and explicit racialized messages that reinforce our perception of self, and distinguish the groups to which we are socially assigned as well as excluded from joining. We are legally required to racially and ethnically self-identify on the U.S. Census, yet biologically we all belong to a single human species. The chapter explores historical and current race-based practices found in U.S. social, legal, and economic systems, which intentionally exclude and marginalize POC and employ the Master Narrative: You are not welcome here.[14] Exclusionary histories that have targeted communities of Color impact the marginalization practices found in the historically White performing arts sector today. For example, the social construction of tokenism or hiring only one employee of Color is psychologically harmful, inhibiting the employee's ability to be his or her authentic self and achieve opportunities in the historically White nonprofit performing arts sector.

Chapter 4, "The Opportunity Structure and the Performing Arts Workforce" examines the ways in which ALAANA performing arts workforce members and ALAANA community stakeholders are precluded from equitable access and opportunities in a predominately White mutually reinforcing ecosystem of intersecting educational, performing arts, and philanthropic organizations. Implicit bias and discriminatory judgements individually and collectively practiced in the ecosystem through White privilege and White fragility, stereotyping and stereotype threat, colorblind racism, and microaggressions impede ALAANA members from equitable access and opportunity in the performing arts workforce. Many POC face systemic structural inequities in early arts education and training, and higher education, which interfere with equitable access to a viable performing arts career path. Within predominately White performing arts organizations, many POC contend with inequitable board and staff recruitment and retention practices, and are witness to undemocratic White-dominated community partnerships with ALAANA-led organizations. Furthermore, funding biases perpetuated by racially and ethnically homogeneous individuals in grant-making institutions sustain unjust philanthropic practices, favoring limited opportunities for POC in the performing arts workforce.

Chapter 5, "The Racial and Ethnic ADEI-Centered Performing Arts Workforce" focuses on ADEI-centered approaches for developing a racially and ethnically diverse performing arts workforce. Respondents of all cultural backgrounds, interviewed for this book, lead the conversation in asking predominately White performing arts organizations to interrogate their core values and their motives for engaging ALAANA communities, demanding that social justice leadership practices be authentic and action oriented.

In a racial and ethnic ADEI-centered performing arts organization, the board and senior staff commitment to social justice or social action engagement[15] is mandatory and communities of Color must be at the center of social justice organizational transformation. Transformative leadership, in historically White performing arts organizations, must be focused on dismantling discriminatory practices, through a dedicated budget; hiring culturally diverse consultants and facilitators who will conduct antiracist training, as well as question, help reframe, and build new recruitment and retention strategies together with culturally plural staff and board leadership. Most importantly, in achieving a transformative racial and ethnic ADEI-centered performing arts workforce, antiracist White performing arts leaders recognize that genuine unity with ALAANA-led multi-party collaborations across intersecting sectors will produce social justice in the entire performing arts workforce.

Chapter 6, "Social Change Champions in the Performing Arts" features articles by two transformative leaders of Color in the higher education and philanthropic sectors: Brea M. Heidelberg and Abid Hussain. Brea M. Heidelberg, program director of the Entertainment & Arts Management program at Drexel University, authors "Teaching Culturally Responsive Performing Arts Management in Higher Education," which discusses the critical role culturally responsive and restorative college education plays in students becoming racial and ethnic ADEI change agents. Abid Hussain, the director of diversity at Arts Council England, authors "The Public Funder's Impact on Racial and Ethnic Diversity in the Arts," revealing his contributions in designing a public sector cultural equity philanthropic model. Both authors share replicative practices in which racial and ethnic ADEI is the central core value and driving force behind the transformative change in their organizations, as well as in in the performing arts field at large.

Notes

1. For purposes of this book, I use the acronym ADEI to represent the term *access, diversity, equity, and inclusion.* I recognize that practitioners and contributors to the book also use the acronym EDI to represent the term *equity, diversity, and inclusion.* In some cases, the term Diversity, Equity, and Inclusion (DEI) is also used. These terms are used interchangeably throughout the book.
2. Tobie S. Stein, "Creating Opportunities for People of Color in Performing Arts Management," *The Journal of Arts Management, Law and Society* 29, no. 4 (Winter 2000): 305.
3. See Chapter 1 for an in-depth examination of the performing arts workforce racial and ethnic demographics.
4. This class was sponsored by the Faculty Resource Network at New York University in June 2016.
5. "Convenience sampling . . . relies on data collection from population members who are conveniently available to participate in the study." Research Methodology, Convenience Sampling, https://research-methodology.net.
6. While face-to-face interviews were the preferred method of data collection, some local New York interviews were conducted by Skype or by phone.
7. The term People of Color (POC) is used by scholars and practitioners throughout this study to identify African, Latinx, Asian, Arab, and Native American (ALAANA) group members who have traditionally been marginalized throughout U.S. history. The terms POC and ALAANA are used interchangeably throughout this book. However, I acknowledge that both POC and ALAANA have been recognized by practitioners and scholars as reductive terms and used either together or alone do not necessarily include members of all historically underrepresented racial and ethnic groups.
8. According to sociologist Ashley W. Doane Jr., "in the U.S., [white] dominant group identity has evolved over time, as the group boundary has expanded—from English Americans to white Protestant Americans to European Americans—in response to changes in intergroup relations and the ethnic composition of the United States." Ashley W. Doane Jr., "Dominant Group Ethnic Identity in the United States: The Role of 'Hidden' Ethnicity in Intergroup Relations," *The Sociological Quarterly* 38, no. 3 (Summer 1997): 391. In my analysis, I intentionally focus on predominately White non-Hispanic group members with European heritage because historically this dominant White ethnic group has had a disproportionate amount of economic, political, and institutional representation and power in U.S. society (see Chapters 1 and 3). I fully appreciate that White non-Hispanic group members with European heritage are not a monolith, and additionally there are other U.S. White non-Hispanic ethnic communities who do not enjoy all

of the privileges of the dominant group. However, in this study race and ethnicity are the salient social identities being analyzed, recognizing that socioeconomic status, religion, gender and gender identity, sexual orientation, national origin, disability status, and additional intersecting social identities play a critical part in power relations and privilege.

9. Asian Pacific Institute on Gender-Based Violence, "Census Data & API Identities," www.api-gbv.org.

10. Perry G. Horse (Kiowa), "Native American Identity," *New Directions for Student Services* 109 (Spring 2005): 63–64; Perry G. Horse, email to author, May 2, 2019.

11. Antonio C. Cuyler, email to author, April 16, 2019.

12. Predominately or Primarily White Organizations (PWOs) are organizations that historically sustain a primarily White power structure, in which the dominant group benefits.

13. There are scholars quoted in this book that do use the social descriptor nonwhite to describe ALAANA community members.

14. In *A Different Mirror: A History of Multicultural America* (2008), author Ronald Takaki establishes that U.S. historical accounts are grounded in a Master Narrative, where White U.S. history takes precedence over multicultural U.S. history. The primary message of the [White] Master Narrative is that the White lens and perspective are historically accurate and that a multicultural perspective of U.S. history has not been included and recognized in an equitable manner. Takaki interrogates the Master Narrative through his remarkable scholarship of multicultural America. Ronald Takaki, *A Different Mirror* (New York, NY: Little, Brown and Company, 2008).

15. Stephanie Burrell Storms, "Using Social Vignettes to Prepare Students for Social Action Engagement," *Multicultural Perspectives* 16, no.1 (2014): 43.

1 Racial and Ethnic Diversity in the Performing Arts Workforce

> I define workforce diversity as an environment where people regardless of race, class, color, and gender all have the equal opportunity to be self-supporting, self-sustained artists.
>
> Black respondent, Workforce Diversity study

Introduction

Workforce diversity, for the purposes of this study and book, is defined as **racial and ethnic diversity** among performing arts workforce participants and stakeholders, including employees, artists, board members, donors, audience members, educators, and community partners.

Racial and ethnic workforce diversity is an inclusive term. It encompasses the leadership process and organizational collective and collaborative management practice of valuing and intentionally recognizing, including, and affirming the representation and engagement of a workforce with a multiplicity of cultural identities, experiences, perspectives, and traditions at every organizational level in the workplace, reflecting the entire community.[1]

According to scholar Antonio C. Cuyler,

> racial and ethnic workforce diversity is part of a quartet that includes racial and ethnic access, diversity, equity, and inclusion (ADEI). Together these intersecting practices embody creative justice or the manifestation of all people living creative and expressive lives on their own terms.[2]

In achieving racial and ethnic access, the historically White performing arts workforce tackles and removes structural access barriers for underrepresented groups found in the career pathway and in recruitment and retention practices. In addition to examining and dismantling its structural access barriers, an inclusive and equitable performing arts organization scrutinizes and disrupts the interpersonal unconscious and conscious racial bias of employees and other stakeholders that also often restricts access, entry, and the full representation, engagement, and retention of participants from historically underrepresented and marginalized groups in ALAANA communities.[3]

Within the workforce diversity conversation, there is recognition that for a performing arts organization to be racially and ethnically diverse, the organization must also value active planning and execution of racially inclusive and equitable or socially just practices in the workplace. The Greater Pittsburgh Arts Council defines inclusion as

> the practice of including and of being included within a group or structure. It highlights the mosaic of individuals offering unique perspectives, with the goal of minimizing tensions between groups and building capacities to get along. Inclusion involves authentic and empowered participation and a true sense of belonging.[4]

Racial equity, according to Fred Blackwell, chief executive officer of The San Francisco Foundation, is

> just and fair inclusion in a society where everyone can participate, prosper, and thrive, regardless of their race or where they live or their family's economic status or any other defining characteristic.[5]

Why Racial and Ethnic Workforce Diversity Matters

Social scientists[6] as well as respondents interviewed for this book recognize that racial and ethnic workforce diversity matters because when multiple perspectives are engaged, cognitive decision-making is strengthened, and better decisions are made throughout organizations. When the workforce is racially and ethnically diverse, cultural pluralism or the respect and high regard for cultural difference[7] is a core value and a community connector. Furthermore, in a culturally diverse organization, policies and programs are created to intentionally remove exclusionary racial and ethnic access barriers and embrace the full inclusion of "'distinctive and creative' cultural traditions"[8] in the workplace. Most importantly, when racial and ethnic access, diversity, equity, and inclusion matters to a historically White performing arts organization, there is an intentional effort among all members to acknowledge systemic racism and actively participate in its elimination.

Workforce Diversity Engages Multiple Perspectives and Strengthens Cognitive Decision-Making

When there is intentional and equitable inclusion of multiple perspectives as well as the recognition that input and engagement of everyone who has been historically underrepresented in an organization matters, the organization is more creative, productive, and more likely to represent the entirety of its community's interests. Various studies have shown that when an organization hires culturally plural employees who have a broad range of perspectives and experiences, the culturally diverse employees will contribute expansive input, inspiring and encouraging their White colleagues to think and act in more innovative ways and "outside the [White] box."[9] For example, a Workforce Diversity study respondent who identifies as both Black and Puerto Rican speaks about the cognitive impact of different perspectives on an organization: "If all members of the human race are represented without regard to whatever [racial and ethnic] boxes one may check, it provides us all with a way to adapt to unfamiliar circumstances. If you can be inclusive and open the door to everyone who has the qualities you're looking for, in terms of work performance, you're going to ensure that everyone in the organization will grow cognitively and have a great opportunity to engage different perspectives."

Workforce Diversity Values Cultural Pluralism

One White respondent, with an ethnic heritage that includes English and German roots, speaks about the need for historically White nonprofit performing arts organizations to intentionally acknowledge and embrace the multitude of ethnic and cultural perspectives within diverse performing arts communities of Color. In other words, in seeking to create a diverse workplace, organizations must adopt cultural pluralism as an organizational value and lens that recognizes that each community culture has a distinct contribution to make to the workplace.[10] When cultural pluralism is a core value, performing arts organizational leaders respect and engage employees, artists, and board members who share a multiplicity of different cultural traditions within a multitude of racial and ethnic communities.

Not everyone in the performing arts sector is conscious of the multiplicity of cultural traditions that reside within socially constructed racial and ethnic groups. As sociologist Edwin M. Schur points out in his work on labeling, there are individuals who presume "that all people are alike," within a racial or ethnic group, but in actuality cultures and traditions vary greatly within racial and ethnic groups.[11] For example, within the Latinx[12] community there are many cultures that thrive. The Pew Research Center identifies the ethnic heritage of the fourteen largest U.S. Hispanic groups: Mexican, Puerto Rican, Salvadoran, Cuban, Dominican, Guatemalan, Columbian, Honduran, Spanish, Ecuadorian, Peruvian, Nicaraguan, Venezuelan, and Argentinean.[13] Within each Latinx ethnic group, there are distinct rich cultural traditions that are learned and practiced in the process of social interaction. Cultural traditions encompass values, standards of beauty, as well as art and culture.[14] When working with artists that identify as Latinx, non-Latinx performing arts managers, who may not be well versed in the rich variety of Latinx cultural traditions, must be cognizant of collaborating closely and in concert with the Latinx artist and the artist's specific ethnic community. This is only accomplished when a non-Latinx arts manager is immersed in respecting, learning, experiencing, and engaging with the cultural perspectives and traditions of the Latinx artist's specific community. For example, one Workforce Diversity study respondent who identifies as White as well as English and German American explained the importance of intentionally working with artists that matter to a specific ethnic community:

> We [historically White organizations] often talk about the White community and the community of People of Color, but depending on the situation, we're also talking about the African American versus the Latinx versus the Asian—the API (Asian and Pacific Islander) communities, and then of course there are many communities within any one of those communities. And it may be for a given project, that the difference between selecting a Puertorriqueña artist or a Chicana artist, makes all the difference to their community.

Workforce Diversity Recognizes That Intersectional Social Identities Are Community Connectors

Broadly defined, a performing arts organization that supports racial and ethnic workforce diversity, not only openly values the shared leadership and contributions of a culturally plural workforce, but also acknowledges and welcomes the involvement of a workforce grounded in the intersecting relationships among race and the socially constructed categories of gender, gender identity, socioeconomic status, age, disability status, religion, and sexual orientation, among others. In a workplace environment that considers racial and ethnic workforce diversity a core value and therefore an organizational priority in its board and staff recruitment, casting, hiring, promotion, and retention practices, organizational decision making, programming, and community relationships, all intersecting social identities are equally acknowledged, accepted, respected, and treated as assets and not deficits to the performing arts organization.[15] With respect to intersectionality or the interrelationships among race, ethnicity, and other social identities, one African American respondent who interviewed for the Workforce Diversity study emphasized how important it is to broadly define workforce diversity:

> I see workforce diversity on a broad spectrum inclusive of race, age, religion, and sexual orientation. I don't believe it's enough to just have racial diversity in an organization. I find that in my position as a marketer, having employees of various ages, cultural, and ethnic

backgrounds only add to my ability to speak to different audiences and ultimately do my job better.

The State of Racial and Ethnic Diversity in the Performing Arts: A Statistical Portrait

Both scholars and practitioners recognize that culturally plural organizational members collectively make better decisions, are cultural connectors with communities of Color, and provide opportunity and access to individuals who have been historically marginalized. But what does the statistical data tell us about the extent to which U.S. nonprofit performing arts organizations[16] are culturally plural and reflect the U.S. population? In addition, to what degree does the nonprofit performing arts workforce replicate the racial and ethnic diversity found in U.S. major metropolitan areas? To what extent are specific performing arts disciplines racially and ethnically diverse? Furthermore, what is the racial and ethnic makeup of the audience members, board members, and funding institutions that provide substantial revenue to the nonprofit performing arts sector? And, how does the racial and ethnic diversity of these revenue sources impact racial and ethnic access, diversity, equity, and inclusion practices in the performing arts workforce?

Do Performing Arts Organizations Reflect the Racial Diversity of the U.S. Population?

According to the United States Census Bureau, the total United States population is currently 60.4% White non-Hispanic, 13.4% Black or African American non-Hispanic, 18.3% Hispanic or Latino, 5.9% Asian non-Hispanic, 1.3% American Indian and Alaska Native non-Hispanic, and 2.7% identify as Two or More Races.[17]

There is statistical evidence that the majority of artists, managers, and board members[18] do not reflect the racial and ethnic diversity of the U.S. population. According to the U.S. Census Bureau, the majority of artists, who may or may not be affiliated with an organization, identify as White non-Hispanic.[19] Of the more than two million artists working in the United States during the period 2006–2010, and of individuals that identify as only one race (excluding Hispanic ethnicity), more than 78% identify as White non-Hispanic, nearly 6% identify as Black or African American non-Hispanic, more than 8% identify as Hispanic or Latino, and more than 5% identify as Asian, non-Hispanic (including Native Hawaiians and Pacific Islanders). Less than 2% of artists identify as non-Hispanic and more than one race.[20]

Scholars Antonio C. Cuyler and Francie Ostrower independently examined the degree to which racial and ethnic diversity is found within the arts workforce. Cuyler's study on racial and ethnic diversity in arts management found that 78% of nonprofit arts managers identify as Caucasian or White American; 6% identify as Black or African American; 7% identify as Chicano, Hispanic, or Latino American; and 3% identify as Asian American. Four percent identify as Multiethnic, and 2% selected the "Other" category.[21]

Ostrower's study, *Diversity on Cultural Boards: Implications for Organizational Value and Impact*, which analyzed the data of more than 400 arts organizations, found that 91% of nonprofit cultural board members were White non-Hispanic; 4% were African American or Black non-Hispanic; and 2% were Hispanic or Latino.[22] From these national statistics, we can conclude that the racial and ethnic representation of most U.S. performing arts organizations does not reflect the racial and ethnic demographics of the United States. Statistics also show that the U.S. performing arts workforce doesn't reflect the racial and ethnic diversity of many major metropolitan areas in the United States.

Racial and Ethnic Diversity of U.S. Metropolitan Areas Is Not Reflected in the Workforce

This country's major metropolitan areas are extremely racially and ethnically diverse and are becoming more so. In the last census, the White population was the minority in 22 out of 100 of the largest cities.[23] In New York, for example, more than two-thirds of the population identify as POC.[24] In Los Angeles county, almost three quarters of the population identifies this way as well.[25] Yet, research shows that the cultural organizations in these two cities are majority-White non-Hispanic, when it comes to its staff and board racial and ethnic demographics. In July 2015, research organization ITHAKA S+R surveyed the extent to which New York City's cultural organizations are diverse (e.g., racial and ethnic diversity, gender). They surveyed 987 New York City cultural organizations (including performing arts organizations), which are funded by the New York City Department of Cultural Affairs (DCLA), representing 36,441 employees and in their report, *Diversity in the New York City Department of Cultural Affairs Community*, found that the racial and ethnic composition of New York City Department of Cultural Affairs grantees is as follows: "In the aggregate, DCLA [grantee] staff is 62% white non-Hispanic and 38% minority. Minority groups with over five percent representation include black or African American (15%), Hispanic (10%) and Asian (8%)." These numbers do not correspond to the United States 2010 Census racial and ethnic population demographics of New York City, where 67% of the population are POC and 33% are White non-Hispanic.[26]

In addition, the DCLA study found that New York City's cultural leaders or senior executives are 74% White non-Hispanic and its board members are 75% White non-Hispanic.[27] Mid-level staff are 68% White non-Hispanic and 55% of junior staff members are staffed by White non-Hispanic employees.[28] The significant difference in racial and ethnic demographics between senior and mid-level and junior managers raises questions about the opportunity for more managers of Color to become senior leaders as White non-Hispanic managers retire in the coming years. But could this goal of promoting mid-level and junior managers to more senior positions be realized when 77% of the respondents to the study believe that there are no barriers for increasing diversity among employees, 74% said there were no barriers for increasing diversity among senior staff members, and 68% believe that there are no barriers to increasing board diversity?[29] If there are no barriers to advancement and recruitment, why are senior managers and board members of cultural organizations in New York City predominately White?

In November 2015, the Los Angeles County Arts Commission funded a study, *The Demographics of the Arts and Cultural Workforce in Los Angeles County*, conducted by DataArts to determine the racial and ethnic diversity of the cultural community's leadership and staff. Their sample included 386 cultural organizations and 3,175 respondents.[30] Sixty percent of cultural workers in Los Angeles County identified as White non-Hispanic and the population of Los Angeles County is 27% White non-Hispanic.[31] In addition, 4% of cultural workers identified as Black or African American, 14% as Hispanic or Latino(a), and 10% as Asian. An additional 4% identified as being More Than One Race or Ethnicity.[32] The senior staff of Los Angeles County cultural organizations identified as 63% White non-Hispanic, while the general staff identified as 53% White non-Hispanic, demonstrating that there is greater racial and ethnic diversity among general staff and an opportunity to promote junior POC to senior level positions. Board members in Los Angeles County cultural organizations were also more likely to identify as White non-Hispanic, as 68% did so. Sixty-six percent of employees who work in performing arts organizations are majority-White non-Hispanic, and this percentage is higher than any other organization type in Los Angeles County.[33] If the performing arts workforce is not racially and ethnically representative of this country's total population as well as the population in major metropolitan areas, to what degree is this lack of racial and ethnic diversity reflected in specific performing arts disciplines?

Performing Arts Disciplines Are Not Racially and Ethnically Representative

Studies on performing arts organizations such as symphony orchestras and regional nonprofit theaters reveal that both fields are historically White and in great need of making racial and ethnic access, diversity, equity, and inclusion a workforce value and priority. The League of

American Orchestras' 2016 *Racial/Ethnic and Gender Diversity in the Orchestra Field* study of more than 800 orchestras found that African American, Hispanic/Latino, Asian/Pacific Islander, American Indian/ Alaska Native musicians constitute less than 15% of the orchestra musician population.[34] The diversity of orchestra musicians increased four-fold during the period 1980 through 2014 (3.4% to 14.2%), and this fact is explained by the increase in Asian and Pacific Islander musicians. The study also reveals that just 2.5% of the musicians are Hispanic or Latino and 1.8% of orchestra musicians are African American.[35] In addition, the percentage of African American and Latino musicians employed by small orchestras is double the percentage of those employed by larger orchestras.[36] Music directors and conductors also are more likely to be white: 21% are identified as people of color.[37] The League study also reports that African Americans comprise 5 to 7% of symphony orchestra staff members, and 3 to 5% are of Hispanic or Latino heritage.[38] Senior managers of color account for 5.2% of symphony orchestra executive positions and board members of color represent 7.8% of all board seats.[39]

The Wellesley Centers for Women and the American Conservatory Theater's report *Women's Leadership in Resident Theaters* found that among 74 League of Resident Theatre (LORT) organizations, during the 2013–2014 season there were no managing directors of Color and only six artistic directors of Color in these nonprofit organizations.[40] The Actors' Equity Association's diversity study found that during 2013–2015, 78.7% of League of Resident Theatres' stage management contracts of one week or longer went to stage managers who self-identified as Caucasian.[41] In addition, "The Count 2.0," which is the Dramatists Guild and Lilly Award's survey of writers whose works are produced at U.S. regional theaters, found that 15.1% of U.S. theater productions were written by playwrights of Color during the 2016–2017 season.[42]

Do Predominately White Revenue Sources Perpetuate a Predominately White Workforce?

Statistically, Predominately White Organizations (PWOs)[43] in the performing arts receive income from White audience members, White board members, and funding sources with predominately White staff. If the nonprofit business model is dependent on revenue sources that are racially homogeneous, to what extent do these resources reproduce and perpetuate a workforce in which racial identity is homogenous as well? While there is no definitive or quantitative evidence that there is a correlation between the racial homogeneity of funding resources and the racial composition of the performing arts workforce, this question and association is worth interrogating as the next set of statistics are revealed.

Let's first look at performing arts audience members. According to the National Endowment for the Arts study, *A Decade of Arts Engagement:*

Findings from the Survey of Public Participation in the Arts, 2002–2012, over 83% of classical music audiences and nearly 80% of ballet audiences were White non-Hispanic in 2012.[44] If an overwhelming percentage of audience members in primarily White nonprofit performing arts disciplines are White non-Hispanic, and they provide the majority of the ticket income, which for many organizations is a significant portion of earned income and total revenue,[45] what financial motivation do PWOs have to question the lack of racial and ethnic diversity among audience members? According to the National Endowment for the Arts study, White non-Hispanic adult attendance to benchmark[46] performances such as symphony and ballet performances declined significantly, while African American and Latinx audience members had the same levels of attendance in 2008 and 2012.[47] In addition to this steady attendance among African American and Latinx audience members, the millennial generation born between 1980 and 2000 is extremely diverse, with more than 44% identifying as POC.[48] To what degree are historically White performing arts organizations recognizing the social and economic impact of current and future racial and ethnic demographic trends? To what degree do primarily White senior managers and their boards acknowledge that cultural pluralism must be a strategic leadership imperative?

The answer to this question is troubling, as the majority of board members and chief executives in nonprofit organizations, as a whole, self-identify as White and don't view demographic diversity, which includes racial and ethnic diversity, in their board recruitment practices as a sector-wide imperative. In BoardSource's *Leading with Intent: 2017 National Index of Nonprofit Board Practices*, the organization found that 90% of chief executives, 90% of board chairs, and 84% of all nonprofit board members self-identified as Caucasian.[49] Furthermore, the organization discovered that only 24% of chief executives and 25% of board chairs believed demographics to be a high priority in their board recruitment practices, and, when asked what they should do to improve their board's overall performance, only 21% of chief executives and 23% of board chairs reported "change or strengthen [board] recruitment practices."[50]

Why do these statistical findings matter? In addition to ticket revenue, nonprofit organizations must raise money from their boards, individual donors, and funding agencies in order to survive. In many performing arts organizations unearned or contributed income accounts for 40% of an organization's revenue.[51] The data has already established that the majority of board members in primarily White nonprofit organizations don't see a need to change or strengthen board recruitment practices. If board members consider racial and ethnic diversity to be a low priority in recruitment practices, how might this cultural value affect the ways in which they distribute their philanthropy to nonprofit organizations?

Individual giving, of which board members are a significant part, accounts for one-third of giving to arts and cultural organizations.[52] The

2017 Helicon Collaborative study *Not Just Money: Equity Issues in Cultural Philanthropy* reveals that it is likely that wealthy individuals who make over $100,000 per year are more likely to be White and that their giving is more likely to be centered on large cultural organizations rather than organizations of Color.[53]

In addition to board members and high net worth individuals, funding agencies, like local arts councils and foundations, are critical to supporting the nonprofit business model. There are approximately 4,500 private and public local arts councils in the United States and 59% of local arts councils fund the arts in their local communities through grants to individuals and/or organizations. In 2019, local government funding to local arts agencies was estimated to be $860 million.[54] According to Americans for the Arts, 91% of the executive directors and chief executives who lead local arts councils identify as Caucasian, White, or European American, non-Hispanic.[55] How might this homogenous group of local arts funders affect the distribution of funding in their communities and what proportion of funding is given to organizations that explicitly serve ALAANA communities? While the distribution of local arts agency funds to arts organizations that represent ALAANA communities is not available, Americans for the Arts reports that among local arts agencies that provide grants and other types of financial support, just 19% have developed their own written diversity guidelines about their grantmaking/funding programs, 17% adhere to a policy developed by someone else (e.g., a parent organization), and 40% have informal considerations but no formal diversity policies for their grantmaking process.[56]

Private foundation staff and board decision makers who create funding policies and practices are also predominately White. The *State of the Work* report of the D5 Coalition, which "advances diversity, equity, and inclusion in philanthropy," revealed that 91.6% of foundation chief executives self-identified as Caucasian, while 82.9% of full-time foundation staff and 67.7% of program officers self-identified as Caucasian. In addition, they reported that racial and ethnic diversity among foundation chief executive officers and program officers remained the same for a five-year period (2010–2015).[57]

According to BoardSource's 2017 *Foundation Board Leadership* report, 40% of foundations have all Caucasian boards and 35% report that they don't have a single POC on their board.[58] Furthermore, 18% of foundation chief executives surveyed are both dissatisfied with the board's racial and ethnic diversity and place a "low or no priority on the demographics in board recruitment."[59] If there is low or no priority placed on racial and ethnic demographics in foundation staff and board recruitment, to what extent are funding priorities centered around cultural equity?

The Helicon Collaborative's *Not Just Money* reports

> that while people of color make up 37 percent of the population, just 4 percent of all foundation arts funding is allocated to groups whose primary mission is to serve communities of color.[60]

Holly Sidford's 2011 study *Fusing Arts, Culture and Social Change* found that of the $2.3 billion that is awarded to nonprofit arts and cultural organizations from foundations, the majority is given to organizations that "focus on Western European art forms, and their programs serve audiences that are predominately white and upper income."[61] In an effort to determine the extent to which "arts funding is distributed by race," the Greater Pittsburgh Arts Council's 2018 study *Racial Equity and Arts Funding in Greater Pittsburgh* found that of the 218 Greater Pittsburgh area arts organizations that received grants from public and/ or private funders during the period 2003–2017, 82% were primarily White non-Hispanic organizations, and 18% were ALAANA-led arts organizations.[62] Furthermore, Greater Pittsburgh ALAANA-led arts organizations received 16% of the grants and 14% of the total funds from private and public sources.[63] The study found that "no funders' distribution patterns reflect both the population demographics of Allegheny County or the City of Pittsburgh, and the breakdown of the area's arts organizations by race."[64]

To what degree does the inequitable distribution of philanthropy create a socially unjust performing arts workforce? Furthermore, if the historically White performing arts sector's senior leadership receives the message that workforce racial and ethnic diversity isn't valued and considered a top priority by racially homogeneous funding sources, how might this affect board and staff recruitment, programming, and equitable community partnerships with ALAANA individuals, organizations, and communities? To what extent are the leadership structure and cultural values of primarily White performing arts organizations reproduced and perpetuated by a funding system that appears to reward primarily White performing arts organizations for the lack of racial and ethnic access, diversity, equity, and inclusion? Again, while there is no statistical evidence that the lack of racial and ethnic diversity is rewarded, staff and board leadership in both primarily White performing arts and philanthropic organizations must interrogate this question and its consequences together with ALAANA communities.

The enormous incongruity of racial and ethnic access, diversity, equity, and inclusion practices found in both the primarily White performing arts workforce and its funding sources demands these questions: If there is such cultural inequity, why does the inequity exist, and why should the predominately White performing arts sector and its funding sources continue to collectively pursue and employ racial and ethnic access, diversity, equity, and inclusion as a field-wide imperative? In order to answer these questions, it is important to first examine the root cause of racial and ethnic inequity in the predominantly White intersecting performing arts and philanthropic ecosystem: Racism.

Name the Root Cause of Racial and Ethnic Inequity in the Performing Arts: Racism

The United States has been battling racism from its very beginning. Racism is the White-dominated power "system of interpersonal, social, and institutional patterns and practices that maintain social hierarchies in which Whites as a group benefit at the expense of other groups labelled as 'non-white'—African Americans, Latinos, Asian Americans, Native Americans, and Arab Americans."[65] Racism works to systemically sustain the dominant group's privileged norms and values within its legal, political, and economic institutions.[66] Institutional racism manifests itself in "practices that operate to restrict—on a racial basis—the choices, rights, mobility, and access of groups and individuals."[67] These institutional practices are regarded as normal and are embedded in the explicit and implicit rules of the organization.[68] Both systemic and institutional racism are internalized within dominant-group individuals as prejudice or premature or unsupported judgements, which leave individuals biased, either consciously or unconsciously, explicitly or implicitly in favor of their own kind, their own way of life.[69] Without the intentional commitment to seek knowledge to interrogate such bias, differential treatment or discrimination based on racial and ethnic categorization and negative stereotypes may be used to justify the marginalization or oppression of people who are unconditionally considered inferior.[70]

Dismantling Racism in the Performing Arts Workforce

Respondents of Color from the Workforce Diversity study share personal experiences concerning the structural segregation of employment opportunities and the discriminating behaviors that often accompany it. The Workforce Diversity study respondents' personal experiences influence the ways in which racial and ethnic workforce access, diversity, equity, and inclusion is viewed as a necessity in the performing arts workforce, as well as the need to find ways to disrupt the systemic, institutional, and individual racist practices and attitudes that have and continue to prevail. In the next section, Workforce Diversity study respondents share unified core values that must exist in order for racial and ethnic workforce ADEI to be achieved in the performing arts workforce: Economic and social equity; art that incorporates the multiplicity of experience; the creation of cultural value for everyone in the community; acknowledgement that communities of Color matter and must be included as thought partners in the workforce; the recognition that sharing all stories will help all of us heal; and the acknowledgement that racial and ethnic access, diversity, equity, and inclusion ensures the survival of the field.

"Everyone Deserves to Have a Piece of the Economic Pie"

Philanthropic institutions can infuse social justice or cultural equity funding as well as provide needed networks and mentoring to change the historically inequitable distribution of resources to historically marginalized communities and organizations of Color. One Workforce Diversity study respondent who identifies as Asian American reflected on how her personal childhood experiences with discrimination impacted the type of work she does and her efforts to disrupt systemic racism by providing funding, leadership, mentoring, and below-market-rate workspace for artists and arts organizations through her nonprofit social enterprise:

> For me, it's deeply personal because I grew up in a world where it was okay to walk by my grandparents, and my parents' Chinese laundry, and to rap on the window, and yell ugly racial epithets, and be protected if you were White. It was endless. Every single day it was something. For my parents or my grandparents to have responded, they would have been arrested, not the perpetrator. I did not want to live in a world like that. I was touched early on by the power of the arts. I figured that the one thing I could do through my own work was to build an infrastructure of leadership, money, and now real estate to support contemporary voices that really represent the America I ultimately want to live in and not the America that I grew up in. So, my commitment is to look at supporting diverse voices in the arts, diverse voices that are represented in small and midsized community-based organizations, and artists working in their own communities, working to create beautiful, lyrical, provocative, idiosyncratic works that have meaning to the people and places where they work and live. And that means supporting them formally and informally. For example, in addition to providing leadership and financial support to a diverse group of artists, I want to mentor a diverse, talented workforce. Also, I look at the gaps in our own organization and ask this question, "Are there particular opportunities in which we could further diversify our workforce, or our board that will help us with our goal of developing below market real estate for the artists we want to serve?"

The Workforce Diversity study respondent's work emphasizes that racial and ethnic ADEI practices are a core value within the respondent's philanthropic culture. In my *Journal of Arts Management, Law and*

Society article, "Creating Opportunities for People of Color in Perform-ing Arts Management," I posit that "organizational culture guides the behaviors of its members and affects everything from who gets hired, promoted, and what decisions are made."[71] Furthermore, "the culture governs what kinds of people are respected and its values set the tone for human resources recruitment and selection strategies within an organi-zation."[72] A culture's core values are the "belief system of an organiza-tion's stakeholders."[73] Not only is the core value of cultural equity, or fair and just distribution of funding, found in the institution's grantmaking practices, but cultural equity guides the Asian American respondent in creating racial and ethnic ADEI leadership practices for the philanthropic organization's workforce and board of directors.

The Asian American respondent recognized above is actively engaged in disrupting the stratified socioeconomic system that prevents some art-ists from finding affordable real estate and making a living in a prosper-ous sector of the economy. The nonprofit arts sector is a large industry; and everyone deserves to participate in its productive economy. The American for the Arts 2017 *Arts and Economic Prosperity 5* study found that the nonprofit arts and culture industry generated $166.3 billion of economic activity during 2015—$63.8 billion in spending by arts and cultural organizations and an additional $102.5 billion in event-related expenditures by their audiences. This activity supported 4.6 million jobs and generated $27.5 billion in revenue to local, state, and federal govern-ments.[74] Furthermore, in "The 2019 Nonprofit Employment Report," Lester M. Salamon and Chelsea L. Newhouse note that nonprofit arts and recreation employment increased from 13.1% of private employ-ment in that field in 2007 to 15.5% in 2016.[75] As was discovered in the previous section, "The State of Racial and Ethnic Diversity in the Per-forming Arts: A Statistical Portrait," not everyone shares equally in this economic piece of the nonprofit arts and cultural pie. The statistics reveal that this booming arts economy is not representative of all people. One Workforce Diversity study respondent who identifies her "cultural his-tory and legacy" as both Nigerian American and from the African Carib-bean Diaspora believes that "workforce diversity in the performing arts should address the social-economic issues that marginalized communities face." The respondent elaborated:

> If we are ever going to start addressing the real social-economic issues that we experience, then everyone needs to have a piece of the pie and be a part of the sectors that are making money. Right? I mean like, that's the truth of it, right? That's why the New York City Mayor's Office of Media and Entertainment has a program that trains and places low income people, 95% of which are POC in entry-level tel-evision and film production jobs.[76] That's why there's this push to get Black and Brown people into [computer] coding now, because tech

is a huge industry. There's an economic argument to be made that's ultimately tied to equality and better social outcomes for everyone, right? One group cannot continue to move forward while everyone else is faltering. We won't address any of these political and social issues that we're dealing with until everybody has an ability to get on the same economic footing.

"Theater That Incorporates the Multiplicity of Experience Is Just Better Theater"

A racially and ethnically diverse staff, board, group of artists, and community that unites with a multiplicity of cultural identities, perspectives, and experiences make the workplace better. In fact, an increase in racial and ethnic diversity in the workplace may promote increased creativity.[77] Social psychologist Charlan Nemeth found that "diversity and confrontation provide the impetus for detecting truths primarily because they stimulate thought."[78] In a 2004 research report on this subject, scholar Anthony Lising Antonio and his colleagues found that "the racial diversity of a student's close friends and classmates may have stronger effects on students' complex thinking than more limited contact with racially diverse members."[79]

One Workforce Diversity study respondent who identifies as Palestinian American has found that a diversity of cultural perspectives is indeed more productive and believes:

> the work is better when there are plural perspectives. If you get ten people who are exactly like you into a room to solve a problem, you essentially have one point of view. So, if everybody's been trained in the same way, comes from the same cultural background, has the same range of experiences, and those people are put together in a room, you're not nearly as likely to get an interesting outcome as if you have ten people in a room, each coming from their own perspectives, training, background, culture, and skillset, being brought to bear on any given question. And in the end, this is why I believe in diversity the most, because in my experience, it makes the work demonstrably better. It makes the world measurably and demonstrably better.

A Workforce Diversity study respondent who identifies as Puerto Rican emphasized that holding different perspectives and viewpoints is essential to telling a good story within a play:

> Theater is about the multiplicity of experience. You don't put two characters onstage who think the same thing. You just don't. That's a boring play. You must create characters with different voices,

different backgrounds, different personalities, and perspectives, and start out from a position where people come from different places. It's important. And if you think about a season the same way you think about a play, you want to ideally have different voices engaging in conversations with each other. It's just objectively better. I don't know how to say it in a different way. It should be a better season.

"The Demographics Are Changing: Organizations Must Create Value for Everyone"

In *Diversity Explosion*, author and demographer William Frey reveals that U.S. youth are already quite racially and ethnically diverse and will be necessary to fortify the aging American labor force, which is predominately White and will decline by 15 million people between 2010 and 2030.[80] In contrast, the U.S. labor force will gain 26 million POC during the same period.[81] According to Frey's research, people of Asian, Latinx, and Multiracial heritage have contributed to three-quarters of the United States population growth during the last ten years and that by 2040, the United States will not have a single racial or ethnic majority.[82] Forty-four percent of the millennial generation, born between 1980 and 2000, are POC.[83] How are the changing racial and ethnic demographics of a young generation impacting the performing arts workforce? To what degree are historically White performing arts organizations creating value to reflect and honor America's changing demographics? To what extent does a historically White performing arts workforce make the effort to recognize and include the multiplicity of vibrant ALAANA community worldviews in programming and workplace practices?

The 2015 National Endowment for the Arts report *When Going Gets Tough: Barriers and Motivations Affecting Arts Attendance* reveals that "among all racial and ethnic groups, non-Hispanic Black and African American individuals most often cited supporting community as a major motivation for attending performances."[84] This finding is significant because it underscores the value of viewing a cultural institution through a specific community's lens or worldview.

One Workforce Diversity study participant who racially identifies as White and culturally and ethnically as Jewish pondered the question of the degree to which predominately White nonprofit organizations are creating value for racially and ethnically diverse communities and the consequences of failing to respond:

> But at its highest and purest notion: How can we foster connections between and among all of us as people? Soon, we will be a country where People of Color will be the majority, and babies being born now are majority-minority. The future is here and it's now. We are a rapidly changing country. The demographers talk about the

browning of America. What does that mean for us culturally and for the arts to continue to be legitimate and valuable? I don't mean financially valuable but in a deeper way we need to reflect the world in which we live, and we need to relate to the world in which we live. Otherwise we run into the danger of having plays that were written a hundred, or two hundred, or three hundred years ago by White men. There's going to be a whole world, a whole population that may not care about them. And maybe that's okay. But if we think it's great work and great art then how do we make sure it speaks to as many people as possible? That to me is the most important question. The second question is, for those companies whose work doesn't speak to a broader community, how are you going to handle the fact that you are going to run out of people walking in your doors? So, there is also an economic imperative to make sure that your work speaks to as many people as possible. The changing demographics will not happen uniformly. Maine and Idaho may be White as the driven snow for a very long time. Texas has already changed. Houston is a majority-minority city. There are a lot of cities around the country that are majority-minority cities already and as each day passes it's going to happen. Performing arts organizations in Texas must deal with this because White people are a shrinking part of the population in major communities in that state. Changing demographics will come to some communities sooner than it comes to others and ignore it at your peril.

One Workforce Diversity study respondent who identifies as Black agrees that "organizations and institutions that continue to cater to really exclusive populations will just have a smaller share of the market." The respondent said,

I've read statistics that say that by 2045 there will be more People of Color in this country than White people. If that is true, in the ways that we think about ethnicity at this exact moment, it would be hard to understand how ballet companies are primarily interested in having only White people go to the ballet. I go to the ballet regularly, but I feel as a Black person, no one who works for ballet companies is saying, you know, "Let's find the Black people who want to come to the ballet." I don't see how that's sustainable in the long run. I mean, you think about the percentage of people who go to the ballet, or who go to the opera, or the philharmonic, or the theater, and it's already a small number. People would rather keep up with the Kardashians. And I think how easy it is to watch reality television on your computer or go to the movies. There's so little effort you must put in to that sort of entertainment, relative to how expensive it is to attend the performances of professional companies. It's already a small group who attends live performances and I think this group will only get much, much smaller. I don't know that my grandkids will have a concept of what live opera is. I don't know that there will be five opera companies in America by the time my grandkids are born because I think it's just not financially viable.

"People of Color Are Your Thought Partners: Give Us a Seat at the Decision-Making Table"

When POC are included in the organizational decision-making process, it signifies that ALAANA members' contributions as "thought partners" matter.[85] "From a business perspective," maintains a Workforce Diversity study respondent who identifies as both Black and African American,

it is wise to have people from different backgrounds sitting at the table, the decision-making table. Let us be your thought partners, too. It is important to have lots of thought partners sitting around a table. While I do not want to be the sole person being asked how to get more Black people to come see our work, I certainly would rather be there, at the table, as the only one [Person of Color], than not be at the table at all. It's important for us to have more arts administrators of Color, because you must have people behind the scenes, helping with the decision-making, so you can reach more audiences of Color, so that you can reach younger audiences. America is changing, and it's going to continue to change racially. And that's just what it is.

Diversity of the workforce plays an integral role in the sustainability and relevancy of the arts. As someone who works in development, I see how audiences and the core donor base are still graying by the day and still are very much White. However, I rarely see strategic efforts made to increase the number of donors or audience members of Color. Is it mentioned in passing? Yes. But the organization I work for has yet to implement anything meaningful to address this issue. The artistic side of the organization I currently work for is quite diverse—racially, ethnically, culturally. However, the administrative side is less so. Of the more than 15 senior managers, three are of Color. None of them work in development or marketing, which are hugely important when it comes to cultivating new audiences and creating inclusive messaging. In addition to having racial and ethnic diversity among artists and senior leadership, diverse development and marketing teams matter too, since we are actively raising the money from various constituency groups and creating the collateral needed to attract diverse audiences. If you have an all-White development and or marketing team, you risk producing materials and a narrative that may not accurately reflect the culture of Color you are trying to reach and embrace.

If organizations (especially "high art," historically White arts organizations) don't make concerted efforts to reach out to diverse populations, then they will continue to be perceived as elitist and exclusive—which are major perceptual barriers to having many People of Color attend ballet, theater, opera, or orchestra performances. (Though it is important to note that many People of Color are interested in seeing artists who look like them and art that is telling a story that they can relate to.) As an administrator of Color, I've got a lot to say. We must have diversity in voices. You must have differences of opinion to help create better thinking. That, again, will move the art, absolutely.

"Sharing All of Our Stories Will Help All of Us Heal"

One Workforce Diversity study respondent who "grew up [identifying as] Black because they put so much emphasis on it [social identity]," believes that diversity in the performing arts is crucial because it will help us heal as a society. The respondent explained,

> I used the arts as a platform to flush out the issues of racism, gender inequality, and ethnicity, and being a Person of Color, I identify with the plight of so many People of Color and their struggles just to be. Just to be, not to do anything else, just to be where they are in their existence. When we have the arts in our lives, we can all tell our stories, and then we'll all learn from sharing those stories with each other. When we can experience the arts as a people, that's when we can heal, that's when we can learn, and that's when we can begin to heal the wounds that need to be healed. Through sharing our stories, we're moving those boundaries and those things that are in the way of seeing that progress.

Another Workforce Diversity study respondent who identifies as Black elaborates on the idea that everyone's story needs to be told, otherwise racial and ethnic segregation will continue to be perpetuated in the U.S. The respondent asserted:

> Workforce diversity tells our story as Americans, and that if we're not culturally diverse on stage, off stage, on camera, behind the camera, then we're telling stories to our children that aren't true, and we're perpetuating more separation of ourselves and our society. If the arts can't get it right, I don't think anybody can. Because we're the people that have the ability. We come to the table. The spirit of artists is a spirit of ensemble. It is the spirit of working together and creating something together. And if we can't do that, that's a problem. Because if we can't do it, then how do we expect it to happen in

the workforce? How do we expect it to happen in the schools? How do we expect it to happen in our neighborhoods and in our communities? So, we must be the leaders of diversity, we must be the leaders in telling the stories of diversity, we must be the leaders in who's being hired and who's being brought to the table. That's the only way, as artists, that we can then create the dialogue, create the conversation, and create the change necessary in our communities for us to become much more diverse. And more importantly, not just more diverse, but more open and more accepting of each other as humans.

"Workforce Diversity Will Ensure the Survival of the Performing Arts Sector"

John Moore's *American Theatre* article, "American Theatre's Leadership Vacuum: Who Will Fill It?," posits that within ten years, 50% of nonprofit theater organizations will have experienced a leadership transition.[86] In planning for the leadership vacuum, and ultimately the survival of the field, what are PWOs doing to make sure that their leadership reflects and will replicate the changing demographics of the United States? And if PWOs choose to remain primarily White, why would leaders of Color want to work in performing arts organizations that are not racially and ethnically accessible, diverse, equitable, and inclusive?

The next two Workforce Diversity study respondents of Color maintain that racial and ethnic workforce diversity will ensure the survival of the field and that the historically White performing arts sector should not fear it.

Respondent #1: "We know from research that workforce diversity creates better organizations, more resilient organizations, and more creative organizations. So, there is real research to back that up, which is great. We need that. Although workforce diversity planning and execution has mostly been done in a corporate environment, I really do think that a workforce diversity strategy is the key to the survival of the nonprofit performing arts field. If we are thinking about long-term sustainability within changing communities and we're not changing ourselves, who is going to support us? How will we be able to evolve as [a field] and as institutions if we don't bring our communities with us?"

Respondent #2: "We shouldn't be fearful of becoming more diverse. I think there's a lot of fear in America right now because we're changing so much, and our racial and ethnic demographics are becoming more diverse every single year. I think that's why there's so much conflict right now in terms of race because there is this inherent fear of marginalization and ultimately the unknown. The majority will become the minority and certain people feel that they won't have a voice anymore and that's not true. I think this fear and how this fear manifests are something that we need to be very conscious of as leaders in performing arts organizations and how can we quell this fear and build the confidence that there is always room at the table."

Conclusion

The historically White performing arts workforce is not collectively representative of the human experience, yet respondents interviewed for this study maintain that racial and ethnic diversity is crucial to the health and survival of the performing arts workforce. A racially and ethnically diverse performing arts workforce collectively committed to social justice or social action engagement[87] will disrupt and dismantle the web of interrelated systemic, institutional, and interpersonal barriers that continue to perpetuate a primarily White nonprofit performing arts sector. When racial and ethnic ADEI is viewed and executed as a core value, predominately White performing arts organizations not only dismantle historic institutional structural barriers and attack individual bias, but also acknowledge and fully embrace the assets and implications of a culturally plural workforce.

Historically, communities of Color only become marginalized through society's social, economic, and legal systems that are embedded in U.S. cultural institutions and interpersonal relations. Racial and ethnic ADEI in the nonprofit performing arts workforce is necessary because all of our stories and legacies are of cultural significance and our country and society cannot afford to develop separately anymore. Everyone deserves to have a piece of the economic pie that is generated by the performing arts economy. Nonprofit performing arts organizations are public organizations and are legally required to be open and accessed by all people.

Furthermore, when performing arts organizations represent and include a multiplicity of stories, voices, and experiences, the art is "just better." Additionally, U.S. racial and ethnic demographics have changed and are continuing to change, and public nonprofit organizations must create value that is representative by including all cultural legacies in every aspect of the performing arts workforce. When historically White performing arts organizations make racial and ethnic ADEI an organizational priority and core value, it signifies that communities of Color matter. If communities of Color really matter, members of ALAANA communities must share leadership power and funding, be recognized, and be intentionally recruited as thought partners in the development of all performing arts organizational policies and practices. This social justice lens and worldview will ensure collective racial healing and warrant the sector's survival. Consequently the historically White nonprofit performing arts sector must not fear what it will take to dismantle its discriminatory practices and create a racially and ethnically accessible, diverse, equitable, and inclusive workforce.

However, the quantitative data presented in this chapter overwhelmingly points to an alarming amount of social injustice based on the underrepresentation or absence of POC in historically White legally and publicly oriented organizations and in the institutions that fund them. The current deficiency of racial and ethnic ADEI practices and policies in the country's historically White performing arts workforce, as well as the inequitable distribution of philanthropy, is rooted in the nation's history of systemic inequity and injustice and its impact on the country's cultural institutions. In the next chapter, Emma Halpern provides a historical exploration and explanation of social injustice in the predominately White performing arts field, as well as a history of the individuals and organizations who fight social injustice by honoring, respecting, and infusing the legacy of social justice practices in the performing arts.

Notes

1. Lee Anne Bell, "Theoretical Foundations for Social Justice Education," in *Teaching for Diversity and Social Justice*, 3rd ed., eds. Maurianne Adams and Lee Anne Bell, with Diane J. Goodman and Khyati Y. Joshi (New York, NY: Routledge, 2016), 3; Daryl G. Smith, *Diversity's Promise for Higher Education*, 2nd ed. (Baltimore, MD: Johns Hopkins University Press, 2015), 77, 272.
2. Antonio C. Cuyler, email to author, April 19, 2019.
3. Annie E. Casey Foundation with Terry Keleher, *Race Equity and Inclusion Action Guide* (Baltimore, MD: The Annie E. Casey Foundation, 2014), www.aecf.org; Xiomara Padamsee and Becky Crowe, *Unrealized Impact* (Promise54, 2017), www.unrealizedimpact.org. The data was collected between November 2016 and March 2017; Smith, *Diversity's Promise*. The term ALAANA is used by scholars and practitioners throughout this book to identify African, Latinx, Asian, Arab, and Native American individuals who have traditionally been marginalized throughout U.S. history. The terms ALAANA and POC are used interchangeably throughout this book. However, I acknowledge that both ALAANA and POC have been recognized by practitioners and scholars as reductive terms and used either together or alone do not necessarily include members of all historically underrepresented racial and ethnic groups.
4. Greater Pittsburgh Arts Council with The Learning and Leadership Committee, *Racial Equity & Arts Funding* (Pittsburgh, PA: Greater Pittsburgh Arts Council, 2018), 13, www.pittsburghartscouncil.org.
5. Kyoko Uchida, "Fred Blackwell, CEO, The San Francisco Foundation: Community Foundations and Racial Equity," *Philanthropy News Digest* (February 2, 2018), https://philanthropynewsdigest.org.
6. According to the National Institutes of Health, "behavioral and social science research is a multidisciplinary set of sciences including psychology, sociology, demography, anthropology, economics, and other social sciences." National Institutes of Health, https://obssr.od.nih.gov.
7. Richard J. Bernstein, "Cultural Pluralism," *Philosophy and Social Criticism* 41, nos. 4–5 (2015): 354.

8. Daniel S. Sanders, "Dynamics of Ethnic and Cultural Pluralism: Implications for Social Work Education and Curriculum Innovation," *Journal of Education for Social Work* 11, no. 3 (Fall 1975): 97.

9. James M. Jones, *Prejudice and Racism*, 2nd ed. (New York, NY: McGraw-Hill, 1997), 534; Jennifer Lee, Frank D. Bean, with James D. Bachmeier, "Ethnoracial Diversity, Minority-Group Threat, and Boundary Dissolution: Clarifying the Diversity Paradox," in *The Diversity Paradox* (New York, NY: Russell Sage Foundation, 2010), 159–60; Katherine W. Phillips, "How Diversity Makes Us Smarter," *Scientific American* (October 1, 2014), www.scientificamerican.com.

10. Gordon W. Allport, *The Nature of Prejudice* (Reading, MA: Addison-Wesley, 1954), 238–39.

11. Edwin M. Schur, *Labeling Women Deviant* (New York, NY: McGraw-Hill, 1984), 29.

12. "Latinx is used generally as a gender-neutral term for Latin Americans, but it has been especially embraced by members of Latin LGBTQ communities as a word to identify themselves as people of Latin descent possessing a gender identity outside the male/female binary." www.merriam-webster.com. For the purposes of this study, participants and scholars also use the social identifiers Latino(s), Latina(s), and Hispanic to describe people of Latin American and Spanish descent.

13. Antonio Flores, "How the U.S. Hispanic Population Is Changing," *Washington, DC: Pew Research Center* (September 18, 2017), www.pewresearch.org; The information presented is based on Pew's tabulations of the 2015 American Community Survey. "Pew Research Center bears no responsibility for the analyses or interpretations of the data presented here. The opinions expressed herein, including any implications for policy, are those of the author and not of Pew Research Center."

14. Norman R. Yetman and C. Hoy Steele, eds., *Majority and Minority* (Boston, MA: Allyn and Bacon, 1974), 12.

15. Bell, "Theoretical Foundations," 3.

16. According to GuideStar.org, an online research database that gathers and disseminates information about all IRS-registered tax-exempt charities in the United States, there are more than 31,000 nonprofit organizations that are classified as performing arts organizations. www.guidestar.org.

17. U.S. Census Bureau, "QuickFacts United States," (2018), www.census.gov. Hispanic and Latino individuals in this survey many be of any race. Population estimates are for 2018. Percentages may not total 100% due to the rounding of percentages required by the Census Bureau's Disclosure Review Board. I acknowledge that data presented in this book may not be comparable due to methodology differences that may exist between different data sources.

18. These statistics include artists, managers, and board members who work for both visual and performing arts organizations.

19. Not all studies cited in this book differentiate between White and White non-Hispanic racial identities.

20. National Endowment for the Arts, "Table 2b: Total Number of Artists by Residence: Race and Ethnicity," *NEA Tables from the EEO 2006–2010 Data*, www.arts.gov. American Indian and Alaska Native artists represent 0.3% of U.S. artists. Percentages may not total 100% due to the rounding of percentages required by the Census Bureau's Disclosure Review Board.

21. Antonio C. Cuyler, "An Exploratory Study of Demographic Diversity in the Arts Management Workforce," *GIA Reader* (October 2015), www.giarts.org.

22. Francie Ostrower, "Diversity on Cultural Boards: Implications for Organizational Value and Impact," (Working Paper, Research: Art Works, Full Listing of Papers by Grantee Organizations, National Endowment for the Arts, 2013), 7, www.arts.gov. The author used data from the 2005 Urban Institute *National Survey of Nonprofit Governance.*

23. William H. Frey, *Diversity Explosion* (Washington, DC: Brookings Institution Press, 2015), 4.

24. New York City Department of Cultural Affairs, "NYC Cultural Affairs Diversity," https://www1.nyc.gov.

25. DataArts, *The Demographics of the Arts and Cultural Workforce in Los Angeles County* (Los Angeles, CA: Los Angeles County Arts Commission, April 2017), 13, www.lacountyarts.org. The data was collected in 2016. Percentages may not total 100% due to the rounding of percentages. On July 1, 2019, the Los Angeles County Arts Commission became the Los Angeles County Department of Arts and Culture.

26. Roger C. Schonfeld and Liam Sweeney, *Diversity in the New York City Department of Cultural Affairs Community* (New York, NY: ITHAKA S+R, 2016), 6–7, 20, https://sr.ithaka.org. The data was collected in 2015; New York City Department of Cultural Affairs, "NYC Cultural Affairs Diversity," https://www1.nyc.gov.
    Additionally, New York City actors do not represent the racial and ethnic diversity of New York City. According, to The Asian American Performers Action Coalition's 2016–2017 report *Ethnic Representation on New York City Stages,* "[New York City] nonprofit theatre companies filled 37% of all roles with minority actors in the 2016–17 season, a significant increase from 31% the season prior." The Asian American Performers Action Coalition, *Ethnic Representation on New York City Stages 2016–2017* (New York, NY: The Asian American Performers Action Coalition, 2019), 13, www.aapacnyc.org.

27. Schonfeld and Sweeney, *Diversity in the New York City,* 21, 27, https://sr.ithaka.org.

28. Ibid., 21.

29. Ibid., 39.

30. DataArts, *The Demographics of the Arts,* 5, 7, www.lacountyarts.org.

31. Ibid., 15.

32. Ibid.

33. Ibid., 21, 23.

34. League of American Orchestras, *Racial/Ethnic and Gender Diversity in the Orchestra Field.* A Report by the League of American Orchestras With Research and Data Analysis by James Doeser, Ph.D. (New York, NY: League of American Orchestras, 2016), 3, https://americanorchestras.org.

35. Ibid.

36. Ibid., 4.

37. Ibid., 5.

38. Ibid., 6.

39. Ibid., 6–7. The League of American Orchestras collected the data on Latino and African American orchestra musicians in 2014 and data on music directors and conductors of color was collected from 2006–2016. Data on African American and Latino orchestra staff was collected between 2010 and 2014 and data on senior managers of color was collected between 2006 and 2014. *Racial/Ethnic and Gender Diversity in the Orchestra Field,* a report by the League of American Orchestras with research and data analysis by James Doeser, Ph.D., was originally published by the League of American Orchestras in September 2016. A portion is here reprinted with permission.

40. Sumru Erkut and Ineke Ceder, *Women's Leadership in Resident Theaters* (San Francisco, CA: American Conservatory Theater; Wellesley, MA: Wellesley Centers for Women, Wellesley College, 2016), 8, www.wcwonline.org. As of 2019, theater directors and researchers Rebecca Novick and Evren Odcikin report that, as of this writing, there are seven artistic directors of Color and no managing directors of Color working in LORT theaters. Rebecca Novick, email to author, April 3, 2019.

41. Actors' Equity Association, data compiled by Russell Lehrer, "Looking at Hiring Biases by the Numbers," *Equity News* (Spring 2017), www.actorsequity.org.

42. Julia Jordan, "The Count 2.0: Who's Getting Produced in the U.S.?" *Dramatists Guild* (2018), www.dramatistsguild.com.

43. The terms Primarily White Organizations and Predominately White Organizations (PWOs) are used throughout this book. Scholars and practitioners use this term to define organizations that historically sustain a primarily White power structure, in which the dominant group benefits.

44. Bohne Silber, Silber & Associates, and Tim Triplett, The Urban Institute, *A Decade of Arts Engagement: Findings from the Survey of Public Participation in the Arts, 2002–2012* (Washington, DC: National Endowment for the Arts, January 2015), 12, www.arts.gov.

45. Americans for the Arts, "Source of Revenue for Nonprofit Arts Organizations," (2016), www.americansforthearts.org.

46. The NEA defines benchmark arts as "jazz, classical music, opera, musical and non-musical plays, ballet, and visits to an art museum or gallery." Silber, Silber & Associates, and Triplett, The Urban Institute, *A Decade of Arts Engagement*, x, www.arts.gov.

47. Ibid., 6.

48. U.S. Census Bureau, "Millennials Outnumber Baby Boomers and Are Far More Diverse, Census Bureau Reports," (June 25, 2015), www.census.gov.

49. BoardSource, *Leading With Intent* (Washington, DC: BoardSource, 2017), 10, https://leadingwithintent.org. The data was collected in 2016.

50. Ibid., 15, 29.

51. Americans for the Arts, "Source of Revenue," https://americansforthearts.org.

52. Holly Sidford and Alexis Frasz, *Not Just Money: Equity Issues in Cultural Philanthropy* (Oakland, CA; and Brooklyn, NY: Helicon Collaborative, July 2017), 11, http://heliconcollab.net.

53. Ibid., 12.

54. Americans for the Arts, "Government Funding to Arts Agencies,"; "2018 Profile of Local Arts Agencies-Executive Summary," (1999–2019), https://americansforthearts.org.

55. Americans for the Arts, *2018 Local Arts Agency Salary Report* (Washington, DC: American for the Arts, 2019), 14, https://americansforthearts.org.

56. Randy Cohen, Graciela Kahn, and Ben Davidson, *The 2018 Profile of Local Arts Agencies* (Washington, DC: American for the Arts, 2019), 30, www.americansforthearts.org. Diversity in this report is not solely defined as racial and ethnic diversity.

57. Christopher Shea, *State of the Work* (Chicago, IL: D5 Coalition, April 2016), 8–9, www.d5coalition.org. According to Kelly Brown, director of D5 Coalition, "Since it [the data] is not drawn from an appropriately structured random sample of foundations but from data drawn from the Council on Foundations' annual survey (2014), it cannot be generalized to the field of philanthropy overall." (Kelly Brown, email to author, December 7, 2018).

58. BoardSource, *Foundation Board Leadership* (Washington, DC: Board-Source, 2018), 6, https://leadingwithintent.org.
59. Ibid., 21.
60. Sidford and Frasz, *Not Just Money*, 7, http://heliconcollab.net.
61. Holly Sidford, *Fusing Arts, Culture and Social Change* (Washington, DC: National Committee for Responsive Philanthropy, October 2011), 1.
62. Greater Pittsburgh Arts Council with The Learning and Leadership Committee, *Racial Equity*, 22, www.pittsburghartscouncil.org.
63. Ibid., 23.
64. Ibid., 33.
65. Lee Anne Bell, *Storytelling for Social Justice* (New York, NY: Routledge, 2010), 13.
66. Ibid., 23.
67. Jones, *Prejudice and Racism*, 14.
68. Smith, *Diversity's Promise*, 39. Please see chapter 2 for a detailed discussion of the history of racial and ethnic systemic racism in the United States and its impact on the performing arts field and its institutions.
69. Allport, *The Nature*, 6, 150.
70. Ibid., 52, 191.
71. Tobie S. Stein, "Creating Opportunities for People of Color in Performing Arts Management," *Journal of Arts Management, Law and Society* 29, no. 4 (Winter 2000): 311.
72. Ibid.
73. Tobie S. Stein and Jessica Bathurst, *Performing Arts Management: A Handbook of Professional Practices* (New York, NY: Allworth, 2008), 52.
74. Americans for the Arts, *Arts & Economic Prosperity 5* (Washington, DC: Americans for the Arts, 2017), 4–6, https://americansforthearts.org/economicimpact.
75. Lester M. Salamon and Chelsea L. Newhouse, "The 2019 Nonprofit Employment Report," *Nonprofit Economic Data Bulletin*, no. 47 (Baltimore, MD: Johns Hopkins Center for Civil Society Studies, January 2019), 13, ccss. jhu.edu. "The data are from the U.S. Bureau of Labor Statistics. There are several years' data covered in the report—2007, 2012, and 2016. The latter is the primary year of analysis, with the two earlier years being used for comparison" (Chelsea L. Newhouse, email to author, February 22, 2019).
76. "City's Media Czar Encourages More Filming in Outer Boroughs," *Crain's New York Business* (June 13, 2016), www.crainsnewyork.com.
77. Lee, Bean, with Bachmeier, "Ethnoracial Diversity," 159–60.
78. Charlan J. Nemeth, "Differential Contributions of Majority and Minority Influence," *Psychological Review* 93, no. 1 (January 1986): 30.
79. Anthony Lising Antonio et al., "Effects of Racial Diversity on Complex Thinking in College Students," *Psychological Science* 15, no. 8 (August 2004): 509; Phillips, "How Diversity Makes Us Smarter," www.scientificamerican.com.
80. Frey, *Diversity Explosion*, 28.
81. Ibid., 250–51.
82. Ibid., 3–4.
83. U.S. Census Bureau, "Millennials Outnumber Baby Boomers," www.census.gov.
84. Margaret E. Blume-Kohout, Sara R. Leonard, and Jennifer L. Novak-Leonard, *When Going Gets Tough: Barriers and Motivations Affecting Arts Attendance* (Washington, DC: National Endowment for the Arts, 2015), 24. The data was collected as part of the 2012 General Social Survey.
85. Smith, *Diversity's Promise*, 274–75.

86. John Moore, "American Theatre's Leadership Vacuum: Who Will Fill It?" *American Theatre* (August 31, 2017), www.americantheatre.org. This statistic is based on a 2015 TCG survey.
87. Stephanie Burrell Storms, "Using Social Justice Vignettes to Prepare Students for Social Action Engagement," *Multicultural Perspectives* 16, no. 1 (2014): 43.

2 Race and Performance
A Brief History

Emma Halpern

> We're having conversations about diversity and inclusion and equity. But I don't know if people understand that this isn't a new topic. . . . I think you start to understand the frustration of someone who's 80 years old, and you tell them, "Well, diversity takes time." They've been watching it for decades.
>
> Theresa Ruth Howard, founder and curator of
> *Memoirs of Blacks in Ballet*[1]

Introduction

The history of social injustice in the American performing arts is really the history of social injustice in America. People of Color have had and continue to face unjust legal, political, educational, and economic systems in this country, and this discrimination has played out in microcosm in the performing arts field. Historically, People of Color have been denied opportunities to work, to train, to engage, and to profit, in the arts and elsewhere in American society. Despite this systemic oppression, arts professionals of Color have also found ways to subvert and resist racist narratives and power structures, using scant resources to create vibrant and influential performing arts institutions of their own.

The following chapter is a brief summary of how arts professionals in marginalized groups have, throughout U.S. history, navigated the live performing arts workplace—the injustices they've encountered as well as the ways in which they've succeeded in practicing their craft, asserting identity, and building community in the face of discrimination and violence.

The Origins of Race in America and American Performance: 1600–1900

People of the African Diaspora[2] have been in the Americas for over 400 years.[3] The importation of kidnapped Africans to the colonies, and then to the newly formed United States, occurred legally through the slave trade until 1808, over half a century before the abolition of slavery.[4] Errol G. Hill and James V. Hatch foreground their comprehensive study *A History of African American Theatre* by outlining the manner in which slavery in the New World shaped modern conceptions of race: "Slavery has been a common human phenomenon for countless years, but not until the modern era was it limited to people of any particular racial group." They write, "Naming the new captives 'slaves' before they left Africa promptly changed their status from human to nonhuman; as 'black slaves' they unwittingly conferred the stigma of inferiority to free Blacks on the basis of skin color."[5] James Baldwin emphasizes this concept in his essay "On Being White . . . and Other Lies," laying out how American notions of Whiteness, as well as Blackness, are rooted in slavery. "No one was white before he/she came to America. It took generations, and a vast amount of coercion, before this became a white country," and he writes, the "people who, as they claim, 'settled' the country became white—because of the necessity of denying the black presence, and justifying the black subjugation."[6]

Indeed, racist depictions of Black characters reflected how the new nation's economic dependence on slavery was central to the formation of the White "American" identity itself. "Black slavery enriched the country's creative possibilities. For in that construction of blackness *and* enslavement could be found not only the not-free but also, with the dramatic polarity created by skin color, the projection of the not-me," writes Toni Morrison. "What rose up out of collective needs to allay internal fears and to rationalize external exploitation was an American Africanism—a fabricated brew of darkness, otherness, alarm, and desire that is uniquely American."[7] That "fabricated brew" seen in racist depictions of Blackness on colonial and post-American Revolution stages promoted American ideas of "otherness," which in turn justified the racist attitudes and behaviors that White audience members engaged in outside of the theater.

Early Examples of Stereotypes and Autonomous Black Performance on U.S. Stages

Specific examples of White actors portraying Black,[8] Asian,[9] or Native American[10] characters in the U.S. are numerous and go back at least as far as 1767.[11] As a rule, People of Color were denied opportunities to perform in these productions and were often portrayed as one-dimensional comic servants,[12] bloodthirsty killers, or "noble savages."[13] New York theaters in the early United States were also frequently segregated, with the Park Theatre, a 2,000-seat venue near City Hall Park that opened in 1798, offering only the worst seats in the upper gallery to Black patrons.[14]

In the face of discrimination and racist misrepresentation, the Black producer William Alexander Brown founded the African Grove Theatre in New York in 1821, six years before the abolition of slavery in that state. The earliest known major African American theater company,[15] the African Grove mostly produced Shakespeare and musical performances, and Brown's 1822 play *Shotaway; or, the Insurrection of the Caribs of St. Domingo*, a retelling of a slave rebellion in the Caribbean, is the first known play written by an African American. The company's work thwarted White notions about theater as an exclusively White institution, particularly concerning Shakespeare,[16] and was able to bring in an audience of both Black and White patrons, creating what Marvin McAllister calls "an invaluable blueprint for an inclusive national theater."[17]

The African Grove was only active for three years, as violent White rioters ultimately made it impossible for the company to continue.[18] The African Grove's premature end is a testament to just how much the company threatened the racist status quo, and the degree to which visibility on the stage symbolically translates to visibility in public life. Brown was working in a national environment that allowed White people to destroy Black institutions with impunity, and the fact that his company was able to survive for as long as it did suggests an extraordinary resistance and demand for the work.

The Ubiquity of Blackface Minstrelsy

Less than a decade after The African Grove Theatre folded, White performer T. D. Rice began performing as Jim Crow,[19] a character that personified a type of Blackface minstrelsy that would remain prevalent for over a century, and whose name would come to denote the dehumanizing and discriminatory laws enacted against Black people in the South. Jim Crow minstrelsy propagated Black stereotypes through comic song and dance, portraying Black characters as grotesque caricatures content with plantation life. These performances propagated a false sense of equity in the way African Americans were thought of and treated by society at large. Poet and critic Sterling A. Brown writes, "If the Negro could be shown as perpetually mirthful, his state could not be so wretched. This is, of course, the familiar procedure when conquerors depict a subject people."[20] In addition to anesthetizing a White audience to the horrors of slavery (and after the Civil War, to the violence and oppression Black people continued to face at the hands of the Ku Klux Klan, the police, and the government), Blackface minstrelsy further stacked the deck against actual Black performers and companies. As Eileen Southern posits, "White blackface minstrels literally pushed black actors off the stage."[21]

Eric Lott notes the degree to which minstrelsy has since permeated American culture, writing,

> The minstrel show has been ubiquitous, cultural common coin; it has been so central to the lives of North Americans that we are hardly aware of its extraordinary influence. . . . From "Oh! Susanna" to Elvis Presley, from circus clowns to Saturday morning cartoons, blackface acts and words have figured significantly in the white Imaginary of the United States.[22]

Minstrelsy became such a widespread form of entertainment, and such a potent shorthand for rationalizing White supremacy, that it would remain embedded in both Black and White performance, as well as in the collective White American conception of race, for generations to come.

Late Nineteenth-Century Black Performers and Producers

Blackface minstrelsy remained so ubiquitous that Black managers and performers began creating their own minstrel shows. In 1865, African American Charles Barney Hicks founded the first major all-Black minstrel show, the Georgia Minstrels, which he toured around the country and Great Britain.[23] For the most part, performers in these shows still applied burnt cork to their faces and maintained the form's racist status quo, but they also included more pathos than the grotesque comic buffoonery seen in White-run minstrel shows. "The early black minstrels were stereotyped depictions of the life and pursuits of black people," writes Henry T. Sampson, who continues:

> Aware that their audiences, mostly whites, were not ready to accept anything of a serious nature from them, these artists . . . put forth a series of selections of a sentimental nature, interspersed with dramatic recitations and sketches, always offset with humor.[24]

By adhering to minstrelsy's racist conventions, these companies were able to produce and tour in one of the few ways that was available to them, but because these were Black-owned and Black-run endeavors, performers could also resist those conventions as much as they thought audiences would allow.

Other African American companies found ways besides Blackface minstrelsy to showcase the considerable talent of their performers. In 1873, the Colored American Opera Company of Washington, D.C., the first known opera company in Washington, performed the comic operetta *The Doctor of Alcantara*. Produced as a fundraiser for its parent organization, the Blessed Martin de Porres church, the company played to Mixed Race audiences and received positive reviews.[25] John W. Isham, a theater producer whose light skin helped him to secure a management job with Barnum and Bailey, founded John W. Isham's Octoroons, an all–African American company with shows that featured a mix of grand opera, comedy, and specialty acts.[26] African American composer and songwriter Bob Cole outlined the goals of companies like Isham's in his 1898 "Colored Actor's Declaration of Independence," where he declared that Black musical theater troupes would write, manage, and produce their own productions and refuse to perform in segregated houses.[27] While some aspects of Cole's document were aspirational, Black producers and managers were already working to bring Black musical theater and vaudeville performances to Black audiences without having to appeal to White managers or theater owners.

Black Opera Singers and the Barriers to Entry in Elite White Performing Arts Disciplines

Nineteenth-century Black performers looking to pursue opera would encounter more hostility than Black minstrels or musical comedy performers. However, much like the African Grove Theatre in the 1820s, there were performers who achieved some success in spite of White opposition. Elizabeth Taylor Greenfield and Matilda Sissieretta Jones were two nineteenth-century Black opera singers who were able to forge distinguished careers. Both were compelled to perform for segregated or all-White audiences, had their appearances scrutinized by White critics,[28] and had to incorporate Stephen Foster numbers[29] and songs like Paul Allen's "A New Coon in Town" into their presentations.[30] Still, both built reputations for performing repertoires of classical music and toured extensively, with Greenfield performing for Queen Victoria,[31] and Jones performing at Madison Square Garden and the White House.[32]

The Founding of White Elite U.S. Cultural Institutions

The accomplishments of Greenfield and Jones are all the more remarkable considering how nineteenth-century America was undergoing a cultural stratification at large, particularly during Jones's lifetime. Opera and Shakespeare, two types of entertainment that were generally enjoyed by the masses earlier in the century, had by the late nineteenth century become the entertainment of the White elite. Lawrence Levine writes, "More and more, opera in America. . . [was] deeply influenced if not controlled by wealthy patrons whose impresarios and conductors strove to keep the opera they presented free from the influence of other genres and other groups."[33]

The founding of the Metropolitan Opera in 1883[34] and Carnegie Hall in 1891,[35] both generously funded by wealthy White families and businessmen, demonstrates how certain types of art became synonymous with wealth and high status during this time. As Keryl E. McCord observes, the founders of these organizations built their institutions with both exclusion and longevity in mind. "The success of their efforts resulted in the separation of the 'high arts' from popular culture," she writes.[36] Those initial investments help account for the dominance that these types of institutions have shown in funding and taste-making arenas, as well as their struggle with diversification and inclusion.[37] At the very moment Jones was trying to break down racial barriers in opera, a culture of arts patronage that was focused on status and homogeneity for wealthy White audiences was taking shape.

Nineteenth-Century Latinx and Asian Performance in the U.S.

While minstrelsy was the dominant form of popular entertainment in most parts of the country at this time, tours of professional Spanish language theater began to have a significant presence on the West Coast and in the southwest. In California, Arizona, and Texas, family audiences attended Spanish language drama, music, comic farce, and holiday *pastorelas*.[38] By the 1860s, there was such a demand for this type of performance that touring troupes were able to put down roots as resident companies across California. These included The Compañía Española de la Familia Estrella, which by 1862 had settled in San Francisco, and The Compañía Española de Angel de Mollá, which was based in Los Angeles and toured periodically to Tucson. These productions were generally family friendly, and many Spanish-speaking communities saw the theater as an important cultural and community outlet.[39] People outside of Mexican and Mexican American communities took note of Spanish-language theater's popularity and professionalism, as Nicolás Kanellos writes, "The Hispanic stage was a strong and important enough institution at that time to attract Anglos into the audiences and to be reviewed in the English- and French-language newspapers."[40]

The mid-nineteenth century also saw an influx of Chinese immigrants to the United States. Between 1848 and 1850, the Chinese population in California rose from virtually zero to 25,000. As the Chinese population increased, so did the demand for affordable Chinese entertainment. The Chinese opera companies that came to the United States did very well in areas with large Chinese populations, catering to Chinese audiences in San Francisco and Portland, Oregon.[41] However, when the Tong Hook Tong Dramatic Company, a Chinese opera troupe originally from the Guangdong Province, brought their show from San Francisco to New York City, they were sorely disappointed. While Western plays that caricatured and exoticized China like *The Yankees in China* (1839) and *Irishman in China* (1842) were popular in New York, East Coast audiences had no familiarity with or interest in performance that was actually rooted in Chinese culture, or performed by Chinese people. Dishonest dealings from New York producers made Tong Hook Tong's situation all the more dire. The company's New York venture failed,[42] foreshadowing the anti-Asian sentiment that would emerge in both American performance and politics later in the century, including through the 1882 Chinese Exclusion Act that banned Chinese immigration.[43] "The bottom line was that 'faux Chinese' or 'simulated Chinese' were more profitable for theatre producers and investors in New York City," writes Esther Kim Lee, who adds, "Unfortunately, this tradition would continue throughout the nineteenth and the twentieth centuries in American theatre."[44]

Race and Performance in Early Twentieth-Century America: 1900–1930

Though slavery had been abolished in 1865 with the ratification of the thirteenth amendment, the Jim Crow laws of the post-Reconstruction-era South ensured that slavery's degradations, impoverishments, and perpetual threats of White violence would endure. The restrictions that began at the end of Reconstruction intensified in the early twentieth century. Over 4,000 lynchings of African Americans were documented between 1877 and 1950, and many more went unrecorded. Many victims had never been accused of any crime, and the White perpetrators (often members of crowds who would bring picnics, take photographs, or take souvenir pieces of the victim's body after they were tortured and killed) were almost never held accountable.[45] The specter of mass, quotidian White terror haunted Black communities in the South and beyond, as incidents of White mobs killing African Americans with impunity were documented from New York to California.[46] With hopes of both securing their physical safety and finding better economic opportunity, over 1.3 million African Americans fled the south between 1900 and 1930 in what became known as the Great Migration.[47]

Early Twentieth-Century Asian Immigration, Performance, and Appropriation

At the same time as the African American Great Migration, a new migration of Asian immigrants was also taking place. From 1850 to 1930, almost one million people from China, Korea, Japan, the Philippines, and India came to the United States.[48] One example of the type of entertainment Asian Americans were consuming during this era was work at the Nippon Kan Theater in Seattle. Built in 1909, Nippon Kan was a venue for Japanese audiences to see Japanese performance, and it presented music, Kabuki, and films, as well as hosted martial arts competitions and community gatherings.[49] At the same time, White audiences were seeing a completely distorted view of Asia, Asians, and Asian Americans at the theater. Melodramas like David Belasco's *Madame Butterfly* (one of the

sources on which Puccini based his opera), offered heroic White pro-
tagonists and Asian female characters who were exoticized and submis-
sive.[50] Escalating anti-Asian sentiment in the U.S. led to the passage of the
Immigration Act of 1924, which banned virtually all Asian immigration,
and with it came a curious phenomenon on White stages: While many
shows before the ban portrayed Asian characters living in the United
States (though still with stereotypical characteristics), shows produced
soon after the ban tended to depict Asian characters far away, living in
their native countries. As Lee writes, "It was as if the Immigration Act of
1924 erased Asian Americans from the national domestic imagination."[51]

The Great Migration and Black Middle Class Philanthropy

While the U.S. was working to curb Asian immigration, African Americans' mass exodus to Northern cities, coupled with the country's
increased urbanization and industrialization, contributed to the formation of a Black middle class. The wealth generated by this new demographic was barely a fraction of what the White founders of the elite
arts institutions had accumulated, as those White families had had the
opportunity to create multigenerational wealth due to the inequities of
slavery and Jim Crow. Still, middle class African Americans participated
in a culture of giving and volunteerism that they had been building since
the late eighteenth century, one focused on community building and combatting racial oppression. "The myriad self-help societies, organizations,
and programs that blacks launched over time should be seen as exercises
in philanthropy," writes Colin Palmer, who adds, "Lacking access to vast
amounts of capital, blacks who were in a position to do so placed their
time, energy, and paltry resources in the service of others."[52]

Out of necessity, combatting violence and providing social services, as
opposed to promoting the arts, were philanthropic priorities for Black
communities. As McCord writes, "[Traditional White philanthropy] is
based in the principle of noblesse oblige; black philanthropy is based
on the concept of taking care of one another to ensure the survival of
the race."[53] While White philanthropy implied large donations from a
few very wealthy individuals, Black philanthropy implied a large number
of small donations from people giving what they could. Additionally,
the "noblesse oblige" that founded the elite White institutions served to
reinforce racial and class differences, while Black philanthropy served to
enhance upward mobility and fight discrimination.

Performing Arts Training at Historically Black Colleges and Universities

Despite limited personal wealth and numerous charitable obligations,
African Americans in the early twentieth century still found ways to

practice and support the arts, most notably through the creation of performing arts programs at Historically Black Colleges and Universities
(HBCUs). Slavery and postbellum segregation restricted most educational opportunities for African Americans, and HBCUs, most founded
shortly after the end of the Civil War (and over 100 of which are still in
operation), offered many students their first access to formal schooling.[54]
As early as 1898, African American faculty members at Atlanta University, North Carolina Agricultural and Technical College, and Tuskegee
Institute were directing students in productions of Shakespeare and original work. Ernest Everett Just founded the Howard University Players in
1911, marking Howard University as a flagship institution for theater
training.[55] Howard philosophy professor Alain Locke recognized the
potential contributions the Players could make to the theatrical canon
as well as towards social change, declaring in 1922 that the school was
a place where "race drama becomes peculiarly the ward of our colleges,
as new drama, as art-drama, and as folk-drama."[56] By 1936, Sheppard
Randolph Edmonds, an African American playwright and educator, had
formed both the Negro Intercollegiate Dramatic Association, which
served five HBCUs based in Washington, D.C., Maryland, and Virginia,
and the Southern Association of Dramatic and Speech Arts, which served
a larger network of Southern HBCUs. Both organizations served to promote the study of theater arts, champion young Black theater artists, and
create inter-collegiate theater communities.[57]

Howard University created particularly rich opportunities in other
performing arts fields as well. In 1927, Maryrose Reeves Allen founded
the group that would go on to be known as the Howard University
Dance Ensemble, which by the 1950s was performing with the National
Symphony Orchestra in Washington and at integrated theaters in New
York.[58] Howard was offering music courses as early as 1870 and established an independent music conservatory in 1914. The School of Music
at Howard would go on to be admitted to the National Association of
Schools of Music in 1942, the first school in the Washington area to gain
admittance.[59] All of these initiatives at Howard and other HBCUs helped
to cultivate rich performing arts traditions in Black communities and to
position many Black artists to create their own opportunities once they
entered the discriminatory White performing arts workforce.

Exploitation and Autonomy in the Jazz World: Duke Ellington's Residency at the Cotton Club

While performing arts programs were developing on HBCU campuses,
the Great Migration was helping to bring jazz music from New Orleans
to other parts of the country. With origins in both the African and Caribbean traditions of enslaved people as well as the music of French, Spanish, and British colonizers, jazz expanded its reach when early pioneers

like Jelly Roll Morton and Joseph "King" Oliver relocated to Chicago in the 1910s.[60] White audiences and listeners took notice as the form gained popularity, though as was the case with vaudeville and opera, Black jazz artists still struggled to be seen as legitimate artists. During Duke Ellington's residency at Harlem's Cotton Club from 1927–1931, his music was frequently referred to as "jungle" music, or described with other language that exoticized the performance. While today the club is remembered for presenting Billie Holiday, Count Basie, and other jazz legends, it was also known during this time for presenting sketches set in "primitive" Africa. The club's featuring of Black artists while having a Whites-only admission policy created an environment where wealthy White audiences could visit Harlem while keeping a safe distance from the people who actually lived there, oblivious and indifferent to the realities of the performers' lives. "The girl you saw doing the squirmy dance . . . was not in the throes of passion. . . . She was working to get that salary to take home and feed her baby," Ellington said in a 1964 interview.[61] The fact that Ellington felt compelled to play The Cotton Club implies how necessary a credential it must have seemed for future success, and how meager other opportunities were for Black performers. "[Most African American musicians] struggled against Jim Crow restrictions to find places to sleep and eat," writes Harvey G. Cohen.[62]

Ellington found many of The Cotton Club's practices offensive, but he was also working in much better conditions than most Black musicians, and was ultimately able to parlay his experience there into a lucrative and satisfying career. In 1943, Ellington debuted "Black, Brown and Beige: A Tone Parallel to the History of the Negro in America" at Carnegie Hall. A 43-minute work, "BB&B" takes listeners on a journey through the Black experience from slavery to the early twentieth century.[63] By presenting a piece at Carnegie Hall that used jazz to tell an African American story in epic fashion, Ellington made a powerful statement about the legitimacy of Black art and its place in elite White arts institutions.

African American Vaudeville and Musical Comedy

In the professional theater world, Black performers working in vaudeville and musical comedy were finding new ways to depict African American life onstage, though minstrelsy remained a component of most performances. A class of African American comedian-managers emerged, including Bert Williams and Ernest Hogan. With funding from White investors, they developed and toured big-budget musical comedies starring all-Black casts, rivaling Broadway in terms of professionalism and production values. "Even in the entrenched mainstream theatrical establishment of New York City, the big shows demonstrated that black producers and performers were capable of things white performers could not reproduce," write Lynn Abbott and Doug Seroff.[64] Black vaudevillian-turned-producer Sherman H. Dudley worked to organize a vaudeville circuit for Black audiences, controlling almost thirty Black theaters in the South, Northeast, and Midwest by 1916.[65] Dudley's dominance in the Black touring world would eventually give way to the Theater Owners Booking Association,[66] whose touring model, now commonly known as the Chitlin' Circuit, brought touring shows to African American audiences throughout the South and Midwest in the 1920s. Henry Louis Gates, Jr. writes of the early Chitlin' Circuit:

> Crisscrossing black America, the circuit established an empire of comedy and pathos, the sublime and the ridiculous: a moveable feast that enabled blacks to patronize black entertainers, . . . They were the kind of melodrama or farce—or as often both—in which nothing succeeds like excess.[67]

Like much Black performance of the nineteenth century, Black musical theater and vaudeville of the early twentieth century still did not speak to the most pressing issues of the Black experience. However, figures like Williams, Hogan, and Dudley also worked to orient White audiences towards a more nuanced understanding of Blackness. Abbott and Seroff write,

> The comedian-producers of the big shows weaned mainstream audiences away from the crude character delineations of nineteenth-century minstrelsy. . . . Still in blackface makeup, black comedians dared to bring forth modern, recognizable characters who spoke more directly to black audiences.[68]

While performance opportunity was certainly important to these performer-managers, social ideology was at play in their work as well.

Some of the racist trappings of musical comedy and vaudeville were also present in the shows produced at The Pekin Theater, Chicago's first Black-owned performance venue, but activism was still a driving force behind the institution. Founded by Robert T. Motts and active from 1904 until Motts's death in 1911, the Pekin had a state-of-the-art facility, an all-Black staff, a professional Black stock company, and a robust repertoire of new musical comedies written and produced in-house. Motts was interested in using his theater to make a positive impact on Chicago's Black community, but through the success of his business as opposed to the content of the performance on stage. Thomas Bauman writes, "As a businessman, Motts saw the content of what was enacted on his stage as a commodity, as a representational means to an institutional end—to gaining the unqualified respect due a prosperous, elegant, and soundly managed enterprise."[69] For Motts, founding an institution that was a major source of Black employment and that served as a civic hub was a political act in and of itself, regardless of how apolitical, or even regressive, the work on stage might be.

Theater Examining the Black Experience

At the same time, Black artists and managers were producing the kinds of dramatic work that had not been successful since the African Grove Theatre. The National Association for the Advancement of Colored People (NAACP) funded a production of Angelina Weld Grimké's anti-lynching play *Rachel*, and its 1916 premiere in Washington, D.C., marked the first time a nonmusical play by a Black playwright—with Black actors—was performed for a wide audience.[70] *Rachel* inspired a series of subsequent anti-lynching plays, which as a genre focused on how a lynching incident would go on to affect the family and community of the person who had been murdered. These plays refute White narratives of Blackness as inherently violent and offer depictions of loving Black families. "According to dominant assumptions, mobs targeted African Americans because they represented an evil that would destroy society," writes Koritha Mitchell; "the dramatists offered their communities scripts that preserve the truth these myths disregarded. They portray black characters leading ordinary lives in domestic interiors where they affectionately sustain each other."[71]

W. E. B. Du Bois and the Krigwa Players

As the Harlem Renaissance of the 1920s began, Black activists and theater professionals articulated the need for a theater that spoke to Black issues and the Black experience. Civil rights activist and scholar W. E. B. Du Bois crystalized this idea in his newspaper *The Crisis* by writing that Black theater must be "about us," depicting an honest portrayal of Black life; "by us," utilizing Black playwrights; "for us," catering primarily to Black audiences; and "near us," reaching those audiences in their own neighborhoods.[72]

Building on some of the ideas in Cole's *Actor's Declaration*, Du Bois's proposal calls for a synthesis of what he might have seen as the most productive aspects of Black performance until that point. His ideal theater combines the high artistic aspirations of the African Grove Theatre, the entrepreneurship of the Black vaudeville and musical theater managers, the civic prominence and accessibility of the Pekin, and the activism of anti-lynching plays with a crucial additional ingredient: The use of theater as a means for the expression and exploration of Black identity.

Du Bois had already been instrumental in creating the NAACP drama committee that had produced *Rachel*,[73] and in 1924, *The Crisis* established a playwriting competition with funding from Jewish philanthropist Amy Spingarn, encouraging writers to "deal with some phase of

Negro history or experience."[74] The Krigwa Players, as the drama wing of the NAACP came to be called, would stage productions of *The Crisis* contest winners through 1927, and as Ethel Pitts Walker notes, their influence was felt across the country almost immediately: "Krigwa . . . proved again that Black audiences treasured their culture and were willing to pay to see it paraded on stage."[75] With little funding or resources, The Krigwa Players initiated a type of Black theater that continues to be practiced and re-invented today.

Race, Labor, and the Integration of Western European–Influenced Performance: 1930–1960

The Harlem Renaissance gave way to the Great Depression. Soon after the stock market crash of 1929, almost half of the African Americans in Harlem were unemployed.[76] In the face of economic crisis, the Apollo Theater opened on 125th Street in 1934, offering live music, comedy, and variety shows to an African American clientele. Owned by White businessmen Frank Schiffman and Leo Brecher, the Apollo became one of the only theaters in New York to employ African Americans backstage, and regularly hosted events for the NAACP and other community organizations.[77] The Apollo's weekly Amateur Night gave a platform to performers who might not otherwise have the means to attempt careers in the performing arts, while also assigning a sense of agency to the audience. Julia L. Foulkes writes:

> Amateur Night gave crucial opportunities to African Americans who had few of them. And the role of the audience in this process was a key part of the Apollo's success, . . . The working and middle classes of Harlem and beyond had both a voice and the power to determine outcomes.[78]

The feeling of ownership that the Apollo instilled in its audiences helped the community to view the Apollo as an indispensable institution. This community investment continues to sustain the organization today, as it is currently run by the nonprofit Apollo Theater Foundation,[79] operating under Black leadership.[80]

The Negro Units of the Federal Theatre Project

During the Depression, however, only a few performing arts professionals were lucky enough to win at Amateur night or to be employed by the Apollo. In an effort to put members of the theater industry back to work, the Roosevelt administration established the Federal Theatre Project (FTP) in 1935 as a program of the Works Progress Administration (WPA). Headed by Hallie Flanagan, the FTP's goals were to provide theater professionals with employment and to bring high-quality theater to communities all over the country. With a budget of $6.8 million, the FTP employed over 12,000 theater artists in over 30 states,[81] including 22 Negro Units nationwide.[82]

In many ways, the FTP's approach to race relations did much to promote equity. The inclusion of Black-specific units had been the suggestion of African American actress Rose McClendon, who thought that their inclusion could ensure funding and visibility for Black artists and Black stories. Flanagan listened to McClendon, and directed her staff to strictly enforce the WPA's anti-discrimination codes, leading the FTP to have fewer incidents of overt discrimination than any other New Deal program.[83] This attitude towards racial equality may have contributed to Congress's termination of the FTP in 1939,[84] as the Special House Committee on Un-American Activities (HUAC) saw integration to be a sign of deviant activity, with Chairman Martin Dies, Jr. maintaining, "Those who are certain that they are for racial and religious tolerance, some of them openly advocate the use of class hatred to achieve some [Communist] objective."[85]

The FTP also provided Black artists, many of whom had no formal arts training, with opportunities to professionalize. As Fannin S. Belcher explains, Black artists in the FTP's Negro theater units

> were securing their first opportunity to have steady employment in their profession, to produce the plays they wanted to produce without bowing to commercial prejudices. . . . The Negro units thought also of the project as a training school.[86]

Noting that most African Americans had little access to theater management training, McClendon also recommended that Negro units start out with experienced White administrators who would then train Black successors.[87] Considering how the history of Black theater management already included vaudeville, musical theater, and political drama at this point in time, it seems doubtful that there were no African Americans capable of filling these supervisory positions. However, this succession plan largely seemed to work. After a year, Harlem unit director John Houseman stepped down, leaving the unit to Black artists Harry F. V. Edward, Augustus J. Smith, and Carlton Moss.[88]

The FTP and Negro theater units offered ample opportunity to African American theater artists and administrators, though not everyone was satisfied with their initiatives. The African American novelist and playwright Richard Wright, who at the time was the Chicago publicist for the FTP, was disappointed by the number of "Negro" adaptations of classic plays by White writers that were being produced, as opposed to new plays by African American playwrights.[89] These adaptations included

Orson Welles's adaptation of *Macbeth* set in Haiti and produced by the Harlem unit,[90] as well as adaptations of *Romeo and Juliet* and *Everyman* in Chicago.[91] Wright notes in his autobiography:

> [FTP] had run a series of ordinary plays, all of which had been revamped to "Negro style," with jungle scenes, spirituals, and all. . . . Contemporary plays dealing realistically with Negro life were spurned as being controversial. . . . Here was an opportunity for the production of a worth-while Negro drama and no one was aware of it.[92]

Statistics support Wright's frustration, as an FTP list of sixty-three Negro unit plays only names sixteen plays that were written by African Americans.[93] Black theater professionals were able to use the FTP as a source of employment, a platform for professionalization, and as a means to play the types of coveted roles they were often denied, although the bias of White supervisors and the threat of HUAC's investigation may have kept the program from fully exploring modern Black life onstage.

Theater in the Face of Anti-Immigrant Sentiment: The Federal Theatre Project's Spanish Language Unit

There was one Latinx unit in the FTP, operating out of Tampa, Florida, from 1936 to 1937. Tampa had been home to a robust Latinx theatrical scene since the 1890s, when the city's Spanish-speaking community (many members of which were Cuban tobacco workers) set up mutual aid societies that housed theater venues in their buildings. These theaters presented professional touring shows and were also home to local companies whose artists worked as cigar rollers during the day.[94] The semi-professional nature of the Tampa theater community made the city an unusual choice for the FTP's sole Spanish language unit, as New York and Los Angeles had larger Latinx theater communities that depended more heavily on full-time theater employment. Nicolás Kanellos writes,

> The [FTP's] basic objective of creating work-relief theatre of a relevant nature would best have been served where the full-time professionals were suffering unemployment, not in Tampa, where many of the artists still gained a good part of their living rolling cigars.[95]

Nonetheless, the unit produced 14 shows in Spanish, mostly musical comedies and revues, including *El Mundo en la Mano*, which earned more recorded profits than any other FTP show in Florida.[96]

While the unit's work was extremely well-received, it was terminated after 18 months, shortly after the Emergency Relief Appropriation (ERA) Act of 1937 was passed. The Act prohibited non-citizens from being employed through government work relief programs. The unit subsequently lost 25 members, including its director Manuel Aparicio, and the rest were integrated into the FTP vaudeville unit.[97] For immigrants in other fields and other areas of the country, the ERA meant the loss of their only means of employment. Members of the Tampa Spanish Unit, however, still had their day jobs as cigar rollers. Furthermore, as Tampa's Latinx theater tradition had never depended on full-time employment in the theater to begin with, the troupe continued to perform, despite losing the FTP's resources.[98]

Black Participation in Western European–Influenced Performance

Integration initiatives were taking place in the performing arts and beyond at this time, albeit gradually. The 1950s saw some of the major events of the civil rights movement, with the Supreme Court striking down segregated schools with the Brown v. Board of Education ruling in 1954. Rosa Parks was arrested for breaking segregation laws the following year, spurring the Montgomery bus boycott. Capitalizing on this momentum, African Americans striving to work in the performing arts disciplines of opera, classical music, and ballet were able to make small gains in the upper echelons of these historically White fields.

In 1955, Marian Anderson became the first African American to sing at the Metropolitan Opera.[99] By the 1950s Anderson had a successful career as a classical concert singer, and her 1939 Easter Sunday performance at the Lincoln Memorial, spurred by the Daughters of the American Revolution's refusal to let her sing at Constitution Hall, had made her an icon of the civil rights movement.[100] The Metropolitan Opera's general manager Rudolf Bing recognized both Anderson's talent and the political statement her casting would make, despite her lack of experience or general desire to perform in opera (as opposed to concert recitals). Bing waited until Anderson's contract was signed before informing his White board of trustees about the hire, knowing that, however resistant they might be to the idea of casting an African American singer, they would be more averse to the scandal that rescinding the offer or firing Bing would create.[101]

Anderson's performance was an unqualified triumph.[102] Still, while Bing's work to secure Anderson's appearance was indeed a milestone in the history of integration in American opera companies, it was not unproblematic. Anderson sang the role of the enchantress Ulrica in Giuseppe Verdi's *Un Ballo in Maschera*,[103] a role that Nina Sun Eidsheim describes as "a gypsy, internationally imagined as other." Bing likely felt that casting Anderson as an "otherized" character would make her appearance at the Metropolitan Opera more palatable to the board, and Eidsheim wonders if the casting caused listeners to "connect the voice of

Anderson with the sight and therefore with the sound of the other, thus confirming the otherness of blackness."[104] Bing also seemed to know that integrating the Metropolitan Opera was, in the long term, a smart strategic decision, and that choosing Anderson as the singer to break the color barrier would endow the hire with an added political symbolism. Wallace McClain Cheatham writes that Bing's decision

> was not made without a complete awareness and understanding of what was going on within the country's personality. . . . The reality being that had Mr. Bing not chosen to integrate his singers voluntarily, pressures from outside forces would have soon forced such a move.[105]

These issues notwithstanding, Anderson's performance paved the way for the Metropolitan Opera debuts of other major African American opera singers of the time, including baritone Robert McFerrin just three weeks after Anderson's debut,[106] and soprano Leontyne Price in 1961.[107]

Black composers and conductors were also making professional strides in the White-dominated classical music profession during this time. In 1930, William Grant Still became the first African American to have a symphony performed by a historically White American orchestra when the Rochester Philharmonic performed his *Symphony no. 1 "Afro-American."* Six years later, with the Los Angeles Philharmonic, Still became the first African American to conduct for a historically White orchestra. Still used classical music as a means to explore the Black experience in a variety of ways, writing arrangements for spirituals and setting the poetry of Black poets Paul Laurence Dunbar, Langston Hughes, and Philippe Thoby-Marcelin to music.[108] He also received commissions for political compositions, writing the orchestral piece *Rhapsody* for a pro-integration group in the South and the choral work *And They Lynched Him on a Tree* for poet Katherine Garrison Chapin, who wrote the lyrics, and her husband Francis Biddle, who went on to become U.S. Attorney General. "They wanted both a white chorus and a Negro chorus crying out against lynching," Still explained in a 1969 interview.[109]

Everett Lee was another African American musician and conductor who was able to forge a mid-century career in spite of discrimination. In 1945, Lee was playing in the New York City Symphony and conducting *On the Town* on Broadway. Frustrated by the discriminatory practices that barred him from auditioning for the New York Philharmonic, Lee formed an interracial orchestra, the Cosmopolitan Symphony Society, in 1947.[110] The orchestra was social justice driven, with the *New York Amsterdam News* writing at the time, "This effort to combine highly competent musicians in a grand orchestral ensemble as a cultural venture deserves the support and good will of every faithful adherent to the principles of our democracy."[111] The Cosmopolitan Symphony Society was a success, playing a classical repertoire as well as new compositions by Black composers. The *New York Times* called the orchestra a "gifted group," and the Cosmopolitan Symphony Society continued to play until Lee went abroad on a Fulbright scholarship in 1952.[112] Both Still and Lee were working in a field that had been aggressively claimed by the White elite, but they were both able to forge careers in classical music and create their own opportunities within the field.

Integration in historically White ballet companies occurred at a similarly incremental rate during this time. Janet Collins, who became the first African American principal dancer at the Metropolitan Opera in 1951, studied with a private dance teacher as a child in 1930s Los Angeles, as local dance studios would not accept a Black student.[113] The Ballet Russe de Monte Carlo rejected Raven Wilkinson multiple times due to racism, until she finally became the company's first African American dancer in 1955. Wilkinson encountered much overt discrimination during her time with the company, as it frequently toured the segregated South. She was told to wear makeup to make her already light skin look whiter and had multiple encounters with the KKK, causing company managers to sometimes keep her from performing in order to ensure her safety.[114] Wilkinson said in a 2014 *Pointe Magazine* interview:

> I didn't want to put the company in danger, but I also never wanted to deny what I was. . . . Some of the other dancers suggested that I say I was Spanish. But that's like telling the world there's something wrong with what you are.

Despite these dangers, Wilkinson stayed with the company for six years, followed by long stints with the Dutch National Ballet and New York City Opera.[115]

Exploring Caribbean and African Roots Through Dance: Katherine Dunham and Pearl Primus

African American dancers were also exploring the dance traditions of their own ancestry in this era. Katherine Dunham and Pearl Primus were both Black dancers, choreographers, teachers, activists, and anthropologists. In 1935, with a grant from the Julius Rosenwald Fund, Dunham embarked on a trip to the Caribbean to study the dance traditions of Jamaica, Martinique, Trinidad, and Haiti. The research she brought back informed the dances she staged for the Negro unit of the Federal Theatre Project's Chicago branch, of which she became the director in 1938, as well as her choreography for Broadway, film, and her own dance company.[116] Born in Trinidad and raised in New York City, Primus was heavily influenced by the modern dance movement,[117] and became a teacher and choreographer with the New Dance Group. She incorporated heavily researched African dance traditions into work that toured nationally and appeared on Broadway, and received a Rosenwald grant to study dance in Africa.[118] Both women regularly incorporated issues of civil rights and social protest into their dances; gave educational, creative, and financial opportunities to Black dancers; served to bring elements of Caribbean and African dance to wide audiences; and worked to demonstrate the high artistry of traditions that both Black and White critics had labeled "primitive" or "folk."[119] By building their own institutions, Dunham and Primus were able to build careers that were not dependent on commercial success and that enabled them to employ other Black theater artists in meaningful work.

Black Drama on Broadway: A Raisin in the Sun

The era closed with the 1959 production of Lorraine Hansberry's *A Raisin in the Sun*, which marked the first appearance of both a Black female playwright and a Black director, Lloyd Richards, on Broadway.[120] *A Raisin in the Sun* received high praise from a wide variety of audiences and critics, both Black and White.[121] James Baldwin notes the play's ability to draw in Black audiences: "I had never in my life seen so many black people in the theater. . . . Black people ignored the theater because the theater had always ignored them."[122] Hansberry died of cancer six years after the play's opening at age 34,[123] but the play's success inspired countless Black theater artists that followed and helped usher in the Black Arts Movement of the 1960s and 1970s.[124]

Race and the Nonprofit Performing Arts Movement: 1960–1985

The mid-twentieth century brought the height of the civil rights movement, with national protests opposing racial segregation, voter suppression, housing discrimination, hiring discrimination, and other injustices. Dr. Martin Luther King, Jr. delivered his "I Have A Dream" speech at the March on Washington for Jobs and Freedom in 1963, and the following two years saw the passage of the Civil Rights Act and the Voting Rights Act.[125] The era also saw the creation of the U.S. federal funding agency, the National Endowment for the Arts (NEA).[126] The NEA's founding in 1965 coincided with President Johnson's larger Great Society program, and arts funding was available under the auspices of national progress.[127] The NEA housed Expansion Arts, a program that for 25 years[128] funded organizations led by People of Color. At its height, Expansion Arts had a budget of $8 million, which it stretched to fund more than 600 arts groups a year.[129] Philip Kennicott of the *Washington Post* writes, "If you want to understand Johnson's cultural agenda, you have to see [the NEA] not as an appendage but integrally related to the War on Poverty and the Civil Rights Act of 1964."[130]

Many nonprofit organizations led by People of Color formed during this time. Between 1961 and 1982, over 600 African American theaters were founded nationwide,[131] many spurred by the Black Arts Movement. Echoing Du Bois's 1920s treatise outlining the need for Black theater that speaks to members of its own community, Black activist Larry Neal articulated the movement's aims in his 1968 essay "The Black Arts Movement," writing:

> Black Art is the aesthetic and spiritual sister of the Black Power concept. As such, it envisions an art that speaks directly to the needs and aspirations of Black America.[132]

Activism and Theatrical Experimentation: The Black Arts Movement and BARTS

Playwright and poet Amiri Baraka (formerly known as LeRoi Jones) was arguably the most prominent theater artist of the movement, and his Black Arts Repertory Theatre and School (BARTS) the most revolutionary company, both in terms of its politics and in its experimentation with theatrical forms. Founded in Harlem in 1965, BARTS produced several of Baraka's plays as well as poetry readings and concerts. The company had a policy of not allowing White people in the building and produced work that at times called for extreme action,[133] with Baraka himself writing in the essay "The Revolutionary Theatre":

> White men will cower before this theatre because it hates them. Because they have been trained to hate. The Revolutionary Theatre must hate them for hating. For presuming with their technology to deny the supremacy of the Spirit.[134]

The company's confrontational practices soon upset its major funder, the community organization Harlem Youth Opportunities Unlimited (HARYOU), causing HARYOU to cancel its support.[135] Larry Neal blamed the fallout on HARYOU's "fearing Black creativity," writing that despite the loss of money, BARTS "proved that the community could be served by a valid and dynamic art."[136] James V. Hatch offers a similar explanation for backlash against BARTS, writing:

> In 1926, W. E. B. Du Bois supervised the formation of the Krigwas [sic], a theatre that was to produce plays *about* Negros, *by* Negroes, *for* Negros, and *near* Negros. The white mass media did not exploit it, and white America remained unthreatened by a separatist art movement. In 1965, LeRoi Jones demanded a theater *about* black people, *with* black people, *for* black people, and *only* black people. This time Caucasian fears rose righteously to denounce "reverse racism."[137]

Regardless of whether BARTS's politics justified HARYOU's decision, BARTS could not make up the funding loss and folded soon after.[138] Despite BARTS's short life, it remained extremely influential in the Black Arts Movement, for both its unwavering commitment to Black nationalism and its rejection of naturalistic theater conventions. After BARTS, Baraka returned to his hometown of Newark, New Jersey, where he founded the theater and community center Spirit House and helped elect Ken Gibson, the city's first Black mayor, in 1970. Though controversial, Baraka remained a prolific artist and activist until his death in 2014,[139] with Hatch writing in a 1974 introduction to Baraka's play *The Slave*, "The metamorphosis of this poet has paralleled the growing consciousness of Afro-America."[140]

Artistic Excellence, Community Engagement, and the Struggle for Funding

Less militant than BARTS but no less politically engaged were the Negro Ensemble Company (NEC), founded by Douglas Turner Ward with a $1.2 million Ford Foundation grant in 1968,[141] and the New Federal Theatre (NFT), founded by Woodie King, Jr. in 1970.[142] Both companies became well known for producing and touring new work by Black playwrights, and launched the careers of many well-known Black artists. During this era, NEC plays received over 40 major theater awards, including a Pulitzer Prize for Drama in 1982 for Charles Fuller's *A Soldier's Play*.[143] The NFT opened over 280 productions between 1970 and 2011, including Ntozake Shange's *for colored girls who have considered suicide/when the rainbow is enuf*[144] and Ron Milner's *Checkmates* on Broadway, starring Denzel Washington and Ruby Dee.[145]

Both companies have survived for far longer than almost any other Black theater company before or since. Still, neither company ever received the kind of foundation support that White nonprofit theaters of the same era were able to secure. The year after *A Soldier's Play* won the Pulitzer Prize, the company lost $50,000 in grant money. In the 1985–1986 season, NFT's funding was cut by $70,000.[146] As of this writing, however, both companies continue to find the means to produce in New York,[147] with NEC recently celebrating its fiftieth anniversary season[148] and NFT working with Castillo Theatre, a program of the arts education and community building nonprofit organization The All Stars Project, as a producing partner since 2007.[149]

East West Players: An Incubator for Asian American and Asian Pacific Theater Makers

People of Color were forming performing arts organizations outside of New York as well during this era. In 1965, the East West Players was founded in Los Angeles.[150] Established by a group of actors who were hungry for roles beyond Asian stereotypes, the company initially served as a showcase for Asian American actors to demonstrate their talents and range to producers. Originally under the artistic direction of the Japanese American stage and film actor Makoto (Mako) Iwamatsu, the company also offered actor training workshops and became an incubator for Asian American playwrights.[151] One such playwright was David Henry Hwang, who in 1988, with his play *M. Butterfly*, became the first Asian American playwright on Broadway.[152]

East West Players currently serves over 10,000 people a year, and the company continues to offer a platform for nuanced representations of the Asian Pacific American experience.[153] Ironically, the company was only able to survive and grow in its early years because Iwamatsu financially supported the organization with money he made playing Asian stereotypes in movies. Lee writes:

> He did not hesitate to use his own money to pay the company's bills. . . . More than once Mako used the money he earned by playing stereotypical roles in Hollywood films to produce Asian American plays that criticized the very same stereotypes.[154]

While Iwamatsu did participate in the propagation of Asian stereotypes in Hollywood, he and his colleagues were able to use those stereotypes as a means to fund their company and build a community that would then work to fight those stereotypes.

Grassroots Political Activism on Broadway: El Teatro Campesino

Also founded in California in 1965, Luis Valdez's El Teatro Campesino created political theater that advocated for California farmworkers and spoke to the Chicana/o experience. Valdez had spent time with both the San Francisco Mime Troupe and union organizer Cesar Chavez,[155] and collaborated with company members to create *actos*, or short sketches, designed to be performed in union halls or on the beds of pickup trucks, promoting the farmworkers' cause.[156] Valdez routinely employed a technique in his work that Brian Eugenio Herrera refers to as "executing the stereotype," where the playwright "enact[s] the stereotype in order to eviscerate and entomb it—which rehearses a core theatrical vocabulary to guide artists in their confrontation with received stereotypes."[157]

The company toured its ensemble-driven work throughout the 1970s, and in 1977, Valdez received a Rockefeller Foundation Grant to develop the play *Zoot Suit* for the Mark Taper Forum. The play was a huge success and went on to become the first play by a Latinx writer to appear on Broadway.[158] Though the play was written for a Predominantly White

Organization, Jorge Huerta observes that *Zoot Suit* is in fact not so different from the activist work the company created as a group. He writes,

> Although [Zoot Suit] has been attributed to Luis Valdez, it demonstrates the work of the collective as well. That magnificent play with music combines elements of the *acto* . . . with Brechtian and Living Newspaper techniques to dramatize a Chicano family in crisis.[159]

As of this writing, El Teatro Campesino remains active in a variety of capacities, producing regularly and working directly with communities.[160] On the occasion of the company's 50th anniversary, Valdez said, "If the last 50 years have taught us anything, it is that theater is a creator of community, and that community is the creator of theater."[161]

Indigenous Performance: Spiderwoman Theater

One additional representative theater group created by artists of Color during this time is Spiderwoman Theater, a company founded by Muriel Miguel in 1975[162] that "present[s] exceptional theatre performance and [offers] theater training and education rooted in an urban Indigenous performance practice." Born in Brooklyn and a member of the Kuna and Rappahannock Nations, Miguel formed the company with her sisters Lisa Mayo and Gloria Miguel. The company's work "bridges the traditional cultural art forms of storytelling, dance, and music and the practice of contemporary Western theater," and often engages with the intersection of misogyny, racism, and classism.[163] Their first piece, *Women in Violence*,[164] focused on the sexism that women, particularly Indigenous women, encountered in the political movements of the 1970s. "[Muriel] was angry as hell because when it came down to really negotiating and talking with the powers that be, no women were allowed in the room," Mayo said in a 1995 interview.[165] *Women in Violence* debuted in New York in 1976, and with a recommendation from El Teatro Campesino's Valdez, toured to Le Festival Mondial du Théâtre in Nancy, France.[166] Over 40 years later, the company continues to create and tour new work,[167] and to mentor young people. In 2010, the group received a Lifetime Achievement Award from Women's Caucus for Art.[168] "Out there, the world said 'No, you can't,'" Muriel Miguel said in an interview for the Theatre Communications Group Legacy Leaders of Color Video Project, continuing, "And we said, 'Oh, yes we can.'"[169]

Identity and Inclusivity in Dance:
Alvin Ailey American Dance Theater and Dance Theatre of Harlem

In the dance world, Alvin Ailey American Dance Theater (Ailey) and Dance Theatre of Harlem (DTH) became homes for African American dancers. Founded in 1958, Ailey's company would become a pioneer in modern dance, presenting new and established works with an emphasis on showcasing Black dancers and speaking to sociopolitical issues of the Black Diaspora. Dance training was equally important to Ailey's vision, and he established an expansive school as well. Ailey sought to emphasize the universality of the Black experience in his work, and integrated his company in 1963, a move for which he was criticized by the more militant wing of the civil rights movement.[170]

Arthur Mitchell approached the historically White ballet world with a similar philosophy, founding Dance Theatre of Harlem with Karel Shook in 1969. New York City Ballet's first Black male principal dancer,[171] Mitchell created a company that both produces world-renowned ballet performances and houses a prestigious training school. Like Ailey, Mitchell built a multiethnic company that promotes Black artists and Black issues while appealing to as large and diverse an audience as possible. Waldo E. Martin writes,

> Both institutions vividly illustrate a multicultural and hybrid view of postwar America from the vantage point of black America. . . . The operative black cultural politics in both of these cases is integrationist, inclusive, and expansive—indeed, in an important sense, global, yet rooted in blackness.[172]

Both companies have seen tremendous growth since their founding and continue to be successful. Martin notes how crucial long-term individual giving has been to both companies, and how having White donors has not seemed to change the companies' values. "It is clear that significant backing from white-identified sources has not diminished the Ailey's and DTH's commitment to African-American dance and African-American dancers," he writes, adding, "Nor has it diminished the stature of both institutions as emblematic of modern African-American concert dance."[173] Martin does, however, acknowledge that, while DTH is certainly successful, Ailey is still larger and better funded. He attributes this to biases that still exist concerning ballet and Black bodies. "Classical ballet remains a very Eurocentric world, far more so than modern dance," he writes, adding that the "physical appearance of ballerinas still reflects highly influential Eurocentric notions of female beauty."[174] Even so, DTH has fundamentally changed the ballet landscape by nurturing and employing Black dancers in the face of a predominately White ballet world.

BARTS, The Negro Ensemble Company, New Federal Theatre, East West Players, El Teatro Campesino, Spiderwoman Theater, Alvin Ailey American Dance Theater, and Dance Theatre of Harlem are just a few examples of organizations led by People of Color to come out of this period, although there are many more that continue to thrive, or like

BARTS, were short-lived but influential. Government and private foundation funding proved instrumental in the shaping of many of these institutions, however, controversy and debate around which organizations receive funding, and how much, would continue into the late twentieth and early twenty-first centuries.

Colorblind and Color Conscious Representation: 1985-Present

While the civil rights movement of the mid-twentieth century won huge gains for African Americans and other marginalized groups, systemic racism remains to this day entrenched in American culture in myriad forms. The 1980s and 1990s saw increased calls for Predominantly White Organizations to be more inclusive in casting and other hiring. A four-year study released in 1986 by Actors' Equity Association found that over 90% of professional American theater productions were staged with all-White casts. In response to those findings, theater artists Clinton Turner Davis, Joanna Merlin, and Harry Newman formed the Non-Traditional Casting Project (NTCP),[175] with a mission to "[promote] inclusive hiring practices and standards, diversity in leadership and balanced portrayals of people of color and with disabilities."[176]

Inclusive and Exclusionary Casting

Seeing itself as both an advocacy group and a resource to help theater makers enact more inclusive hiring practices, the NTCP co-produced the First National Symposium on Non-Traditional Casting with Actors' Equity in New York that same year,[177] identifying non-traditional casting as "the casting of ethnic, female or disabled actors in roles where race, ethnicity, gender or physical capability are not necessary to the characters' or play's development."[178] The NTCP also advocated for more representation backstage and in administrative roles, as Brandi Wilkins Catanese writes:

> The NTCP recognizes American theater as a microculture reflective of larger social practices that produce and sustain racial hierarchies. The organization's polyvalent mission reflects its awareness that true cultural diversity cannot be localized: artistic choices must be complemented by business practices, the distribution of authority, and other types of institutional reform.[179]

The Non-Traditional Casting Project saw the lack of opportunity for artists of Color onstage as indicative of a larger pattern of exclusionary hiring practices that pervaded all areas of the performing arts.

The NTCP promoted a variety of approaches to non-traditional casting, including "colorblind casting," or "blind casting," when "all actors are cast without regard to their race, ethnicity, gender or physical capability."[180] While few arts leaders publicly voiced resistance to the NTCP's push for more inclusive casting, translating talk into action proved extremely difficult, with NTCP co-founder and playwright Harry Newman writing in 1989:

> As [theater professionals] realize that . . . they would have to change and expand the way they have been working, that more than talk is required, hesitations are often voiced. It is still considered a great idea—for everyone else.[181]

Seventeen hundred projects had used the NTCP as a casting resource by 1997,[182] though this was still only a small dent in the problem of underrepresentation in the American theater. NTCP co-founder and director Clinton Turner Davis wrote in a 1997 open letter to the American theater community:

At some point we have to stop talking. . . . Isn't it action that we have come to accept as the driving force of good theater—*action*, not talk? Why has it taken so long for these so-called artistic leaders to identify and implement the actions they should take?[183]

A Renewed Call for Funding

At the same time, foundations and arts agencies began to divert funding from organizations led by People of Color to Predominantly White Organizations, funding their diversity initiatives, including "colorblind casting." "The nineties found financial support shifted away from ethno-specific arts programs in favor of funding the agglutinated Other . . . the multi-cultural experience," writes Paul Carter Harrison.[184] In one example, Arena Stage, a Predominantly White Organization in Washington, D.C., received $1 million from the NEA, $200,000 from the Ford Foundation, and $100,000 from the Myer Foundation to fund the theater's Cultural Diversity Program in the 1990s.[185]

African American playwright August Wilson famously linked the issues of nonprofit funding inequity and colorblind casting in his landmark essay, "The Ground on Which I Stand," originally given as a keynote speech at the 1996 Theatre Communications Group Conference. In the speech, Wilson admonishes colorblind casting as a tool for propagating the universality of White stories, and draws on some of the same ideas put forth by Bob Cole in the late nineteenth century, W. E. B. Du Bois in the 1920s, and Larry Neal and the Black Arts Movement in the 1960s and 1970s, stressing the need for Black theaters that speak to and about Black communities. Wilson writes: "Black theatre doesn't share in the economics that would allow it to support its artists. . . . We do not need colorblind casting; we need theatres. We need theatres to develop our playwrights."[186]

From Colorblind to Color Conscious

Other tactics promoted by the NTCP besides "colorblind casting" included "cross-cultural casting," when "the entire world of a play is translated to a different cultural setting," and "conceptual casting," when "an ethnic, female or disabled actor is cast in a role to give a play greater resonance."[187] While the terms "non-traditional casting" and "colorblind casting" have often been used interchangeably, "colorblind casting" was the only one of the NTCP's suggested strategies that overlooked an actor's race within the context of the character or the production's larger theme or story.[188] In contrast, "cross-cultural casting" and "conceptual casting" take a "color conscious" approach, acknowledging racial difference and the history of injustice that difference represents. Because of this distinction, "color conscious" is the preferred type of casting approach as of this writing. Jessica Gelt writes in a 2017 *Los Angeles Times* article that the

> shift from "colorblind" to "color-conscious" may be attributed partly to the growing diversity of stories being produced. . . . In eras past, when the vast majority of tales unfolding onstage were written by white playwrights about white characters, it took colorblind casting for an actor of color to be seen.[189]

Catanese notes that "colorblind casting" does little to put the stories of marginalized people on stage, writing, "An uncritical deployment of colorblind casting invites the question of whether race is truly irrelevant in American performance practices, or if the rhetoric of color blindness only diminishes the value of nonwhite cultures, while leaving whiteness intact."[190]

George C. Wolfe and Inclusion at The Public Theater

As producer of New York's Public Theater (The Public) from 1993 through 2004,[191] African American director and playwright George C. Wolfe addressed issues of inclusivity at the Predominantly White Organization, including casting, on multiple fronts. The Public's founder Joseph Papp had already begun various inclusion initiatives, including a Shakespeare repertory ensemble made up entirely of actors of Color in 1979.[192] Building on Papp's work, Wolfe engaged a diverse group of playwrights,[193] including African American Suzan-Lori Parks, whose play *Topdog/Underdog* premiered at The Public and later transferred to Broadway and won the Pulitzer Prize.[194] Wolfe wrote in a 1995 NTCP newsletter, "I hate the word diversity. . . . The need to come up with a term to express the inclusion of people is based on the absurd fact that in America, European culture is held up as the only true legitimate culture."[195] Wolfe also hired African American marketing professional

Donna Walker-Kuhne. Kuhne served as The Public's director of marketing and audience development from 1993 through 2002 and started a range of audience development initiatives to bring multicultural communities to The Public. These included distributing free tickets to Shakespeare in the Park in all five boroughs;[196] opening The Public up for events from numerous multicultural arts organizations including the Nuyorican Poets Café, Asian American Writers' Workshop, and American Indian Community House;[197] and public school outreach, which enabled over 8,000 students to attend performances at the theater.[198] By the time Wolfe left The Public, he had produced many critically acclaimed hits, ensured the theater's post-Joseph Papp stability, and taken strides in making the theater a more accessible institution.

Identity and Intersectionality: Yellow Face and Teenage Dick

Conversations around representation have continued into the twenty-first century. *M. Butterfly* playwright David Henry Hwang's *Yellow Face* premiered at Center Theatre Group/Mark Taper Forum in Los Angeles in 2007, in association with East West Players and The Public Theater. A satire with a fictionalized version of Hwang himself as the protagonist, *Yellow Face* explores issues of race, identity, and authenticity, both within and outside of the theater industry. Esther Kim Lee connects the play's examination of performed identity to the roles that Hwang has been compelled to perform in real life. She writes:

> Hwang has been tapped to speak on behalf of Asian American theatre. . . . [He] found his unofficial role as Asian American spokesperson uncomfortable. He also recognized the irony of being pigeonholed and labelled as "an Asian American playwright" while having written plays . . . questioning that very label.[199]

In 2018, Ma-Yi Theater Company, a theater whose mission is to "develop and produce new and innovative plays by Asian American writers,"[200] forged an intersectional collaboration through their production of Michael Lew's play *Teenage Dick*. The play, which is a reimagining of Shakespeare's *Richard III* where Richard is a contemporary high school student with cerebral palsy, was commissioned by The Apothetae, a company "dedicated to the production of works that explore and illuminate the 'Disabled Experience,'"[201] and presented by The Public Theater.[202] "[We] found that the advocacy work that Gregg does on behalf of the disabled community dovetails well with what I'm trying to do for the Asian-American community,"[203] Lew said of Apothetae artistic director Gregg Mozgala, who also played Richard in the premiere.[204] Lew further highlights his intentions regarding intersectional representation in an author's note in the script, writing,

> Cast disabled actors for Richard and Buck [a character who uses a wheelchair]. They exist and they're out there. Also cast diverse actors. This includes both racial as well as gender diversity; depending on the actors cast, you may adjust pronouns accordingly.[205]

Both *Yellow Face* and *Teenage Dick* work to expand hegemonic definitions of an Asian American play. *Yellow Face* does this by confronting the "pigeonholing" that Hwang experienced head on. *Teenage Dick* defies pigeonholing all together, as Lew, an Asian American playwright, centers his play on a disabled experience, as opposed to an Asian or Asian American experience. Both of these works refute stereotypical notions about who an Asian American playwright should be or what they should write about. The fact that East West Players and Ma-Yi Theater Company were able to collaborate with Predominantly White Organizations on the premieres for *Yellow Face* and *Teenage Dick*, respectively, suggests the potential and capacity for Predominantly White Organizations to put stories by People of Color on their stages. It also underlies the crucial role that organizations led by People of Color play in cultivating artists of Color, developing work, and forging partnerships that are truly all inclusive.

Conclusion

A cursory knowledge of the history of racial and ethnic diversity in the U.S. performing arts workforce demonstrates that many of the same injustices, debates, and regressions that we see today, as well as acts of resistance and expressions of autonomy, have occurred before. The struggles that performing arts professionals of Color currently face have pervaded the field since the origins of our country, and the call for representation and inclusivity can be seen time and time again, from Bob Cole in the 1890s to W. E. B. Du Bois in the 1920s to Amiri Baraka in the 1960s to August Wilson in the 1990s. Whether the arts leaders of today will take the necessary action to create a performing arts landscape that truly offers equal opportunity and representation remains to be seen, but understanding the history that brought us to this moment is a crucial first step.

This chapter has only covered the tiniest fraction of that history, leaving countless stories of injustice and resistance untold. Histories of marginalized people in the performing arts remain relegated to the margins of both U.S. performing arts history and American history in general. The work of historians Errol G. Hill, James V. Hatch, Esther Kim Lee, and Jorge Huerta, to name just a few, brings these stories to the forefront and decenters Whiteness in performing arts history narratives. It is imperative that historians and theater artists continue to tell and share these stories and compile a more complete history of racial and ethnic access, diversity, equity, and inclusion in the performing arts, so that we can better comprehend the past and, in so doing, better understand the present. Through the continued writing, publishing, and teaching of the performing arts histories of historically marginalized people, we can finally start to build a historical narrative that is truly inclusive of all Americans.

Notes

Many thanks and much appreciation to Martine Kei Green-Rogers, Brian Eugenio Herrera, Stefanie A. Jones, Sara Morgulis, Brisa Areli Muñoz, and Dan Venning. I am extremely grateful for the generous feedback, guidance, and support you've offered during the writing of this chapter.

1. Jennifer Stahl, "Why Philadelphia Was an Early Hub for Black Ballerinas," *Dance Magazine* (October 23, 2017), www.dancemagazine.com/philadelphia-blacks-in-ballet-2498575619.html?share_id=2958281.
2. In discussing the African Diaspora, the Museum of the African Diaspora refers to "the migrations of Africans to the New World via the Transatlantic Slave Trade, and the contemporary [migration] that has happened since." "About Us," *Museum of the African Diaspora*, www.moadsf.org/about-us/our-mission.
3. Eric Herschthal, "What We Get Wrong About the Roots of Slavery in America," *Washington Post* (February 19, 2019). While the first known instance of African people being brought to an English colony in the present-day U.S. occurred in Virginia in 1619, Herschthal notes that the prominence that event is often given in historical narratives oversimplifies the story of slavery, "suggest[ing] a certain timelessness to anti-black prejudice, when in fact racism developed over time, and was as much a consequence of slavery as it was a cause of it."
4. Aliya Semper Ewing, "Last Known U.S. Slave Ship, the Clotilda, Said to Have Been Discovered in Alabama," *The Root* (May 25, 2019), www.theroot.com/last-known-u-s-slave-ship-the-clotilda-said-to-have-1835026448. Slavers continued to import kidnapped Africans into the U.S. even after the practice was banned. The last known slave ship, the Clotilda, transported 110 kidnapped Africans to the U.S. in 1860.
5. Errol G. Hill and James V. Hatch, *A History of African American Theatre* (New York, NY: Cambridge University Press, 2010), 2, 8.
6. James Baldwin, "On Being White . . . and Other Lies," in *The Cross of Redemption: Uncollected Writings*, ed. Randall Kenan (New York, NY: Vintage Books, 2010), 167.
7. Toni Morrison, *Playing in the Dark: Whiteness in the Literary Imagination* (Cambridge, MA: Harvard University Press, 1992), 38.
8. Jeffrey H. Richards, *Drama, Theatre, and Identity in the American New Republic* (Cambridge: Cambridge University Press, 2005), 217.
9. James Moy, *Marginal Sights: Staging Chinese in America* (Iowa City, IA: University of Iowa Press, 1993), 9.
10. Joyce Flynn, "Academics on the Trail of the Stage 'Indian': A Review Essay," *Studies in American Indian Literatures* 11, no. 1 (1987): 1–2, 11.
11. Moy, *Marginal Sights*, 9.

12. Richards, *Drama, Theatre, and Identity*, 218.
13. Flynn, "Academics on the Trail," 1–2, 11.
14. Jonathan Dewberry, "The African Grove Theatre and Company," *Black American Literature Forum* 16, no. 4 (1982): 128.
15. Marvin McAllister, *White People Do Not Know How to Behave at Entertainments Designed for Ladies and Gentlemen of Colour* (Chapel Hill, NC: University of North Carolina Press, 2003), 1.
16. Shane White, *Stories of Freedom in Black New York* (Cambridge, MA: Harvard University Press, 2002), 72, 86–87.
17. McAllister, *White People Do Not Know*, 9.
18. White, *Stories of Freedom*, 93–94, 124.
19. Eric Lott, *Love and Theft: Blackface Minstrelsy and the American Working Class* (New York, NY: Oxford University Press, 1993, 2013), 83–84.
20. Sterling A. Brown, "Negro Character as Seen by White Authors," *The Journal of Negro Education* 2, no. 2 (1933): 188.
21. Eileen Southern, "The Origin and Development of the Black Musical Theater: A Preliminary Report," *Black Music Research Journal* 2 (1982): 5.
22. Lott, *Love and Theft*, 5.
23. Athelia Knight, "He Paved the Way for T. O. B. A," *The Black Perspective in Music* 15, no. 2 (1987): 154.
24. Henry T. Sampson, *Blacks in Blackface: A Sourcebook on Early Black Musical Shows*, 2nd ed. (Lanham, MD: Scarecrow Press, 2014), 2–3.
25. Jacqueline Trescott, "From Church to Stage: Black Opera Company Was the City's First," *Washington Post* (February 24, 2007).
26. Sampson, *Blacks in Blackface*, 50.
27. Daphne Brooks, *Bodies in Dissent* (Durham, NC: Duke University Press, 2006), 220.
28. Nina Sun Eidsheim, "Marian Anderson and 'Sonic Blackness' in American Opera," *American Quarterly* 63, no. 3 (2011): 648.
29. Alex W. Black, "Abolitionism's Resonant Bodies: The Realization of African American Performance," *American Quarterly* 63, no. 3 (2011): 625.
30. John Graziano, "The Early Life and Career of the 'Black Patti': The Odyssey of an African American Singer in the Late Nineteenth Century," *Journal of the American Musicological Society* 53, no. 3 (2000): 565, 587.
31. Black, "Abolitionism's Resonant Bodies," 625.
32. Graziano, "The Early Life and Career," 568–69.
33. Lawrence W. Levine, *Highbrow/Lowbrow: The Emergence of Cultural Hierarchy in America* (Cambridge, MA: Harvard University Press, 1988), 102.
34. "Our Story," *The Metropolitan Opera*, www.metopera.org/about/the-met.
35. "About Carnegie Hall," *Carnegie Hall*, www.carnegiehall.org/About.
36. Keryl E. McCord, "The Challenge of Change," *African American Review* 31, no. 4 (1997): 606.
37. Robin Pogrebin, "It's a Diverse City, But Most Big Museum Boards Are Strikingly White," *New York Times* (August 22, 2017).
38. Nativity pageants traditionally performed at Christmas time in Mexico and Latin America, as well as in Latinx communities in the United States. Emma Halpern, "'La Pastorela': Hope for the Holidays," *American Theatre* (November 29, 2018), www.americantheatre.org.
39. Nicolás Kanellos, *A History of Hispanic Theatre in the United States: Origins to 1940* (Austin, TX: University of Texas Press, 1990), 3–6, 11, 14.
40. Ibid., 16.

41. Esther Kim Lee, *A History of Asian American Theatre* (New York, NY: Cambridge University Press, 2006), 9.
42. John Kuo Wei Tchen, *New York Before Chinatown: Orientalism and the Shaping of American Culture 1776–1882* (Baltimore, MD: The Johns Hopkins University Press, 1999), 86–90, 124.
43. Kat Chow, "As Chinese Exclusion Act Turns 135, Experts Point to Parallels Today," *National Public Radio* (May 5, 2017), www.npr.org/sections/codeswitch/2017/05/05/527091890/the-135-year-bridge-between-the-chinese-exclusion-act-and-a-proposed-travel-ban.
44. Lee, *A History*, 10.
45. "Legacy of Lynching," *Equal Justice Initiative*, www.eji.org/racial-justice/legacy-lynching.
46. "Lynching in America," *Equal Justice Initiative*, https://lynchinginamerica.eji.org/explore.
47. Stewart E. Tolnay and E. M. Beck, "Black Flight: Lethal Violence and the Great Migration, 1900–1930," *Social Science History* 14, no. 3 (1990): 348.
48. Lee, *A History*, 10.
49. David A. Takami, *Divided Destiny: A History of Japanese Americans in Seattle* (Seattle, WA: University of Washington Press, 1998), 28.
50. Douglas Kerr, "David Henry Hwang and the Revenge of Madame Butterfly," in *Asian Voices in English*, eds. Mimi Chan and Roy Harris (Hong Kong: Hong Kong University Press, 1991), 120–21.
51. Lee, *A History*, 13–14.
52. Colin Palmer, "Topics in Black American Philanthropy Since 1785," *Center for the Study of Philanthropy, City University of New York, Curriculum Guide* 3 (Spring 1998): 1.
53. McCord, "The Challenge of Change," 606.
54. Christopher M. Brown and James Earl Davis, "The Historically Black College as Social Contract, Social Capital, and Social Equalizer," *Peabody Journal of Education* 76, no. 1 (2001): 31–33.
55. Hill and Hatch, *A History*, 257–58.
56. Alain Locke, "Steps Toward the Negro Theatre," *The Crisis* 25, no. 2 (December 1922): 67.
57. David Krasner, "The Theatre of Sheppard Randolph Edmonds," *New England Theatre Journal* 16 (2005): 21, 26.
58. Blair Ruble, "Misty Copeland to Dance Swan Lake at DC's Kennedy Center," *The Root* (April 15, 2015), www.theroot.com/misty-copeland-to-dance-swan-lake-at-dc-s-kennedy-cente-1790859344.
59. "Howard University Department of Music," *Howard University*, http://music.coas.howard.edu/mission/index.html.
60. Joseph Gustaitis, *Chicago Transformed: World War I and the Windy City* (Carbondale, IL: Southern Illinois University Press, 2016), 211–12, 223.
61. Harvey G. Cohen, "The Marketing of Duke Ellington: Setting the Strategy for an African American Maestro," *The Journal of African American History* 89, no. 4 (2004): 296–97.
62. Ibid., 297.
63. David Brent Johnson, "History as Symphony: The African-American Experience in Jazz Suites," *National Public Radio* (February 21, 2013), www.npr.org/sections/ablogsupreme/2013/02/21/172619827/history-as-symphony-the-african-american-experience-in-jazz-suites.

64. Lynn Abbott and Doug Seroff, *Ragged But Right: Black Traveling Shows, 'Coon Songs,' and the Dark Pathway to Blues and Jazz* (Jackson, MS: University of Mississippi Press, 2007), 38.
65. Knight, "He Paved the Way," 153, 163–64.
66. Ibid., 172.
67. Henry Lewis Gates, Jr., "The Chitlin Circuit," *New Yorker* (February 3, 1997), 49.
68. Abbott and Seroff, *Ragged but Right*, 81.
69. Thomas Bauman, *The Pekin: The Rise and Fall of Chicago's First Black-Owned Theater* (Urbana, IL: University of Illinois Press, 2014), xiii–xvi.
70. Koritha Mitchell, *Living With Lynching* (Urbana, IL: University of Illinois Press, 2011), 10.
71. Ibid., 2.
72. W. E. B. Du Bois, "Krigwa Players Little Theatre: The Story of a Little Theatre Movement," *The Crisis* 32 (July 1926): 134.
73. Mitchell, *Living With Lynching*, 10.
74. "The Amy Spingarn Prizes in Literature and Art," *The Crisis* 29, no. 1 (November 1924): 24.
75. Ethel Pitts Walker, "Krigwa, a Theatre By, For, and About Black People," *Theatre Journal* 40, no. 3 (1988): 355–56.
76. Cheryl Greenberg, *'Or Does It Explode?' Black Harlem in the Great Depression* (New York, NY: Oxford University Press, 1991), 10.
77. John Edward Hasse, "Impresario Frank Schiffman," in *Ain't Nothing Like the Real Thing: How the Apollo Shaped American Entertainment*, eds. Richard Carlin and Kinshasha Holman Conwill (Washington, DC: National Museum of African American History and Culture Through Smithsonian Books, 2010), 84, 86.
78. Julia L. Foulkes, "Ain't Nothing Like the Real Thing: How the Apollo Shaped American Entertainment" (exhibition and book review), *The Public Historian* 33, no. 3 (2011): 158.
79. "Apollo Theater History," *Apollo Theater*, www.apollotheater.org/about/history.
80. "Apollo Executive Team," *Apollo Theater*, www.apollotheater.org/about/leadership.
81. "The WPA Federal Theatre Project, 1935–1939," *Library of Congress*, www.loc.gov/collections/federal-theatre-project-1935-to-1939/articles-and-essays/wpa-federal-theatre-project.
82. Jo Tanner, "Classical Black Theatre: Federal Theatre's All-Black 'Voodoo Macbeth,'" *American Drama and Theatre* 7 (Winter 1955): 50.
83. Ronald Ross, "The Role of Blacks in the Federal Theatre, 1935–1939," *The Journal of Negro History* 59, no. 1 (1974): 41–42.
84. "Coast to Coast: The Federal Theatre Project, 1935–1939," *Library of Congress*, www.loc.gov/exhibits/federal-theatre-project/final-curtain-legacy.html.
85. U.S. Congress, Special House Committee on Un-American Activities, "Investigation of Un-American Propaganda Activities in the U.S.," Hearings 75th Congress, 3rd Session, (November 22, 1938), 4: 2428.
86. Fannin S. Belcher, "The Place of the Negro in the Evolution of the American Theatre, 1767–1940," (Ph.D. dissertation, Yale University, 1945), 419–20.
87. Ross, "The Role of Blacks," 46–47.
88. Lorraine Brown, "A Story Yet to Be Told: The Federal Theatre Research Project," *The Black Scholar* 10, no. 10 (1979): 72–74.

89. Richard Wright, *American Hunger* (1944; reprinted New York, NY: Harper and Row, 1977), 113.

90. Tanner, "Classical Black Theatre," 52.

91. Hill and Hatch, *A History*, 319–20.

92. Wright, *American Hunger*, 113.

93. Hill and Hatch, *A History*, 316.

94. Robert Francis Mardis, "Federal Theatre in Florida," (Ph.D. dissertation, University of Florida, 1972), 154, 163–65, 168.

95. Kanellos, *A History of Hispanic Theatre*, 156.

96. Mardis, "Federal Theatre in Florida," 190, 192–93.

97. Kanellos, *A History of Hispanic Theatre*, 157–59.

98. Ibid., 159–60.

99. Howard Taubman, "Marian Anderson Wins Ovation in First Opera Role at the 'Met,'" *New York Times* (January 8, 1955).

100. Jess Righthand, "When Marian Anderson Sang at the Lincoln Memorial, Her Voice Stunned the Crowd, and Her Gold-Trimmed Jacket Dazzled," *Smithsonian.com* (April 8, 2014), www.smithsonianmag.com/smithsonian-institution/when-marian-anderson-sang-lincoln-memorial-her-voice-stunned-the-crowds-her-gold-trimmed-jacket-dazzled-180950454.

101. Wallace McClain Cheatham, "African-American Women Singers at the Metropolitan Opera Before Leontyne Price," *The Journal of Negro History* 84, no. 2 (1999): 171–73.

102. Taubman, "Marian Anderson."

103. Ibid.

104. Eidsheim, "Marian Anderson," 663.

105. Cheatham, "African-American Women Singers," 173.

106. NPR Staff, "Marian Anderson's Groundbreaking Met Opera Moment," *National Public Radio* (January 7, 2015), www.npr.org/sections/deceptivecadence/2015/01/07/375440168/marian-andersons-groundbreaking-met-opera-moment.

107. Harold C. Schonberg, "Opera: Two Debuts in 'Il Trovatore;' Franco Corelli and Miss Price," *New York Times* (January 28, 1961).

108. "William Grant Still, 1895–1978," *Library of Congress*, www.loc.gov/item/ihas.200186213.

109. Eileen Southern and William Grant Still, "William Grant Still," *The Black Perspective in Music* 3, no. 2 (1975): 165–76.

110. Carol J. Oja, *Bernstein Meets Broadway: Collaborative Art in a Time of War* (New York, NY: Oxford University Press, 2014), 190–94.

111. Noel Straus, "Everett Lee to Present Mixed Symphony Group," *New York Amsterdam News* (October 25, 1947).

112. Oja, *Bernstein Meets Broadway*, 194–96.

113. Jessie Milligan, "Natural Ballerina," *Chicago Tribune* (October 19, 2000).

114. Lindsey Bever, "Misty Copeland's Mentor: The Courageous Black Ballerina Who Defied Racism," *Washington Post* (July 1, 2015).

115. Margaret Fuhrer, "An Interview With Raven Wilkinson," *Pointe Magazine* (June 2, 2014).

116. The Katherine Dunham Collection at the Library of Congress, https://memory.loc.gov/diglib/ihas/html/dunham/dunham-timeline.html.

117. Anna Kisselgoff, "Pearl Primus Rejoices in the Black Tradition," *New York Times* (June 19, 1988).

118. Jennifer Dunning, "Pearl Primus Is Dead at 74; A Pioneer of Modern Dance," *New York Times* (October 31, 1994).

119. Anna Kisselgoff, "Pearl Primus Rejoices,"; and The Katherine Dunham Collection at the Library of Congress, https://memory.loc.gov/diglib/ihas/html/dunham/dunham-timeline.html.
120. Imani Perry, *Looking for Lorraine: The Radiant and Radical Life of Lorraine Hansberry* (Boston, MA: Beacon Press, 2018), 73, 97.
121. Brooks Atkinson, "A Raisin in the Sun," *New York Times* (March 12, 1959).
122. James Baldwin, "Sweet Lorraine: Introduction," in *To Be Young, Gifted and Black*, ed. Lorraine Hansberry (New York, NY: Vintage Books, 1969), xviii.
123. Ben Keppel, *The Work of Democracy: Ralph Bunche, Kenneth B. Clark, Lorraine Hansberry, and the Cultural Politics of Race* (Cambridge, MA: Harvard University Press, 1995), 22.
124. James Edward Smethurst, "The Black Arts Movement," in *A Companion to African American Literature*, ed. Gene Andrew Jarrett (Oxford: Blackwell Publishing, 2010), 302.
125. "Events," *Civil Rights Digital Library*, http://crdl.usg.edu/events/?Welcome.
126. The National Endowment for the Arts is "the independent federal agency whose funding and support gives Americans the opportunity to participate in the arts, exercise their imaginations, and develop their creative capacities." "About the NEA," *National Endowment for the Arts*, www.arts.gov/about-nea.
127. Philip Kennicott, "The Great Society at 50: Lyndon B. Johnson's Cultural Vision Mirrored His Domestic One," *Washington Post* (May 20, 2014).
128. Hill and Hatch, *A History*, 417.
129. National Endowment for the Arts, "Annual Report 1979," 51–52, 54.
130. Kennicott, "The Great Society at 50."
131. Andrzej Ceynowa, "Black Theatres and Theater Organization in America, 1961–1982: A Research List," *Black American Literature Forum* 17, no. 2 (1983): 84.
132. Larry Neal, "The Black Arts Movement," *The Drama Review: TDR* 12, no. 4 (1968): 29.
133. Daphne S. Reed, "LeRoi Jones: High Priest of the Black Arts Movement," *Educational Theatre Journal* 22, no. 1 (1970): 54, 58.
134. LeRoi Jones (Amiri Baraka), "The Revolutionary Theatre," *Liberator* 5, no. 7 (1965): 4.
135. Reed, "LeRoi Jones," 54.
136. Neal, "The Black Arts Movement," 32.
137. James V. Hatch, ed., and Ted Shine, consultant, *Black Theater, U.S.A.* (New York, NY: Free Press, 1974), 773.
138. Reed, "LeRoi Jones," 54.
139. Star-Ledger Staff, "Amiri Baraka, Legendary Poet Who Never Abandoned Newark, Dead at 79," *Star-Ledger* (January 9, 2014).
140. Hatch and Shine, *Black Theater*, 812.
141. Donald M. Morales, "Do Black Theatre Institutions Translate into Great Drama?" *African American Review* 31, no. 4 (1997): 635.
142. Kalamu Ya Salaam, "Black Theatre-The Way It Is: An Interview With Woodie King, Jr.," *African American Review* 31, no. 4 (1997): 647.
143. "Administrative History," Negro Ensemble Company Records, Schomburg Center for Research in Black Culture, *The New York Public Library*, 13.
144. Marcus Baram, "New Federal Theatre Celebrates 40th Anniversary with Star-Studded Gala," *HuffPost* (May 16, 2011).

145. "Checkmates," *Internet Broadway Database*, www.ibdb.com/broadway-production/checkmates-4515.
146. Hill and Hatch, *A History*, 431.
147. BWW Desk, "New Federal Theatre Present Annual Ntozake Shange Readings Series," (June 1, 2019), www.broadwayworld.com/off-off-broadway/article/New-Federal-Theatre-Presents-Annual-Ntozake-Shange-Readings-Series-20190601; and BWW Desk, "Negro Ensemble Presents 'IMMINENTLY YOURS by Karimah," (May 16, 2019), www.broadwayworld.com/off-off-broadway/article/Negro-Ensemble-Presents-IMMINENTLY-YOURS-by-Karimah-2019051646.
148. "Negro Ensemble Company to Kick Off 50th Anniversary Season With Day of Absence," *BroadwayWorld*, www.broadwayworld.com/off-off-broadway/article/Negro-Ensemble-Company-to-Kick-Off-50th-Anniversary-Season-with-DAY-OF-ABSENCE-20161103.
149. "About Castillo," *Castillo Theatre*, www.castillo.org/about-usa.
150. "About," *East West Players*, www.eastwestplayers.org/about-us.
151. Yuko Kurahashi, *Asian American Culture on Stage: The History of the East West Players (Studies in Asian Americans)* (New York, NY: Routledge, 1999), xix, 16–18, 27.
152. Lee, *A History*, 1.
153. "About," *East West Players*, www.eastwestplayers.org/about-us.
154. Lee, *A History*, 49.
155. Elizabeth C. Ramírez, *Chicanas/Latinas in American Theatre: A History of Performance* (Bloomington, IN: Indiana University Press, 2000), 60.
156. "Our History," *El Teatro Campesino*, http://elteatrocampesino.com/our-history.
157. Brian Eugenio Herrera, *Latin Numbers: Playing Latino in Twentieth-Century U.S. Popular Performance* (Ann Arbor, MI: University of Michigan Press, 2015), 140–41.
158. "Our History," *El Teatro Campesino*.
159. Jorge Huerta, "The Legacy of Luis Valdez and El Teatro Campesino: The First Fifty Years," *HowlRound Theatre Commons* (December 5, 2015), https://howlround.com/legacy-luis-valdez-and-el-teatro-campesino.
160. "Calendar," *El Teatro Campesino*, http://elteatrocampesino.com/calendar.
161. "50th Anniversary," *El Teatro Campesino*, http://elteatrocampesino.com/50th-anniversary.
162. "Timeline," *Spiderwoman Theater*, www.spiderwomantheater.org/timeline.
163. "About Spiderwoman Theater," *Spiderwoman Theater*, www.spiderwomantheater.org/blank-mpvle.
164. "Timeline," *Spiderwoman Theater*.
165. Ann Haugo, "Native Playwrights' Newsletter Interview: Lisa Mayo," in *American Indian Theater in Performance: A Reader*, eds. Hanay Geiogamah and Jaye T. Darby (Los Angeles, CA: University of California Press, 2000), 339.
166. Gaye Jeffers, "Muriel Miguel: Tell Stories That Are Important to You," *Southern Theatre* 60, no. 2 (Spring 2019), 22.
167. Expositor Staff, "Material Witness, Addressing the Searing Issue of Violence Against Indigenous Women at Debaj May 1," *Manitoulin Expositor* (April 29, 2019).
168. "About Spiderwoman Theater," *Spiderwoman Theater*, www.spiderwomantheater.org/blank-mpvle.

169. "Muriel Miguel's #LegacyLeaders Video," *Theatre Communications Group*, www.tcg.org/EDI/EDIInitiative/LegacyLeaders/MurielMiguel.aspx.
170. Jennifer Dunning, "Alvin Ailey, a Leading Figure in Modern Dance, Dies at 58," *New York Times* (December 2, 1989).
171. "Our History," *Dance Theatre of Harlem*, www.dancetheatreofharlem.org/our-history.
172. Waldo E. Martin, *No Coward Soldiers: Black Cultural Politics in Postwar America* (Cambridge, MA; and London: Harvard University Press, 2005), 93–95, 98.
173. Martin, *No Coward Soldiers*, 98.
174. Ibid., 95–96.
175. Ana Deboo, "The Non-Traditional Casting Project Continues into the '90s," *TDR* 34, no. 4 (1990): 188.
176. "Mission & What We Do," *Alliance for Inclusion in the Arts*, http://inclusioninthearts.org/about/mission. The NTCP later changed its name to Alliance for Inclusion in the Arts, and operated under that name until it ceased operations in 2017.
177. Deboo, "The Non-Traditional Casting Project," 188.
178. Clinton Turner Davis and Harry Newman, eds., *Beyond Tradition: Transcripts from the First National Symposium on Non-Traditional Casting* (New York, NY: Non-Traditional Casting Project, 1988), v.
179. Brandi W. Catanese, *The Problem of the Color[blind]: Racial Transgression and the Politics of Black Performance* (Ann Arbor, MI: University of Michigan Press, 2011), 11.
180. Davis and Newman, eds., *Beyond Tradition*, vi.
181. Newman, "Holding Back," 27, 36.
182. Hill and Hatch, *A History*, 461.
183. Clinton Turner Davis, "Non-Traditional Casting (an Open Letter)," *African American Review* 31, no. 4 (1997): 591.
184. Harrison, "The Crisis of Black Theatre Identity," 573.
185. Hill and Hatch, *A History*, 462.
186. August Wilson, "The Ground on Which I Stand," Speech delivered at Princeton University (June 26, 1996), republished in *American Theatre* (June 20, 2016).
187. Davis and Newman, eds., *Beyond Tradition*, vi.
188. Catanese, *The Problem*, 12.
189. Jessica Gelt, "Authenticity in Casting: From 'Colorblind' to 'Color Conscious,' New Rules Are Anything But Black and White," *Los Angeles Times* (July 13, 2017).
190. Catanese, *The Problem*, 34.
191. Robin Pogrebin, "Wolfe Is Leaving Public Theater," *New York Times* (February 12, 2004).
192. Eleanor Blau, "Papp Starts a Shakespearean Repertory Troupe Made Up Entirely of Black and Hispanic Actors," *New York Times* (January 21, 1979).
193. Patrick Pacheco, "Forget Jelly, George Is Jammin," *Los Angeles Times* (November 20, 1994).
194. Adam Hetrick, "Suzan-Lori Parks Named Public Theater Master Writer Chair," *Playbill* (October 27, 2008).
195. George C. Wolfe, *New Traditions* (1995), http://inclusioninthearts.org/projects/archive/contributors/playwrights-on-diversity/george-c-wolfe-1995.
196. "Bio," *Walker International Communications Group*, https://walkercommunicationsgroup.com/bio.
197. Donna Walker-Kuhne, email to author, May 30, 2019.

198. "Bio," *Walker International Communications Group.*
199. Esther Kim Lee, *The Theatre of David Henry Hwang* (London: Blooms-bury Methuen Drama, 2015), 107–9.
200. "About," *Ma-Yi Theater Company*, http://mayitheater.nyc/about.
201. "Home," *The Apothetae*, www.theapothetae.org.
202. "Teenage Dick," *Ma-Yi Theater Company*, http://mayitheater.nyc/onstage/teenagedick.
203. "An Interview with TEENAGE DICK Playwright Mike Lew," *Artists Rep*, www.artistsrep.org/explore/news-center/articles/an-interview-with-teenage-dick-playwright-mike-lew.
204. "Teenage Dick," *Ma-Yi Theater Company.*
205. Mike Lew, *Teenage Dick* (New York, NY: Dramatists Play Service, 2019), 4.

3 Race, Identity, and Social Relations

I might be called Black, I might be called Latino, I might be called Brown, call it whatever you want to, but the thing is, it's other people calling me, it's not because I call myself that way.

Workforce Diversity Study Respondent

Introduction

The Workforce Diversity study respondent's experience of possessing a racial identity that is shaped by "others" is reinforced by the social science literature. Social behaviorist George Herbert Mead maintains that the "self is a reflection of the complete social process."[1] Our racial and ethnic identities are formed in childhood, as young as three years of age. Throughout our lives, we are bombarded with implicit and explicit racialized messages that reinforce our perception of self, and distinguish the groups to which we are socially assigned as well as excluded from joining. We are legally required to racially and ethnically self-identify on the U.S. Census, yet biologically we all belong to a single human species. This chapter explores historical and current race-based practices found in U.S. social, legal, and economic systems, which intentionally exclude and marginalize People of Color and employ the Master Narrative: You are not welcome here.[2] Exclusionary histories that have targeted communities of Color impact the marginalization practices found in the primarily White performing arts sector today. For example, the social construction of tokenism or hiring only one employee of Color is psychologically harmful, inhibiting an employee's ability to be his or her authentic self and achieve opportunities in the historically White nonprofit performing arts sector.

The Social Construction of Race and Identity

One's racial and ethnic identity is socially constructed, determined, and learned through interactions with others. In *What Does It Means to Be White?: Developing White Racial Literacy*, author and educator Robin

DiAngelo, posits that socially constructed identities, although "not inherently true, are agreed upon by society. And once society agrees to this meaning, it becomes real in its consequences for people's lives."[3] According to social identity theorists, "people tend to categorize themselves as similar or different from others based on shared identity-relevant traits, such as race and gender."[4] "Racial identity," according to Ali Michael, co-founder and director of the Race Institute for K-12 Educators, "is about how one feels and understands about being the race that one is within a society that is structured by racism."[5]

Racial Identities Are Formed in Childhood

As young as three years old, a child is socialized or learns from his or her parents, teachers, and peers that race is pivotal to one's definition of self and skin color will influence and effect the ways in which she or he may be treated.[6] Psychologists Derald Wing Sue and David Sue also found that White children between the ages of three and five have already learned to differentiate among people with different skin tones and ascribe positive ethnocentric or superior meanings to their own racial group and negative or inferior meanings to people outside their racial membership group.[7] In their study of multiethnic day care centers, sociologists Debra Van Ausdale and Joe R. Feagin reveal that young children of Color "create their own exclusive play groups, perhaps as a defensive reaction to white exclusion they had felt inside and outside the pre-school setting."[8]

Racial and Ethnic Identities Are Socially Constructed Categories

Racial identities are indeed socially constructed categories based most often on perceived differences in skin color and other physical features by others, and these differences are deemed to be important by some who hold the dominant status in the U.S.[9] As one Workforce Diversity study respondent stated: "I could be considered Afra-Latina, bi-racial, or Black, depending on how other people want to categorize me, but overall as a Person of Color, I know I represent a variety of backgrounds and experiences that uniquely define me."

Ethnic identities are also socially created and reproduced through an environment in which group members feel bound together through common ties that are shared and distinct cultural characteristics such as values, language, nationality, food, definitions of beauty, religion, art, and history.[10] An ethnic group's shared culture, values, and belief systems determine its behaviors and attitudes, and are learned. One's ethnic identity and membership in an ethnic group is transferred through a family's traditions and rituals.[11] Racial and ethnic identities are not separate from each other. ALAANA (African, Latinx, Asian, Arab, and Native

American) communities have a multiplicity of rich cultural ethnic traditions. Those who self-identify as White non-Hispanic group members with European heritage are considered the dominant racial and ethnic group in the United States.[12] They also share a multiplicity of rich cultural ethnic traditions. While ALAANA group members and members of the White non-Hispanic European American group may share similar characteristics such as nationality and religion, these similarities are not salient when it comes to the distribution of power and economic relations among members who are not considered a part of the dominant group.[13] For example, according to the Pew Research Center analysis of data from the U.S. Census Bureau, in 2014, black college-educated adults earned significantly less money than their white counterparts ($82,300 vs. $106,600). In 2013,

> the median net worth of households headed by white [adults] was roughly 13 times that of black household heads ($144,200 for whites compared with $11,200 for blacks).[14]

The reasons for this economic disparity, according to Black respondents, surveyed by the Pew Research Center, are failing schools, racial discrimination, and lack of jobs. Only 36% of White respondents surveyed by the Pew Research Center believed that racial discrimination accounts for the financial disparity between Black and White racial groups.[15]

Seventy percent of the Pew Research study Black respondents and 36% of White respondents do believe that racial discrimination plays a part in the financial disparity between Black and White racial groups.[16] Psychologist Gordon W. Allport, who authored *The Nature of Prejudice*, writes that

> [discrimination is active] and excludes all members of the group in question from certain types of employment, from residential housing, political rights, educational or recreational opportunities. Segregation is an institutionalized form of discrimination, enforced legally or by common custom.[17]

These discriminatory behaviors and practices are grounded in systemic racism or "ideologies, attitudes, and institutions that are created to preserve white advantage and power."[18]

Racial and Ethnic Identification in the United States Census: It's the Law

The mapping of racial distinctions is law of the land in the United States. As far back as 1790, the United States Census, which counts the U.S. population, has identified people according to their racial and ethnic identities: "Through 1950, census-takers commonly determined the race of the people they counted. From 1960 on, Americans could choose their own race."[19] This information along with other demographic information is used by the federal government to determine "the distribution of Congressional seats to states, including legislature districts, and school district assignment areas; where to build new roads and schools, and locate job training centers; and the allocation and distribution of more than $675 billion to local, state, and tribal governments each year for neighborhood improvements, public health, and education."[20]

"Starting in 1997, the U.S. Office of Management and Budget required federal agencies, [including the U.S Census Bureau], to use a minimum of five race categories to collect data on race: White, Black or African American, American Indian or Alaska Native, Asian, and Native Hawaiian or Other Pacific Islander."[21] The 2000 and 2010 U.S. Census Bureau's questionnaires also included a sixth category: "Some Other Race."[22] "The 2010 Census question on race included 15 separate response categories and three areas where respondents could write in detailed information about their race. Seven of the 15 response categories are Asian groups and four are Native Hawaiian and Other Pacific Islander groups."[23] These "race categories," according to the U.S. Census Bureau, "generally reflect a social definition of race recognized in this country and are not an attempt to define race biologically, anthropologically or genetically. In addition, it is recognized that the categories of the race question include race and national origin or sociocultural groups."[24] It is interesting to note that the 2010 U.S. Census White and African American race categories are not linked to various national or sociocultural origins, while the American Indian category requests the name of the tribe and the Asian racial categories are subdivided according to country of origin (e.g., Japanese, Chinese, Filipino, Vietnamese). National Public Radio correspondent Hansi Lo Wang writes:

> For the 2020 census, the Census Bureau is planning to include language so that anyone who identifies as white or black/African-American must share their non-Hispanic origins with the government. As past censuses in recent decades have done, the 2020 census will ask everyone to share their Hispanic/Latino origins.[25]

The U.S. Census doesn't classify the Latino or Hispanic origin category as a race. The *Overview of Race and Hispanic Origin: 2010*, published by the U.S. Census Bureau, defines Hispanic or Latino origin as the "heritage, nationality group, lineage, or country of birth of the person or person's parents or ancestors before their arrival in the United States. People who identify their origin as Hispanic or Latino, or Spanish may be any race."[26] In the U.S. Census, the term Hispanic or Latino is considered an ethnicity, and is linked to "a person of Cuban, Mexican, Puerto Rican,

South or Central American, or other Spanish culture or origin, regardless of race."[27] Although the Hispanic category is not considered a racial category in the U.S. Census, the Pew Research Center's 2015 survey found that 67% of Hispanic adults describe their Hispanic background as part of their racial background."[28] Pew also found in their 2014 National Survey of Latinos that Latino adults also racially and ethnically identified in multidimensional ways: 34% identified as Mixed Race; 25% as Indigenous; 24% as Afro Latino, Afro Columbian, or Afro Mexican.[29]

How Do You Self-Identify?

Reducing one's racial and ethnic identity to a single box, accompanied by a limited amount of space in which to write about one's historically assigned social category in the U.S. Census, can be riddled with emotion and resistance from People of Color who are not comfortable with and affected by the socially constructed categories of race and ethnicity that are imposed upon them. For example, in response to the Workforce Diversity interview study qualitative question, "How do you self-identify with regard to your race and ethnicity?" the qualitative answers of the following three Latinx respondents involved detailed multifaceted explanations that were not limited to "check the box."

> Respondent #1: "'How do I self-identify?' That's a hard question. My family is Puerto Rican on both sides. They've been in New York City on both sides for multiple generations, so we identify as Nuyorican, which is its own ethnic group: Puerto Ricans from New York City are very different from Puerto Ricans from Puerto Rico.
> "The concept of race and ethnicity and diversity is super complicated and loaded. For example, I'm married to a Filipina woman from the States, and her family is from the Philippines and that makes our sons Puerto Rican and Filipino. Potentially, there is also a staggering mix of Spanish and Native American heritage, but we don't really know [our heritage] on the Puerto Rican side. My children are Asian on the Filipino side. We don't know how to answer the Census for any of us."

> Respondent #2: "I'm a Latina. And, you know, that's not a race, [laughs] even though people often list it as one. In the U.S., if you're Latina, you're not White. You know, when I'm in Latin America, I'd be described as 'white-skinned' or 'light-skinned.' And in Latin America, they would call me 'blanca.' These things have different meanings in a way, there. I don't think of myself as 100% European; I know that my ancestors were of multiple races and ethnicities. In the U.S., I think my work gets seen as a 'Latina playwright,' you know? Even though my skin color's white, I don't identify as

White in the U.S., in like Anglo. But skin color, yes, my skin color's white. But culturally and ethnically, I don't identify with White culture in the U.S.; I identify more with Latino cultures because that's my background."

Respondent #3: "I don't like identifications. I don't like labels, and I have been called everything under the sky. Some people say I'm four-in-one, five-in-one, three-in-one. I was raised in a household with people that looked very different, very different races, and that was not a conversation that actually defined my future. In fact, all of them completely contributed to my future and had great hopes for me. What I'm doing on this planet is representing them. I don't define their races because, I mean, this is the way I look. I'm the sum total of all of them, even if they came from three different continents and are three different races. I feel very uncomfortable with all this discussion about [the differences in] skin color and culture."

Three Latinx respondents had very different perceptions of their racial and ethnic identities in contrast to the social categories that are presented on the Census and society in general. The first Workforce Diversity study respondent, while having Puerto Rican heritage knows that the cultural experience he had growing up in the U.S. was different than the one he would have had if he had been raised in Puerto Rico. Furthermore, since the respondent also does not know the entire history of his racial and ethnic background, which may include Native American and Spanish heritage, how do he and his wife, who has Filipina heritage, answer the questions for their multiracial and multiethnic children on the Census? The second Workforce Diversity study respondent experiences racial identity differently, depending upon the cultural context or social norms of the country where the respondent is located. In Latin America, the respondent would be considered "blanca" or "white-skinned"; in the U.S., the respondent is not considered White and is labelled by others as a "Latina playwright." In reality, the respondent recognizes that her ancestors were of multiple races and ethnicities. However, given the cultural context of "being White in America," which we will later discuss, the respondent chooses to identify and is categorized by others as Latina in the United States. The final Workforce Diversity study respondent rejects all racial and ethnic categories or labels altogether and believes that every human is the sum total of all lived experiences.

Regardless of rejecting socially imposed racial and ethnic categorization, the Latinx respondent is still legally obligated to racially and ethnically self-identify in the U.S. Census. And even though the current U.S. Census states that its "race categories" reflect "a social definition of race recognized in this country and are not an attempt to define race biologically, anthropologically, or genetically,"[30] the 1790 U.S. Census's original race categories, "free white males and free white females," and "slaves,"[31] were grounded in scientific racism, paving the way for historical race-based discrimination in an ecosystem of U.S. social, legal, economic, educational, and cultural institutions.

Scientific Racism: Paving the Way for Historical Race-Based Discrimination

Racial and ethnic group divisions serve a purpose in society. Racial and ethnic group classifications are created and exploited by the dominant group to gain and protect their privilege and power.[32] Exploitation theory posits that "race was seized upon as a God-given, not a man-made, category to justify the discrimination practiced."[33] In *Economy and Society*, German sociologist Max Weber wrote that

> race creates a "group" only when it is subjectively perceived as a common trait: This happens when . . . some common experiences of members of the same race are linked to some antagonism against members of an obviously different group. . . . Every highly privileged group develops the myth of its natural, especially its blood, superiority.[34]

The Race Biology Narrative Is Fallacious

One way for race to be "subjectively perceived as a common trait" is by creating and delineating categories of physical appearance such as skin color and then oppressing people with the skin color deemed to be inferior. In *An American Dilemma*, a study of Black and White race relations published in 1944, Swedish economist and sociologist Gunnar Myrdal contends that the

> race doctrine of biological inequality between whites and Negros offered the most convenient solution. . . . A belief the natural inequality . . . is necessary to justify the caste system which succeeded slavery as the social organization of the Negro-white relations.[35]

And for more than 500 years,[36] the fallacious race doctrine of biological inequality continues to be debated, oppressing and excluding People of Color from privilege and power in U.S. society.[37]

Scientific racism was created in the eighteenth century and was rampant throughout the nineteenth and twentieth centuries, the impact of which continues to this day. In *The History of White People*, American historian Nell Irvin Painter gives an impressive and thorough historical account of the scientists who created and fought scientific racism. For example, American anthropologist and physician Samuel George Morton

(1799–1851) measured the cranial capacity of his subjects and concluded that "Caucasians"[38] were the most intellectually superior and "Ethiopians" the most cerebrally inferior. These findings were used to support the enslavement of African Americans in the United States.[39]

Among those who disputed these racist scientific theories were anthropologists Franz Boas, M. F. Ashley Montagu, Ruth Fulton Benedict, and Gene Weltfish. In 1894, German American anthropologist Franz Boas (1858–1942) disputed this scientific racist theory and "questioned the evolutionary view of human races that equated whiteness with development and civilization. [He believed] that environment and culture, rather than race shaped people's bodies and psyches."[40] Further resistance to this racist scientific doctrine was supported by British-American anthropologist M. F. Ashley Montagu (1905–1999) who wrote, *Man's Most Dangerous Myth: The Fallacy of Race*, and warned: "Race is the witchcraft of our time. The means by which we exorcise demons. It is a contemporary myth. Man's most dangerous myth."[41] Additionally, American anthropologists Ruth Fulton Benedict (1887–1948) and Gene Weltfish (1902–1980) who co-authored *The Races of Mankind* state, "The differences did not arise because people were white or black, but because of differences in income, education, cultural advantages, and other opportunities."[42]

"We All Belong to a Single Species"

Despite the scientific evidence forged by anthropologists in the nineteenth and twentieth centuries to combat racist science, there still appears to be a need for today's scientists to prove and confirm that pure races with superior intellectual genes do not exist. Furthermore, "there is no national, religious, linguistic or cultural group or economic class that constitutes a race."[43] In 1996, the American Association of Physical Anthropologists published a statement in the *American Journal of Physical Anthropology* that stated that

> all humans living today belong to a single species, Homo sapiens, and share a common descent. . . . There is great genetic diversity within all human populations. Pure races in the sense of genetically homogeneous populations, do not exist in the human species today, nor is there any evidence that they have ever existed in the past. . . . The human features which have universal biological value for the survival of the species are not known to occur more frequently in one population than in any other. Therefore it is meaningless from the biological point of view to attribute a general inferiority or superiority to this or that race. . . . The genetic capacity for intellectual development is one of the biological traits of our species essential for its

survival. This genetic capacity is known to differ among individuals. The peoples of the world today appear to possess equal biological potential for assimilating any human culture. Racist political doctrines find no foundation in scientific knowledge concerning modern or past human populations.[44]

Historical Race-Based Discrimination in the United States

Nevertheless, racist political doctrines have been used to maintain historical White privilege in the United States. Beginning with its early laws, the 1790 Naturalization Act restricted U.S. citizenship to "any alien being a free white person."[45] This country's founders and leaders were convinced that People of Color were inferior to people of White, English Anglo-Saxon heritage. President Thomas Jefferson, principal author of the Declaration of Independence, who owned more than 250 Black slaves by 1822,[46] wrote this chilling sentence about Indigenous people: "'We would never cease pursuing them with war while one remained on the face of the earth.'"[47] During the nineteenth century, the U.S. government broke treaties with sovereign tribal nations, ended the authority of tribal chiefs, and stole millions of acres of land, destroying the lives of many hundreds of thousands of Native people in the process.[48] Lewis Cass, Secretary of War under President Andrew Jackson, wrote "'The Indians are entitled to the enjoyment of all the rights which do not interfere with obvious designs of Providence, and with the just claims of others.'"[49] In 1838, President Martin Van Buren forcibly removed the Cherokee people from their land and more than 4,000 died in what is now known as the Trail of Tears.[50] Furthermore, The Indian Appropriations Act of 1871, signed into law by President Ulysses Grant, stated: "'No Indian nation or tribe within a territory in the United States. shall be acknowledged or recognized as an independent nation, tribe, or power with whom the United States may contract by treaty.'"[51] Additionally, Native families were forced onto reservations, and Native children were mandated to attend government-funded boarding schools with the intent to strip away their tribal identities, demanding that they learn English. In 1978, the "Indian Child Welfare Act gave Native American parents the legal right to deny their children's placement in off-reservation schools."[52] Reparations from the federal government, according to the Poverty and Race Research Action Council, have taken the form of cash payments, land, and tribal recognition.[53] But despite these reparations, people of Native heritage remain among the most impoverished groups[54] in the United States today.

Along with oppressing Native American and Indigenous people, the United States has historically instituted many other discriminatory race-based practices against many ALAANA communities. For example, the 1882 Chinese Exclusion Act limited Chinese immigrants from coming to the United States and barred those living here from becoming United

States naturalized citizens. In 2012, one hundred and thirty years after the 1882 Chinese Exclusion Act was formally enacted, there was a formal apology from the United States Congress.[55]

Furthermore, during World War II, the United States placed approximately 120,000 individuals of Japanese heritage in internment camps. It is estimated that over two thirds of those interned were Japanese American citizens, many of them losing their belongings, land, and businesses in the process.[56] In 1988, more than 100,000 Japanese American survivors were each paid $20,000 by the federal government.[57]

The Master Narrative: You Are Not Welcome Here

In *A Different Mirror: A History of Multicultural America*, American historian Ronald Takaki maintains that the United States is engaged in a "Master Narrative of American History." The Master Narrative supports the "popular but inaccurate story that our country was settled by European immigrants, and Americans are white. . . . Not to be 'white' is to be designated as the 'Other'—different, inferior, and unassimilable."[58] Here is another example of the Master Narrative at play. During the Great Depression era, it is estimated that up to two million people of Mexican descent between 1929 and 1944 were deported from the United States, the majority of whom were United States citizens or legal residents.[59] While there have been no reparations to date, the state of California issued an apology in 2006, almost eighty years later.[60]

People who self-identify as African American and as members of the African Diaspora have long suffered the effects of the Master Narrative. While in 1868, the Fourteenth Amendment to the U.S. Constitution guaranteed citizenship to "all persons born or naturalized in the United States," and in 1870, the Fifteenth Amendment granted African American men the right to vote,[61] Jim Crow laws passed by Southern states beginning in 1875, began almost one hundred years of deplorable discrimination and segregation of African American individuals in education, employment, housing, freedom of assembly, and voting rights.[62] In 1954, the Supreme Court decision Brown v. Board of Education made segregation in the schools unconstitutional. Furthermore, The Civil Rights Act of 1964, Voting Rights Act of 1965, and Fair Housing Act of 1968 made it illegal to discriminate based on race and other protected categories in public accommodations, employment, voting, sale, rental, and financing of property and housing.[63]

Exclusionary Histories Breed Marginalization Practices in the Performing Arts Sector

The United States' legacy of historical injustice against People of Color is reflected in the performing arts workforce today. For example, in Los

Angeles, which has the second largest Native population in the United States, only 0.4% of the cultural workforce identify as Indigenous.[64] Randy Reinholz, a member of Oklahoma's Choctaw Nation, and co-director with his wife Jean Bruce Scott of Native Voices at the Autry in Los Angeles discusses the reasons for the lack of Indigenous representation the historically White cultural workforce:

> Spiderwoman [Theater], Hanay Geiogamah, Tomson Highway, Bill Yellow Robe were a generation before [us] and they were allowed in the back door of the theatre occasionally. But Native Americans were mostly told, "You can't act because there aren't plays by Native Americans, and you can't write because there are no Native actors." So, there was a prejudice, and a self-fulfilling prophecy by well-resourced theatre institutions, that Native Americans simply weren't part of the discussion or part of the reflection.[65]

Another example of the master cultural narrative lies in the programming of ALAANA artists within primarily White performing arts organizations. Many respondents of Color interviewed for this study point to the race-based programming practice of relegating "ethnic programming," to one month of the year. For example, one African American respondent shared the following:

> Artists [of Color] are put into a category. They say, "If you're Black, we're only going to do your play in February." That's it. And I've heard theaters say, "Well, we already booked so-and-so's play, so that's it. We can't do another one." There's eleven other months. Could we look at those? There's a lack of breadth in realizing that the story of a particular culture is not relegated to a month.
>
> In fact, while I was working at one organization, the Asian American community told me: "Do not do our plays in May. We do not want to be relegated to Asian Pacific American Heritage Month. Please, don't do that." So that's part of the challenge that artists [of Color] have, is just not having enough bandwidth to play with an arts center at different times.

Historically White performing arts organizations also program work they believe specific community members of Color want to see without including the community members in the decision-making process. An East Asian American respondent warns that predominately White performing arts organizations must

> not invest in stereotypes of what you think audiences of Color will go and attend. For example, while a Chinese acrobat group is of Chinese origin, this doesn't guarantee that you will get Chinese Americans

into your theater. Have you asked the Chinese American or Chinese people who are living in your community if this is something they really will go and watch, or have you just made dangerously racist and insulting assumptions about a whole community? Yes, the acrobats are Chinese, but no, that's not the way to sell tickets. Even the best of us can fall prey to prejudices and unconscious bias. It is so important to be conscious of these biases when programming a season, especially with the aim of being more inclusive.

The current Master Narrative about people of Mexican heritage eerily mimics the Great Depression era, and is alive and well in predominately White performing arts organizations that reside in Latinx communities. For example, a Workforce Diversity study respondent who identifies as Latina reported this experience:

> There is a new center that just opened in an area that is largely Hispanic. It's a huge looming white building and it's not welcoming at all. They have all-White volunteers standing at each entrance and it's not welcoming. There's already a wall for the Hispanic communities to enter this brand-new performing arts center.

The African Diaspora and White Social Relations in the Performing Arts

There is great evidence that people who identify as African American and individuals whose background encompasses the "rich cultural heritage of the people of Africa and African descendant cultures all across the globe"[66] and identify as members of the African Diaspora face great discrimination and injustice in the United States and throughout the White-dominated performing arts industry today. According to the Workforce Diversity study respondents who identify as African American and of the African Diaspora, the injustice is generated through a dominant White Eurocentric cultural system of values, beliefs, attitudes, and behaviors constricting the opportunities for engagement and acceptance of African American artists, managers, employees, board members, organizations, and communities.

Structural access barriers such as those found in recruitment and employment, programming, community partnerships, and educational training reinforce these Eurocentric cultural values and are embedded and entrenched in historically White performing arts institutions, limiting choices, access, and mobility among African American community members. The historically White institutional structural barriers that African American and African Diaspora respondents in the Workforce Diversity study experience and observe include limited access to employment and education opportunities through the perpetuation of

White-member homogeneous networks; a resistance to form authentic and equitable community partnerships with ALAANA-led organizations and communities of Color; programming decisions that are based on stereotypes about the types of programs African American and people of the African Diaspora want to attend; and the lack of opportunities to be cast, to direct, and to assume leadership roles in primarily White performing arts organizations. In addition to institutional access barriers, the personal bias of individuals within primarily White performing arts institutions also influences the types of professional roles Black individuals are able achieve and are perpetuated by microaggressions or acts of disrespect that consciously and unconsciously question the authenticity of achievements. All of these access barriers raise serious doubt about whether everyone is invited to fully participate.

Homogeneous Networks Create Limited Access to Education and Employment Opportunities

One African American respondent believes that historically White performing arts organizations favor European culture and that within the European culture there are those who want to keep a closed system, reserving room for those with specific education and particular homogeneous networks. The respondent stated:

> I believe there are so few African Americans in the performing arts because the performing arts, usually, is a European art. And, it is controlled by European education, which perpetuates that culture. Because, most people in America who are in power emigrated from Europe into America, and they carry on that tradition. And, it's very hard for an African American who is really working in this business to gain a foothold because his series of associates are not Europeans. The majority of those people who control power, the leadership and the boards, are not at all interested in African American culture, unless it's a play that's won every award on Broadway or Off-Broadway. Then it would be brought in and defined as safe for their subscribers.

Sociologist Cynthia Fuchs Epstein and her colleagues observe that a group controls employment opportunities by recruiting members like themselves. They maintain homogeneous recruitment networks through self-selection and by making sure that their recruits have similar education and training to accept the requisite behaviors and attitudes associated with their new organizational culture.[67] By maintaining homogeneous networks, primarily White performing arts organizations reserve opportunities for insiders, thereby reducing their anxiety associated with people who are perceived as outsiders, not "safe for subscribers," and therefore not welcome.

Inequitable Community Partnerships

If African American plays or African American artistic programming are not deemed "safe for subscribers," then how does this impact the ways in which historically White organizations include the perspectives of ALAANA-led performing arts organizations and communities of Color within programming decisions? One Workforce Diversity study respondent who identifies as Black Afro Caribbean shared this experience:

> [When they rent] to a Culturally Specific[68] group, they're opening the door, inviting these people in, and then walking out. Even though they're renting this space to a Culturally Specific arts organization, they're not staying for the conversation. They're not trying to figure out how to include them.

The respondent of Black Afro Caribbean heritage believes that predominately White performing arts organizations make little effort to engage ALAANA-led performing arts organizations and communities of Color as legitimate stakeholders who have valid interests and responsibilities for the success of the organization.[69] Weber maintains that if one believes he or she is a legitimate stakeholder, there is the need to justify this favored status through naming others as disadvantaged or not legitimate. This binary view of advantage for White performing arts stakeholders and disadvantage for ALAANA-led performing arts organizations who are not viewed as stakeholders is validated through the dominant norms and traditions of a society that regulates racial and ethnic social norms and traditions.[70] If an ALAANA-led performing arts organization isn't viewed as a legitimate stakeholder, it's defensible to rent rather than to provide a permanent and inclusive home on the primarily White performing arts series.

If a Primarily White Organization wants an authentic and trusting relationship with an ALAANA-led organization, the PWO must do more than simply rent space: That gesture in and of itself does not constitute a trusting relationship because there is no conscious long-term commitment, on the part of the historically White organization, to engage and share power with communities of Color through providing ALAANA-led programming opportunities.

Programming, Casting, and Directing Racial Stereotypes

If staff and board members of a predominately White performing organization don't intentionally engage and share power with ALAANA-led performing arts organizations and communities of Color, programming choices will reflect the absence of ALAANA perspectives. Additionally, without the genuine attempt to know the attendance motivations of the entire community, negative assumptions or stereotypes about culturally diverse communities may be made. In my research on occupational stereotyping, I found that "Stereotyping which involves the labeling in the magnification of one or two attributes out of proportion to others is used by insiders as a mechanism of control to preserve the in-group's majority status [or position] and their privileged allocation of resources, rewards, and power."[71] One Workforce Diversity study respondent who identifies as White worries that the [White] performing arts managers making the programming decisions for the artistic season automatically exclude the local African American community as audience members because "there are stereotypes that certain types of programming are suitable or not suitable for certain types of audiences." This stereotype, made by the dominant members of the historically White organization, is likely based on a stereotype of the African American community without involving the multiple perspectives of the African American community in the decision-making process.

Is the exclusion of African American community members in programming and hiring always a conscious choice by staff and board members of primarily White performing arts organizations? One White respondent, interviewed for the Workforce Diversity study, believes that until an African American cast member spoke candidly, the respondent was unconsciously casting the African American actor in small token stereotypical roles. He admits:

> I've casted him in five or six plays and he came to me last year and said, "I always play a slave, or a butler, or a vigilante. I want to play something else." I hadn't thought of that; my thinking had been "I'm casting him." And he was right. His next casting assignment was as a romantic lead. No one wants to be the token.

Directors of Color are also overlooked in the PWO hiring process, when it comes to interpreting American plays written by White playwrights. One African American respondent posited why: "I probably know more about Eugene O'Neill, more about Tennessee Williams, than any White director working in the American Theater. They aren't going to hire me to do that. They don't want my interpretation of that." And why not hire an African American director to direct a play written by a White American playwright? Did O'Neill or Williams stipulate the racial status of the director? Of course not! Sociologist Robert Merton, wrote that in the insider doctrine, it is perceived that "one must be one to understand one."[72] In other words, if the insider doctrine is applied to this situation where race is salient, only White directors can interpret the intentions of White playwrights. But the "insider doctrine is fallacious," writes Merton, because we do not inhabit just a single status. "Different situations call for different statuses."[73] The Workforce Diversity study respondent above identifies as African American, and is also a director, and a scholar of American theater. The respondent brings all of his inter-related statuses and experiences to the interpretation of the play, and the cast and audience are the richer for it. In other words, the "multiplicity of identity matters."[74]

If primarily White performing arts organizational members truly adhere to the insider doctrine, to what degree are they willing to employ ALAANA artists as actors and directors for roles that are tradition-ally reserved for those who identify and are perceived as White? One Workforce Diversity study respondent who identifies as African Ameri-can believes that these risks are not likely to be taken. The respondent believes the insider doctrine will be maintained in this way:

> No matter how much you fight to get into a White-run, board-con-trolled theater, there are too many impediments. Too many blocks. Too many. If you get past the artistic director, you must deal with the chairman of the board. The chairman of the board and other board members are bringing so much money into the institution, that they conclude, "No, this can't happen. We're not going to take that risk." And then another board member will make this statement, "I like this guy, but he's not qualified." He's never going to say, "That direc-tor has got too many impediments to overcome."

Individual Bias and Microaggressions

Institutional barriers that restrict access to career opportunities are accompanied by individual bias that manifests itself in discriminatory behaviors. A Workforce Diversity study respondent of Color reports hav-ing experienced microaggressions such as overtly being questioned about the quality of the work. Furthermore, if the respondent is included in the racial and ethnic access, diversity, equity, and inclusion conversation, the respondent becomes distrustful of the reason. The distrust is grounded in the ongoing theoretical discussion of racial and ethnic access, diversity, equity, and inclusion that doesn't seem to produce an active resolution that is just. The respondent explains,

> One of the things that I notice in terms of speaking about the racial divide is that people that look like us are always questioned. It doesn't matter how many degrees that I have. It doesn't matter how many orchestras I have conducted. It doesn't matter how many commissions I have done, how many awards I have received. I'm always doubted. People that are in positions of power let you know, or you are not included in certain things. When you are called to be included, then you get suspicious because you know that if you're going to be part of such board, and you look at the composition of

the board, you realize that you are going to become a target on that board. The whole "diversity" thing has never been solved yet. That goes for the workforce, that goes for academia, that goes for the performing arts. For me, it's very tragic that *Hamilton* had to exist, or that *West Side Story* is recreated over and over, or that *Porgy and Bess* is the only opera where many singers of Color sing. In other words, there's something that we're perpetuating. We keep saying that we are going to straighten out this whole thing, but I don't think that I can straighten out the whole thing. I think that this is something that has to be taken care of by everybody as a responsibility.

If everyone in a Primarily White Organization takes responsibility for racial and ethnic access, diversity, equity, and inclusion, every White employee would have to make a commitment to antiracist and multicultural competency training or exposing his or herself to the historical injustices that have been imposed among ALAANA artists, managers, employees, board members, organizations, and communities. Empathy and exposure are essential to understanding how the social construction of race division is created, perpetuated, and justified in society, organizations, and individuals. In deconstructing or dismantling the Master Narrative, primarily White performing art organizations must examine the extent to which their organizational structures and corresponding practices privilege some at the expense of negating others. However, it's difficult to "scrutinize the belief system critically when through the generations, strengthened by tradition and community consensus, a public opinion among whites is formulated which is plainly opportunistic in the interest of the majority group."[75] It's much easier to ignore the inequities and socially construct a narrowly defined vision of diversity in which ALAANA artists, managers, employees, and board members are recruited as "the only one."

The Social Construction of "The Only One"

When an artist, manager, employee, or board member of Color is the "only one" in a historically White organization, he or she may feel the pressure to represent his or her entire race or sometimes other culturally diverse people in meetings, committees, and anything else that corresponds to "diversity work" within a primarily White performing arts organization. This places enormous pressure on the ALAANA staff, board, or community member who can be made to feel as though this extra unpaid work, which often goes unnoticed, is relegated to the token ALAANA member in an organization. Many respondents of Color interviewed for this book have experience being hired as the only Person of Color in the organization. Although there isn't a formal job description that denotes what is expected of a Person of Color when being hired as the "only one," there may be an understanding and an expectation on the part of the employer who is White, and the employee of Color that he or she will assume a role that will have additional responsibilities based on his or her racial identity and what that identity implies within a Primarily White Organization. In being assigned this "only one" role, the respondents of Color question the degree to which they are really wanted as full members of the organization, or even qualified for the formal job that was advertised. One playwright of Color interviewed for this study lamented that being the one Person of Color limits his ability to take risks and make certain artistic choices in his plays. Still other Workforce Diversity study respondents of Color reported that they don't bring their entire selves to work because they don't feel safe to share their ideas or fully express themselves, fearing they will confirm the stereotypes their White counterparts already have about them. Furthermore, it's exhausting to feel as though one is expected to represent and speak on behalf of an entire race of people, while at the same time feeling the responsibility to call out White colleagues who make offensive and insensitive remarks and decisions. Sometimes the pressures are so great that Workforce Diversity study respondents of Color admit they try their best to assimilate and to avoid confrontations based on their "only one" racial status. And while trying to assimilate is one alternative, there are ALAANA employees and board members who see their presence as an opportunity to attack the ignorance that exists and impact change in the organization. What resonates for many Workforce Diversity study respondents of Color is the need to carry the burden of their "only one" racial and ethnic status on behalf of their own communities of Color, who support them and want their voices to be heard and represented. In addition, there is great suspicion that the Predominately White Organization will see this token appointment as the end result of their total commitment to diversifying the organization.

Since the majority of People of Color interviewed for this study experienced the harmful effects of the "only one" status, it's important to recognize that achieving equitable representation of ALAANA artists and managers, in an organization that has been primarily White, fuels empowerment among POC and creates a safe place to be authentic. In the following section, the Workforce Diversity study respondents of Color detail the impact this socially constructed "only one" racial and ethnic status has had on their professional and personal lives.

"Do They Really Want Me Here?"

One Workforce Diversity study respondent of Color stated:

> When you are the only one, you think: "Am I really here because I'm qualified for this job and they want me here, or [was I hired] for

show?" You feel like you have to be on your best behavior, be success-ful in what you do, assimilate yet represent yourself as well as people who look like you. This is a lot of responsibility for one person to bear, and in many ways unfair because you didn't necessarily ask to be that person. This is something that I have experienced many times in my career as an East Asian American artist as well as an arts man-ager. It's a double-edged sword. While it breaks down initial barriers of making your White workforce more diverse, it does isolate the person who is breaking down this barrier. Performing arts organiza-tions that are looking to be more diverse need to strongly reflect on the overall organizational structure and think about whether they are hiring or promoting someone just to fill a quota or if they truly think this person is right for the job. And, if they don't think this person is right for the job, what are they as an organization doing to make the candidate right for the job or what hiring processes are they imple-menting so that they are hiring People of Color to not just fill a quota but also because they are the best talent.

In order to really transform the racial and ethnic diversity of an organ-ization, which is predominately White, the leadership would have to acknowledge that hiring one Person of Color is not only psychologically and socially isolating, but could place doubt in the mind of the recruit that her skill set is relevant to the organization. In an organization, where the above respondent is the only one Person of Color, what is the likeli-hood that she would feel comfortable bringing her entire self to work, and taking innovative risks that true leadership requires? The next Work-force Diversity study respondent recognizes as a playwright of Color, who is often the "only one," he must acknowledge the impact of this limited and constricted status on his work and his ability to take artistic risks in a primarily White performing arts organization.

"It Limits My Ability to Take Artistic Risks"

Another respondent shared this:

Writers of Color know that there is a limited space for them. Going hand in hand with that is that now you know you're the one who's lucky enough to be selected. You know that you carry the burden of speaking for the entirety of your race or your people and that sucks. That really sucks. It prevents you in some ways from being able to take risks. What if I want to tell the story of a fundamentally con-flicted Black woman onstage? You realize that this is the only Black woman this [primarily White] theater company is going to cast this year or for the next three years, and do I really want [to write the] Black character as a murderer or grappling with complex issues and

being sad all the time? You know you have these challenges of carry-
ing all the weight in these [predominately White] environments: It's
limiting and it's constricting. and it makes for less effective art.

By consciously choosing not to take the risk to tell the story of a Black
woman who is a murderer, the respondent is avoiding the possibility that
a primarily White audience will confirm the stereotype they may already
have of a Black person who could also be a murderer. In evading stereotype threat, the playwright eliminates the threat, the risk associated with
the threat, and the possibility of creating an innovative and powerful
play.

Stereotype Threat: "It Doesn't Feel Safe to Be the Only One"

Scholar Daryl G. Smith maintains that "a group that experiences widely
known negative stereotypes with respect to performance is more likely to
underperform when attention is drawn to the salient identity."[76] Under-
performance is a way to avoid stereotype threat or the likelihood that the
stereotype will be confirmed. For this reason, many respondents of Color
don't speak up, share and challenge ideas, and bring their entire selves
to work, lest they confirm the negative stereotypes that White colleagues
have of them. For example, one Workforce Diversity study respondent
notes that in being the "only one," she must be aware that in essence she
is representing more than herself in encounters with her White colleagues:

> I've had that experience of being the only one and for me, personally,
> it was pressure. I had to represent a people, and in doing so, I had to
> be very mindful of not displaying those stereotypes of that group of
> people. For example, I may not agree with something being discussed
> at a meeting and if I disagree, I may be perceived as an "angry Black
> woman." There is pressure to represent your race in a positive way.

Both avoiding and experiencing stereotype threat is a reality for many
of the respondents of Color interviewed for this book. The following two
respondents are colleagues of different racial and ethnic backgrounds,
working together in a predominately White performing arts organization. In an interview where both colleagues are present in the same room,
they both discuss the concept of a safe and equitable workplace space
for a Person of Color, when stereotype threat is rampant in the organizational culture.

> Respondent #1: "I've experienced a tremendous amount of personal
> agita around [the experience of being the only one Person of Color].
> Also, for me, often times it feels like it's not a safe place: A place
> where I've been able to speak freely about things that are real issues.

When it's not a safe space, I don't know who's really on my side or who really can understand what I'm speaking and talking about. The challenge always is having to determine how much of me I can actually bring into the room? How threatening will my ideas be to my White counterparts and my White colleagues? Because of the perception of like, 'You want to take over!' Or like, 'You're stirring the pot!'"

Respondent #2: "I totally concur with what my colleague is saying, and I think his personal experience is really valuable for this question. As a [White] director, I have been told by staff of Color, in one-on-one meetings, that they have not felt like they could express themselves in the way that they feel is how they want to express themselves, for fear that it's going to be interpreted differently. This is the feedback I've gotten from staff [of Color] who adapt themselves. They essentially choose to not be themselves so as to not come across as seeming too aggressive, too opinionated. I'm thinking of the Black males on my team in particular. I think we [White managers] can pat ourselves on the back and say, 'There's diversity at this table.' But since the numbers are small, these staff aren't necessarily feeling empowered to be themselves, you know."

Again, the avoidance of stereotype threat or not being perceived as "too aggressive or opinionated" is at play here and the White manager admits that this power dynamic exists between White employees and employees of Color. Antiracist White performing arts organizational members must strive to see these potential oppressive workplace communication dynamics through the lens of People of Color who often feel they aren't accepted as full participants in a predominately White space.

"It's a Lonely Existence and I Am Not the Spokesperson for My Race"

Workforce Diversity study respondents of Color stressed that being asked to represent an entire race of people is unreasonable and objectionable. How is it possible for any one person to know everything there is to know about entire group of people when there is such a multiplicity of experiences and perspectives? Two respondents of Color shed light on how it makes them feel when they are placed in the position of being the sole voice for everyone who shares their racial or ethnic background:

Respondent #1: "Well, I think most people say it's a very lonely existence if you're the only person there. Part of the objection that people [of Color] have is not that they got the job (because we're all happy to be the only one if that's the job), but then expected to be the spokesperson as if you know every single thing [about a particular group of people]. 'Why do all Puerto Ricans do. . .?' I don't know. I've never seen Puerto Ricans do that; none of the Puerto Ricans I know do that. You're not really the keeper of that knowledge and so that makes it hard."

Respondent #2: "I can't think of any area in life where there should be only one Person of Color. It's just ridiculous. And to me it indicates a laziness and [it's] insulting that you didn't even bother to look, and you think you have sufficiently fulfilled what diversity looks like by having this only one [Person of Color]. And the person who's the only one is just as uncomfortable. Because now you're expecting me to represent the entire race. How can I possibly do that? I was at a dinner a while ago with a group of professors from an Ivy League school and the conversation got around to the African American student protests about a statue being removed. The professors looked at me and said, 'What do you think?' And I said. 'I haven't a clue. I don't represent Black America. But I can tell you what I think about humanity.' So, I just shifted the conversation. I'm not going to represent all of the Black people in the world, but I'll tell you what I think about how we should treat each other as people."

"You Have to Speak Up and Attack It With a Sense of Humor"

The next Workforce Diversity study respondent of Color also agrees that he is not the "keeper of all knowledge" when it comes to speaking for a specific racial or ethnic group. On the other hand, he and two more respondents also feel a responsibility to speak up or interrupt a situation that is offensive or inequitable in an employment setting. It is imperative for both employees of Color and White antiracist allies to speak up and make their White colleagues aware of the insensitive and disrespectful language that is harmful to members of ALAANA communities. Respondents of Color note that having a sense of humor helps in these "teachable moments."

Respondent #1: "I was brought into an organization specifically to help diversify them in terms of both ethnicity and age and bring in young, emerging writers. And I was the only Person of Color upstairs. And how does that put me in a place to speak on behalf of every African American person in the United States, and every Asian person in the United States, and every Latino in South America? I am the one who was expected to speak up, and I felt a responsibility to speak up—to say hey, this marketing language might be offensive. Or, this programming choice that you're making does not accurately represent a whole wide group of people and there's a long history of you guys not representing these people. If there is a

Person of Color in that organization, they become sort of the police of that. It's an extra burden of feeling like if I don't do this no one else is going to do this."

Respondent #2: "Being the only one of anything makes you the object of more scrutiny because people are looking for you to represent things, whether it's your color, or your sex, or your ideals, or what you stand for. It takes more of an effort to move past that and to deal with it straight on so that people are aware that you're aware of how they're treating you. I'm one of those people that won't let people get away with that. I usually attack it with a sense of humor, but I attack it, nonetheless."

Respondent #3: "I have become very comfortable in being the token Black person at an organization. I've attended several events and department meetings where I have been the only Black person in the room, and that's fine, I'm comfortable with that. However not everyone is comfortable with taking on that responsibility, or confident enough to own their voice and speak up in an environment like that. It's a skill that we should all have but one that needs to be cultivated and supported. It's challenging and requires a lot of self-reflection, conviction, and belief in yourself. As the token Black, you're expected to represent the Black community and know all things related to that culture. I've often been asked, 'I'm looking for a marketer who's a Person of Color. Do you know of anyone?' I respond, 'Oh me too. If you find them let me know!'"

"It's Exhausting Work and I Am Tired of Educating You"

"Why," another respondent asks, "do so many White people make assumptions that one Black person knows everything about the experiences of an entire group of people?" The next Workforce Diversity study respondent shares some important insights about how exhausting the additional educational work is, and its effect on her identity:

When you are the "only one," you are the only person in the room, and everybody is coming to you and asking for your opinion for your entire race of people. I go through that (whispers) every day. And I am not the only one who experiences this problem in organizations. You want to help educate people because they just don't know, but at the same time, I'm tired of educating people. I have those moments where I'm like, "Am I really having this conversation again? Do I really have to explain this again? I am only giving you my opinion. An African American man may have a very different opinion about this, and he probably will, because he is a man and his experiences are different.

I am not a part of the racial majority, so I can't answer to why that is, but why are so many White people asking questions about Black people to one Black person—as if we can speak for the entire race? I know it's well intended, (chuckle) when people ask me to speak on behalf of the other, what, thirteen, fourteen million Black people in this country, but, I can't! Everyone's worldview is shaped by their own experiences.

The Pressure to Assimilate and "Eat Pizza"

When you are the only Person of Color in a primarily White performing arts organization, there is also pressure to adopt the cultural values of the dominate culture or assimilate. States antiracist educator Julie Kailin, "The assimilationist myth that 'we are a nation of immigrants,' negates qualitatively different historical experiences and treatment of people of color, who were either invaded or forced here in chains."[77] In this next section, two Workforce Diversity study respondents of Color commiserate with each other about the pressure to assimilate in their organizations, even during lunchtime.

> Respondent #1: "I don't know if you felt this as well, but I feel like there was a sense of needing to assimilate [in my organization]: You had to eat a certain type of lunch or talk a certain way. It's sad that there's that pressure to not to only represent your race, or your heritage, or your culture, but also having to dismiss some of it too. You don't want to be different, or you don't want to insult [your co-workers], or have too much attention on yourself as a different person."

> Respondent #2: "Every time I brought home cooked Caribbean food, my co-workers would ask me, 'What is that?' I would respond, 'It's food. You want to taste?' Every time. I then told myself, 'Okay, I'm just going to eat pizza.'"

> In her ethnographic work *Antiracist Education*, author Julie Kailin maintains that "the dominant paradigm of assimilation in education says, 'You can join us, but you must be just like us.' This means that if you are different, you cannot discover who you are. Assimilation involves a destruction of memory."[78]

"I Feel the Burden of Responsibility"

The following three Workforce Diversity study respondents of Color feel an enormous responsibility to succeed in their performing arts leadership positions. Even though it's an impossible task to represent the interests of an entire community of people, performing arts leaders of Color feel a responsibility to their own ALAANA communities as discussed in the following section:

> Respondent #1: "I'm one of only a very small handful of People of Color running a large not-for-profit theater in this country. I feel a great deal of support. I don't actually scare very easily. But the one thing I'm genuinely afraid of is failing the very communities that have so believed in this appointment. I feel a tremendous responsibility to not failing folks who really want this to go well. I feel the burden of responsibility there."

> Respondent #2: "When I got my first job in the arts, I was one of the first staff members at my organization to come from a Pakistani background; I was definitely the first person of Muslim faith that some of my colleagues had worked with. I now hold a senior leadership role within my organization. I'm one of a few diverse faces within the organization at that level, it's beginning to change for the better slowly. Being a visible leader of Color comes with additional responsibilities and expectations from the communities you serve and represent. People of Color who are artists, for example, see you as the person who will be speaking on their behalf, you carry their hopes and their expectations within the organization as well as your own."

> Respondent #3: "At the end of the day that's exactly how I feel. There is a sense of responsibility that goes with being the first or the only. You want to show up well, not only for yourself, but for those who may be coming after you. You understand the damage stereotypes can do, so you think about legacy. Early on and for some time I was the only African American and the only woman! Back then people looked to you to be a spokesperson, and to reflect the sentiments of an entire community. African Americans are not a monolith. We're very diverse and have sub-cultures in our community. I consciously embrace diversity and inclusion. My friends come from many different cultures, perspectives, and lived experiences. I see myself as a bridge, someone who wants to bring people together, and care most about values. I dispel myths, stereotypes, and look for the genuine. That's just something that I've carried with me my entire life."

"We Already Have 'One,' So We Are Now a Diverse Organization"

Workforce Diversity study respondents of Color worry that once primarily White performing arts organizations hire one Person of Color, the "diversity quota" and all that it implies is fulfilled. For example, by hiring one staff member who is a Person of Color, the historically White organization is automatically exempt from the possibility that their actions are racist, sexist, or offensive. In addition, as this respondent of Color has experienced:

> Hiring one Person of Color oftentimes relieves organizations of the pressure and of the obligation to continue to make strides toward diversifying their organization, simply because now they've got "one." I want to say it's a double-edged sword. It has many ramifications for the person who's the only one. There is a sense of tremendous pressure on that person to be that representative. Many of us who are Persons of Color have a "tax" on our lives. There are multiple expectations that come to you: To be on all the committees; to have all of the wisdom about what ought to be happening with your group; to be the shining example of the group. Then there are implications for the organization or the employer: Once they have now gotten "the one," that is a sign that they have arrived, that maybe they don't have to work as hard anymore, in terms of the ability to recruit and continue to bring people of diverse backgrounds into the organization.

Another respondent agrees:

> So, from my personal experience, it's very detrimental. In some ways, [having only one Person of Color or member of one community] makes it even harder for an institution or an organization to grow in the right ways in terms of really being more inclusive. Because they figure, "Well, we've got our bases covered. We've got our token. Direct all things 'race-related' to this person. Whatever they say, we're good."

"A Safe Place to Be My Authentic Self"

In being the only Person of Color in a historically White organization, there are often great pressures to avoid standing out or to confirm stereotypes, and to assimilate. In her work on gender tokenism, sociologist Rosabeth Moss Kanter argues that "a group becomes balanced when there is a typological ratio of about 60:40. Culture and interaction reflect this balance."[79] The more representation there is, the more likely it is that ALAANA employees and board members will feel a greater freedom to be themselves, challenging any negative stereotypes that White colleagues may have of them.[80] When People of Color see themselves holistically represented in an organization, they recognize there is freedom to develop an occupational identity that encompasses the cultural values and traditions of their own ALAANA communities, benefitting the non-profit performing arts sector as a whole. The following Workforce Diversity study respondent of Color substantiates the impact that not being the "only one" had on her occupational development:

> When you're the only Black person in an all-White environment, you feel handicapped, as if you only have one arm. When you are in a situation where you are with others who look like you, you feel like you have two arms. You don't feel like you're the only one. You don't feel singled out. It gives you more power; it gives you more voice. It's hard when it's just you.
>
> When I was at grad school, I was the only one Black student in my class during the first semester. During my second semester, another Black woman came. By my second year, there were two more Black women. By then, we were a powerful group, this powerful team. We fueled each other; we fed each other, academically, emotionally, and spiritually. I felt I had a safe place to be my authentic self. I felt I could talk about things in a way I couldn't talk about with my [White] classmates because I felt different than them. For example, I came in with this Southern dialect because my parents are from the South; [my White classmates] were from the Northeast. I would pronounce certain words, they would say, 'What? What did you say?' They made me self-conscious and at times I did not talk as much. I didn't experience that with my Black girlfriends. Having them around me, I felt empowered and valued. I felt like I was in the right place and I didn't feel alone.

Conclusion

A person's identity or self is formed through social interaction with others. One learns early in childhood that the color of his or her skin impacts his or her social position or status in the socially constructed racial hierarchy of social relations. ALAANA racial and ethnic identities are social categories and are laced with histories and compelling stories of social, economic, and political oppression, discrimination, as well as resistance and resilience. The Master Narrative and its exclusionary fallacious historical stories influence the dearth of racial and ethnic access, diversity, equity, and inclusion centered practices in the performing arts workforce today. There are some predominately White cultural organizations that relegate culturally diverse stories to one month; value a Master Narrative in which ALAANA group members are not treated as legitimate stakeholders and feel unwelcome as patrons, employees, board members, and community partners.

Assumptions or negative stereotypes are made by historically White organizations about the type of person that should be cast or direct a production and when POC break through these racial and ethnic access barriers, they are still made to feel as though their contributions aren't good enough.

Some predominately White performing arts organizations have created another social category or position in which a member of the ALAANA community is the "only one" in the organization. Having only one Person of Color in a historically White performing arts organization is simply unacceptable, especially when primarily White organizational members recognize and name what this status signifies and inflicts upon People of Color. By perpetuating the "only one" status in a performing arts organization, the Predominately White Organization is maintaining an opportunity structure that privileges the people that dominate the sector. Furthermore, Primarily White Organizations, within the intersecting performing arts, educational, and philanthropic sectors, collectively perpetuate an inequitable ecosystem that reserve career, educational, and philanthropic opportunities for insiders in a predominately White performing arts sector.

However, when People of Color see themselves reflected in culturally plural education and community institutions, there is a greater optimism and expectation that opportunities will be open to them—to their entire selves.

Historically White performing arts organizations have the ability and power to dismantle and transform their discriminatory workforce cultures so that People of Color are not isolated and are instead respected and recognized as essential leadership assets. But will predominately White leaders in the performing arts and the intersecting sectors of education and philanthropy intentionally and collectively interrogate and transform the practices and structure of their predominately White institutions so that culturally diverse perspectives replace the "only one" perspective? In the next chapter, the opportunity structure in the performing arts sector is examined, as well as the racialized systems, institutional structures, and personal practices that sustain those opportunities.

Notes

1. Charles W. Morris ed., George H. Mead, *Mind, Self, & Society* (Chicago, IL: University of Chicago Press, 1934), 144.
2. In *A Different Mirror: A History of Multicultural America* (2008), author Ronald Takaki establishes that U.S. historical accounts are grounded in a Master Narrative, where White U.S. history takes precedence over multicultural U.S. history. The primary message of the [White] Master Narrative is that the White lens and perspective are historically accurate and that a multicultural perspective of U.S. history has not been included and recognized as

legitimate. Takaki interrogates the Master Narrative through his remarkable scholarship of multicultural America. Ronald Takaki, *A Different Mirror* (New York, NY: Little, Brown and Company, 2008).

3. Robin DiAngelo, *What Does It Mean to Be White?* (New York, NY: Peter Lang, 2012), 17.

4. Katherine L. Milkman, Modupe Akinola, and Dolly Chugh, "What Happens Before? A Field Experiment Exploring How Pay and Representation Differentially Shape Bias on the Pathway Into Organizations," *Journal of Applied Psychology* 100, no. 6 (2015): 1681.

5. Ali Michael, *Raising Race Questions* (New York, NY: Teachers College, 2015), 60.

6. Debra Van Ausdale and Joe R. Feagin, *The First R* (New York, NY: Rowman & Littlefield, 2001), 26–27, 92.

7. Derald Wing Sue and David Sue, *Counseling the Culturally Diverse*, 6th ed. (Hoboken, NJ: Wiley, 2013), 331.

8. Van Ausdale and Feagin, *The First R*, 184.

9. Norman R. Yetman and C. Hoy Steele, eds., *Majority and Minority* (Boston, MA: Allyn and Bacon, 1974), 10.

10. Lee Anne Bell, Michael S. Funk, Khyati Y. Joshi, and Marjorie Valdivia, "Racism and White Privilege," in *Teaching for Diversity and Social Justice*, 3rd ed., eds. Maurianne Adams and Lee Anne Belle, with Diane J. Goodman and Khyati Y. Joshi (New York, NY: Routledge, 2016), 134; Yetman and Steele, eds., *Majority and Minority*, 10, 12.

11. David R. Clemons, J. Coleman Heckman, and Suzette Lamb, "The Wheel of Influence," in *Teaching About Culture, Ethnicity, and Diversity*, ed. Theodore M. Singelis (Thousand Oaks, CA: Sage, 1998), 188.

12. See Preface, endnote 8.

13. Lisa J. Dettling et al., "Recent Trends in Wealth-Holding by Race and Ethnicity: Evidence from the Survey of Consumer Finances," *FEDS Notes* (Washington, DC: Board of Governors of the Federal Reserve System, September 27, 2017), https://federalreserve.gov; Richard L. Zweigenhaft, "Who Represents America, Then (1972) and Now (2016): Race Ethnicity, Gender, and Class in the U.S. Congress," in *Who Rules America?* ed. G. William Domhoff (October 2018), https://whorulesamerica.ucsc.edu.

14. Pew Research Center, *On Views of Race and Inequality, Blacks and Whites Are Worlds Apart* (Washington, DC: Pew Research Center, June 27, 2016). The White and Black respondents surveyed are non-Hispanic. "Pew Research Center bears no responsibility for the analyses or interpretations of the data presented here. The opinions expressed herein, including any implications for policy, are those of the author and not of Pew Research Center."

15. Ibid.

16. Ibid.

17. Gordon W. Allport, *The Nature of Prejudice* (Reading, MA: Addison-Wesley, 1954), 14–15.

18. Feagin, Vera, and Batur, *White Racism* (2001), 17, cited in Barbara Trepagnier, *Silent Racism*, 2nd ed. (Boulder, CO: Paradigm, 2010), 19.

19. Pew Research Center, "How Census Race Categories Have Changed Over Time," (June 10, 2015), www.pewsocialtrends.org. "Pew Research Center bears no responsibility for the analyses or interpretations of the data presented here. The opinions expressed herein, including any implications for policy, are those of the author and not of Pew Research Center."

20. U.S. Census Bureau, "What We Do," www.census.gov/about.

21. Karen R. Humes, Nicholas A. Jones, and Roberto R. Ramirez, "Overview of Race and Hispanic Origin: 2010," *2010 Census Briefs* (Washington, DC: U.S. Census Bureau, March 2011), 2, www.census.gov.

22. Ibid.

23. Ibid.

24. Ibid.

25. Hansi Lo Wang, email to the author, November 16, 2018; Hansi Lo Wang, "2020 Census Will Ask Black People About Their Exact Origins," *NPR* (March 13, 2018), www.npr.org; Hansi Lo Wang, "2020 Census Will Ask White People More About Their Ethnicities," *NPR* (February 1, 2018), www.npr.org.

26. Humes, Jones, and Ramirez, "Overview of Race and Hispanic Origin," 2, www.census.gov.

27. Ibid.

28. Kim Parker et al., "Chapter 7: The Many Dimensions of Hispanic Racial Identity," in *Multiracial in America: Proud, Diverse and Growing in Numbers* (Washington, DC: Pew Research Center, June 2015), www.pewsocial-trends.org. "Pew Research Center bears no responsibility for the analyses or interpretations of the data presented here. The opinions expressed herein, including any implications for policy, are those of the author and not of Pew Research Center."

29. Ibid.

30. Humes, Jones, and Ramirez, "Overview of Race and Hispanic Origin," 2, www.census.gov.

31. National Geographic, "1790 Census," www.nationalgeographic.org.

32. Bobbie Harro, "The Cycle of Socialization," in *Readings for Diversity and Social Justice*, 3rd ed., eds. Maurianne Adams, Warren J. Blumenfeld, Carmelita Castañeda, Heather W. Hackman, Madeline L. Peters, and Ximena Zúñiga (New York, NY: Routledge, 2013), 49.

33. Allport, *The Nature*, 209–10.

34. Max Weber, *Economy and Society*, Guenther Roth and Claus Wittich, eds. (Berkeley, CA: University of California Press, 1978), 385, 953.

35. Gunnar Myrdal, *An American Dilemma* (New York, NY: Harper & Brothers Publishers, 1944), 87–88.

36. More than five hundred years of racialized America coincides with Christopher Columbus's 1492 voyage where he wrote, "As soon as I arrived in the Indies, on the first Island which I found, I took some of the natives by force. . . . " Howard Zinn, *A People's History of the United States* (New York, NY: Harper and Collins, 1980), 1; Many members of the African Diaspora mark 2019 as the "400th anniversary of the [1619] arrival of Africans in the English colonies, at Point Comfort, Virginia," *400 Years of African-American History Commission Act*, 115th Congress, Public Law 115–102 (January 8, 2018), 131 STAT, 2248, www.congress.gov.

37. Vivian Chou, "How Science and Genetics are Reshaping the Race Debate of the 21st Century," *Harvard University Blog* (April 17, 2017), http://sitn.hms.harvard.edu.

38. In Morton's *Crania Americana*, he described the Caucasian race as "characterized by naturally fair skin . . . distinguished for the facility with which it attains the highest intellectual endowments. . . . The Ethiopian race [is] characterized by a black complexion . . . present[ing] a singular diversity of intellectual character, of which the far extreme is the lowest grade of

humanity." Samuel George Morton, *Crania Americana*, (Philadelphia, PA: J. Dobson, 1839), 5, 7.

39. Morton, *Crania Americana*; Samuel George Morton papers 1832–1862, Library Company of Philadelphia, University of Pennsylvania; Nell Irvin Painter, *The History of White People* (New York, NY: W. W. Norton & Company, 2010), 191–194.
40. Painter, *The History of White People*, 231.
41. M. F. Ashley Montagu, *Man's Most Dangerous Myth: The Fallacy of Race* (New York, NY: Harper & Brothers, 1952), 1.
42. Ruth Benedict and Gene Weltfish, *The Races of Mankind* (New York, NY: Public Affairs Committee, 1961), 15.
43. "AAPA Statement on Biological Aspects of Race," *American Journal of Physical Anthropology* 101, no. 4 (December 1996): 569–70 © Wiley Periodicals is the copyright owner and this citation is granted with permission from Wiley.
44. Ibid. © Wiley Periodicals is the copyright owner and this citation is granted with permission from Wiley.
45. 1790 Naturalization Act, First Congress, Session II (March 26, 1790), 103, https://legisworks.org.
46. Takaki, *A Different Mirror*, 62.
47. Ronald Takaki, *A Different Mirror* (Boston, MA: Little, Brown and Company, 1993), 47.
48. Timothy Egan, "The Nation; Mending a Trail of Broken Treaties," *New York Times* (June 25, 2000), www.nytimes.com; Member of the Cherokee Nation of Oklahoma and anthropologist Russell Thornton writes: "The already decimated American Indian population in the United States declined even further during the nineteenth century from about 600,000 in 1800 to a mere 250,000 between 1890 and 1900." Russell Thornton, *American Indian Holocaust and Survival* (Norman, OK; and London: University of Oklahoma Press, 1987), 133.
49. Lewis Cass, excerpted from "Removal of Indians," *North American Review* (January 1830), 4–5, https://nationalhumanitiescenter.org.
50. Museum of the American Cherokee Indian, "Trail of Tears," www.cherokee-museum.org.
51. Takaki, *A Different Mirror*, 102.
52. American Indian Relief Council [Northern Plains Reservation Aid], "History and Culture Boarding Schools," www.nativepartnership.org.
53. Poverty and Race Research Action Council, "American Indian Reparations," (December 12, 1994), https://prrac.org.
54. Valerie Wilson and Zane Mokhiber, "2016 ACS Shows Stubbornly High Native American Poverty and Different Degrees of Economic Well-Being for Asian Ethnic Groups," *Working Economics Blog* (Washington, DC: Economic Policy Institute, September 15, 2017), www.epi.org.
55. Kat Chow, "As Chinese Exclusion Act Turns 135, Experts Point to Parallels Today," *National Public Radio* (May 5, 2017), www.npr.org; "House Passes Rep. Judy Chu's Resolution of Regret for the Chinese Exclusion Act," (June 19, 2012), https://chu.house.gov.
56. Taylor Weik, "Behind Barbed Wire: Remembering America's Largest Internment Camp," *NBC News* (March 16, 2016), www.nbcnews.com; Ronald Takaki, *A Different Mirror* (New York, NY: Little, Brown and Company, 2008), 343–44.

57. Bilal Qureshi, "From Wrong to Right: A U.S. Apology for Japanese Internment," *NPR* (August 9, 2013), www.npr.org; National Archives, "Japanese Relocation During World War II," www.archives.gov; Takaki, *A Different Mirror*, 18; Eric L. Ray, "Mexican Repatriation and the Possibility for a Federal Cause of Action: A Comparative Analysis on Reparations," *The University of Miami Inter-American Law Review* 37, no. 1 (Fall 2005): 183.

58. Takaki, *A Different Mirror*, 4.

59. "Officials and Leaders Gathered for Historic Ceremony Recognizing Forced Removal of Mexican Americans During the Great Depression," *MALDEF* (2009), www.maldef.org; Adrian Florido, "Mass Deportation May Sound Unlikely, But It's Happened Before," *NPR* (September 8, 2015), www.npr.org; Ray, "Mexican Repatriation," 171.

60. "Officials and Leaders Gathered for Historic Ceremony," www.maldef.org; Elaine Woo, "Raymond Rodriguez, Who Drew Attention to the Deportation of Mexicans in the 1930s, Dies at 87," *Washington Post* (July 8, 2013), www.washingtonpost.com.

61. Library of Congress, "14th Amendment to the U.S. Constitution," www.loc.gov; Library of Congress, "15th Amendment of the U.S. Constitution: Primary Documents in American History," https://guides.loc.gov.

62. Myrdal, *An American Dilemma*, 580.

63. William H. Frey, *Diversity Explosion* (Washington, DC: Brookings Institution Press, 2015), 109.

64. Rob Weinert-Kendt, "Raising Native Voices, Then Amplifying Them," *American Theatre* (March 20, 2018), www.americantheatre.org; DataArts, *The Demographics of the Arts and Cultural Workforce in Los Angeles County* (Los Angeles, CA: Los Angeles County Arts Commission, April 2017), 13, www.lacountyarts.org; Tina Norris, Paula L. Vines, and Elizabeth M. Hoeffel, "The American Indian and Alaska Native Population: 2010," *2010 Census Briefs* (Washington, DC: U.S. Census, 2012), 11, www.census.gov.

65. Weinert-Kendt, "Raising Native Voices," www.americantheatre.org.

66. "About Us, Our History," Museum of the African Diaspora, www.moadsf.org.

67. Cynthia Fuchs Epstein et al. (1995) cited in Tobie S. Stein, *Workforce Transitions from the Profit to the Nonprofit Sector* (New York, NY: Kluwer Academic/Plenum Publishers, 2002), 21.

68. A Culturally Specific group is an ALAANA-led organization that explicitly serves communities of Color.

69. Cambridge Dictionary, "Stakeholder," https://dictionary.cambridge.org.

70. Weber, *Economy and Society*, Roth and Wittich, eds., 953–54.

71. Stein, *Workforce Transitions*, 19.

72. Robert K. Merton, "Insiders and Outsiders," *American Journal of Sociology* 78 (1972): 15.

73. Ibid., 24.

74. Daryl G. Smith, *Diversity's Promise for Higher Education*, 2nd ed. (Baltimore, MD: Johns Hopkins University Press, 2015), 287.

75. Myrdal, *An American Dilemma*, 102.

76. Smith, *Diversity's Promise*, 231.

77. Julie Kailin, *Antiracist Education* (New York, NY: Rowman & Littlefield, 2002), 131.

78. Ibid., 196.

79. Rosabeth Moss Kanter, "Some Effects of Proportions on Group Life: Skewed Sex Ratios and Responses to Token Women," *American Journal of Sociology* 82, no. 5 (March 1977): 987.
80. Smith, *Diversity's Promise*, 37.

4 The Opportunity Structure and the Performing Arts Workforce

> The fates of human beings are not equal. Men differ in their states of health, wealth, or social status. . . . In every situation he who is favored feels the never ceasing need to look upon his position as in some way "legitimate," upon his advantage as "deserved," and the other's disadvantage as being brought about by the latter's "fault."[1]
>
> Max Weber, *Economy and Society* (1922)

Introduction

This chapter examines the ways in which ALAANA members are precluded from equitable access and opportunities in a predominately White mutually reinforcing ecosystem of intersecting educational, performing arts, and philanthropic organizations. Implicit bias and discriminatory judgements individually and collectively practiced in the ecosystem through White privilege and White fragility, stereotyping and stereotype threat, colorblind racism, and microaggressions impede ALAANA members' equitable access and opportunity in the performing arts workforce. Many People of Color face systemic structural inequities in early arts education and training, and higher education, which interfere with equitable access to a viable performing arts career path. Within predominately White performing arts organizations, many People of Color contend with inequitable board and staff recruitment and retention practices, and encounter undemocratic White-dominated community partnerships with ALAANA-led performing arts organizations and communities of Color. Furthermore, funding biases perpetuated by racially and ethnically homogeneous individuals in grantmaking institutions sustain unjust philanthropic practices, favoring limited opportunities for People of Color in the performing arts workforce.

The Opportunity Structure and the Performing Arts Workforce: Perpetual and Systemic

In a White-dominated workforce opportunity structure, "both women and People of Color are concentrated into types of jobs and barred from entry into those jobs reserved for White men."[2] Kanter argues that occupations create a "homosocial reproduction" of themselves, which perpetually and systemically allow select advantaged participants the educational and employment opportunities or access to pass though.[3] Social justice educator Lee Anne Bell maintains that

> white-dominated institutions restrict . . . employment and educational opportunities [of people of color], while enhancing opportunities for white people. . . . [Those who enjoy these advantages] use a distorted lens in which the structural privileges they enjoy, and the cultural practices of their group are taken to be universal, superior, and deserved.[4]

"You Can't Audition for the Role of Snow White"

One Workforce Diversity study respondent gave a poignant example of how she was excluded from the performing arts opportunity structure as it related to her being cast as the lead in a production of *Snow White*:

> I remember when I was an actress early on, I went to audition for a production of *Snow White*, and they told me: "Sorry, you can't audition for the role of Snow White." And I responded, "Well, why not?" "And they nervously said, "Because Snow White is . . . Snow White, but you can audition for the Evil Stepmother." Because I was of Color, I was routinely typecast and ineligible to be seen for certain roles. And I'm sure that had a little bit to do with me stepping away from the performing arts field, just because it felt like the opportunities weren't going to be there for me. There were a few productions that took risks though and I was cast in a pretty popular show at the time that eventually ran for 10 years Off-Broadway. I was the first and only Black woman to play a lead character in that show—and the role itself was not race-specific, but it had always been predominantly cast with White actresses.

Those who dominate the nonprofit performing arts workforce opportunity structure create educational, training, and employment opportunities for those who fit the "Snow White" role. These opportunities are regulated through hegemony where "roles and rules, institutional norms, historical accounts, and social practices of dominant groups come to be accepted as the natural order. The advantages of the dominant group and the disadvantages of the marginalized group are normalized through language, ideology, and cultural practices."[5]

In examining the opportunity structure in the performing arts workforce, it's important to first explore the ways in which the White members of the dominant group, across all sectors of the economy, collectively learn and unconsciously internalize society's biased racial attitudes and beliefs, adopting and protecting White privilege practices through creating and perpetuating negative stereotypes against marginalized groups, and producing the socialized behaviors of colorblind racism and micro-aggressions against People of Color.

Implicit Bias: Unconsciously Internalizing Racialized Beliefs

Those who enjoy privilege or educational and employment advantages are not necessarily consciously aware that the primarily White workforce opportunity structure favors them and that they make use of this advantage to exploit those who are considered outsiders. In their study, *Exploring Racial Bias Among Biracial and Single-Race Adults: The IAT*, Pew Research Center used Harvard University's Implicit Association Test (IAT) to "explore the extent to which single-race white, black, and Asian [adults] have a subconscious bias for or against their own or another race."[6] In this 2015 study, Pew found that "about one half of all single-race white [adults] automatically preferred white [adults] over black [adults]."[7] Furthermore, "57% of single-race white [adults] with a two-year college degree or more education favored white over Asian [adults], compared with 46% of those with less formal schooling."[8] Additionally, Mahzarin R. Banaji and Anthony G. Greenwald, who first developed the IAT,[9] conclude that "IAT scores correlated moderately with discriminatory judgements and behavior."[10] For example, Patricia Clark and Eva Zygmunt found in a study of majority-White early childhood and elementary school teachers, who took the IAT test, that 96% of the teachers preferred students of European decent and light skin tones. However, when the same teachers received the results of the test, 33% of the teachers questioned the accuracy of the results and 26% of the teachers affirmed that the results didn't coincide with their beliefs.[11] It is possible to believe that one is not biased; becoming self-aware that socialization contributes to one's biases is uncomfortable and often met with avoidance.[12]

What accounts for the cognitive dissonance or psychological disparity between the test results and beliefs among the primarily White teachers in Clark and Zygmunt's study? In *Outline of a Theory of Practice*, French social theorist Pierre Bourdieu maintains that the ability to perform actions without conscious intention is based on habits that are unknowingly engrained in individuals based on historical conditions and social interaction with others.[13] He called it habitus. "Habitus is an endless capacity to engender products—thoughts, perceptions, expressions, actions—whose limits are set by the historically and socially situated conditions of its production."[14] In his work *Social Intelligence*, psychologist Daniel Goleman writes: "Once a negative bias begins, our lenses become clouded. We tend to seize on whatever seems to confirm the bias and ignore what does not."[15] The degree to which implicit bias becomes active discrimination is determined by those who have privilege or power within the ecosystem of U.S. social, cultural, economic, educational, and political institutions.

White Privilege and White Fragility

Throughout U.S. history, European culture and Whiteness have become the norm, the standard within U.S. systems and institutions. Sociologist Ruth Frankenberg writes, "Whiteness is a location of structural advantage, of race privilege."[16] Additionally, sociologist Nirmal Puwar contends that "white supremacy . . . is a matter of social, political, cultural, and economic privilege, based on a legacy of colonial conquest."[17]

The prevailing cultural values regarding what it means to be White in the U.S. are an essential component of the power structure and power relations in society and are ingrained in White-member dominated institutions though habitus or habit. Whether it's conscious or unconscious, being White in America affords a degree of comfort, respect, acceptance, and the ability to make judgements or assumptions about individuals who are deemed different. Sociologist Allan G. Johnson maintains, "to have privilege is to be allowed to move through your life without being marked in ways that identify you as an outsider, as exceptional or 'other' to be excluded, or to be included but always with conditions."[18] As Peggy McIntosh writes in her article, "White Privilege: Unpacking the Invisible Knapsack," White privilege is an "invisible package of unearned assets that I can count on cashing in each day, but about which I was 'meant' to remain oblivious."[19]

In the Workforce Diversity study, one African American respondent shares a story of White privilege and the differential racial treatment he experiences when hailing a cab:

> If I'm standing on 5th Avenue, or 57th Street, or any of the major areas of New York, and a White person says to me, "Good bye, it was a wonderful lunch, I'm going to get a cab," he or she would not in any way feel that that cab was not going to stop. That White person is privileged, feels he or she deserves that cab, that cab is going to stop, and it does. For the majority of African Americans, that cab would keep going. It's not going to stop for them. When a White person takes advantage of his Whiteness and doesn't even think twice that the average African American can't even get a cab— that is White privilege.

During the research conducted for this study, a White performing arts manager and his Black colleague are seated next to each other for the interview and the White manager discusses the White privileged advantage that he has over his colleague of African descent:

> I have this really big black backpack. Right? At times it can look really oversized, like really packed with all sorts of stuff; I've never been stopped or frisked by subway security because of it. Now what if my Black male colleague decided to wear my backpack on the way back through the subway? What might happen? I believe he would be scrutinized. Things that I have would be viewed differently on a Person of Color, and that's a privilege I partake of, or benefit from.

Another Workforce Diversity study respondent who identifies as Caucasian questions her own White privilege when she is made aware of the everyday experiences of her daughter:

> My oldest daughter identifies as Black and she has the fairest complexion among her Black friends. There's a pizza shop in their school neighborhood that they call the racist pizza shop, but they keep going there because it has the cheapest slices. She's had this experience where her friends have been overlooked when a White woman comes into the store: The White woman gets served first even though the kids paid already. My daughter has wondered to me, "Would [I be treated differently in the pizza shop] if I was not standing next to my friends?" I mean the point is there's a conversation I've been trying to have within that context and to really understand how my own experience is different from my children's experiences, and how I can actively talk to them about that in a way that is meaningful and supportive.

The privileged or dominant group has a vested interest in maintaining its privilege and does so through organizational structures. Weber maintains that an organizational structure is a "specific way of distributing powers of command."[20] He stipulates that the dominant group, who holds the power in an organizational structure, believes it is legitimate, deserving, and favored. In this binary paradigm, the dominant group believes that the subordinate group brings about its own marginalized status. "The dominating group," according to Weber, has a "personal interest in the continuance of domination by virtue of their own participation and the resulting benefits."[21] In historically White performing arts organizations benefits include maintaining valuable homogeneous networks and structuring hiring practices that sustain European-based artistic expression. One Workforce Diversity study respondent who identifies as White emphasized this point:

> I do have a network that leads to the things that access opportunity. I am one to two people away from any answer that I would

want. I feel that even if it's someone I don't know; I could just call them anyway. And I also think it's a deeply-rooted source of inequity. Because those who have greater networks, those who are born plugged in versus work to be plugged in, are just advantaged in whatever structure, whatever power structure they're operating in.

White Fragility: Protecting White Privilege

Protecting the White privileged status and "networks that access opportunity" may produce what scholar Robin DiAngelo coined White fragility or assuming a defensive posture when one's privilege is questioned or threatened.[22] In a *National Geographic* article titled "The Rising Anxiety of White America," Jamie Longazel, associate professor at John Jay College of Criminal Justice, states, "We know in sociology when community identity is challenged or questioned in some way, the community asserts and defends that identity."[23] Members of the dominant group in Primarily White Organizations may protect or defend their Whiteness, and the privilege that accompanies it, by stereotyping People of Color and labelling them outsiders.

Stereotyping: Labelling People of Color Outsiders

One Black respondent interviewed for this study has personally experienced White fragility, which produces negative stereotyping of People of Color in the workplace. He explained:

> There is a fear among White leadership that [if they hire you] you will "Blacken up the place," or bring more people of darker skin into an organization that's predominantly White. And some of that is true, people tend to hire people that look like them. But in bringing someone different in, there's a fear of "Am I safe? Will I have my job?" And with that fear of not being safe or the threat of losing one's job comes the need to stereotype.
>
> There's the myth or the notion of the "angry Black man." There have been times when I've been in a room where something happened, and the room gets really quiet suddenly because they are thinking, "Oh, is he about to go postal?" And that's not the situation at all. It's like, "We can agree to disagree, we can speak. You can tell me what's on your mind and I'm going to tell you what's on mine. And we're going to settle it like human beings and keep it moving."
>
> The stereotypes of a sister that's always late, or the angry Black man, or the person who doesn't speak English and won't understand what's being done are based on fear. Our names can even sometimes be intimidating. Like when I go up for a position, I don't use my African name when I'm first meeting with someone. I use my full name because it's easier to pronounce, and it's less threatening. Because

when you see my African name, you automatically know what I am. Using another part of my name gives me the ability to get through the door first, let them see who I am, let them see what I'm all about and then we begin.

Why would a Person of Color's name be intimidating to White members of Primarily White Organizations and how is this attitude learned? Where does the stereotype of the "angry Black man" originate? In a study of 107 White American mothers, 70% chose a colorblind approach and did not speak to their children about race in early childhood, believing that if they spoke about race, their children would develop bias. In this study psychologist Brigitte Vittrup warns, "Without [learning] specific language, children likely will not get the intended message . . . influencing children's attitudes and intercultural interactions in the long term."[24] In the absence of conversations, children may be misinformed and may rely on stereotypes.[25] According to Allport, "A stereotype is an exaggerated belief associated with a category. Its function is to justify (rationalize) our conduct in relation to that category."[26] Social psychologists Galen W. Bodenhausen and Robert S. Wyer contend that "in the absence of behavioral evidence . . . stereotypes provide coherence, simplicity, and predictability."[27]

Avoiding Stereotype Threat

One aspect of stereotyping is the possibility of stereotype threat, where an ALAANA job applicant feels the threat of being viewed through the lens of a negative stereotype by a predominately White organizational employer. For example, the following Black respondent interviewed for the Workforce Diversity study reacts to both the spoken and unspoken assumption that, based on his race, he won't fit in and he won't be comfortable being the only one Person of Color in a predominately White performing arts organization:

> There are times when I've gone up for certain positions where I have to prove right off the bat that I'm perfectly comfortable in an environment where I'm the only Person of Color. That's not an issue for me, I've done it before. At the end of the day, I just want to work, and I just want to be a phenomenal artist. For me, work has no color: Let's just tell the stories that need to be told.
>
> I recently had an interview and the second question they asked was, "Tell me about all of the plays that you've directed, and what kind of plays do you like to direct?" And I went through them. It's a Predominately White Organization, and there's only one Person of Color working [there] and he works in the box office. My resume is kind of eclectic, but it's a lot of work of Color. In answering their

question, I'm very quick to make sure that I can direct an August Wilson play, but I also love Chekhov, Shakespeare, and Ibsen. So, I must prove to them that if I come, I'm not coming with an ulterior motive or agenda, which is to change things up. I'm not just here to do Black theater, I'm here to just do theater.

Colorblind Racism: "What Kind of Plays Do You Like to Direct?"

The Black respondent is asked by the White interviewer the seemingly colorblind statement, "What kind of plays do you like to direct?" Whether conscious or unconscious, this question is not colorblind, but is perceived to imply or assume that because the candidate is Black, his experience and interest lie in only directing Black plays. In avoiding stereotype threat, the Black directing candidate feels that he must counter the unspoken or implicit stereotype by insisting that he has experience directing the White European canon. Does the White interviewer even realize that the interview question, while seemingly colorblind, supports the underlying notion that a White director who has experience with the White European theatrical cannon is preferred?

Sociologist Nirmal Puwar states, "It's easier for those who are racially in a position of privilege to dismiss the importance of race."[28] If one adheres to the colorblind ideology when it comes to race, one can state without feeling guilt or shame that opportunity is meritocratic and is not based on racism.[29] Since the civil rights movement of the 1960s, it is widely known that the outward expression of overt racist remarks is considered deplorable. Social psychologist Evan P. Apfelbaum and his colleagues maintain in their article, "Racial Color Blindness," "No form of race-based consideration is acceptable in a lawfully egalitarian society."[30] Subsequently, if one doesn't openly consider, acknowledge, or "see" race, how can one act in a biased manner? Naming race is not acceptable, according to the colorblind ideology, so often racialized language is coded in the form of "what kind of plays do you like to direct?" or "the neighborhood is bad," or the voice is intentionally lowered when the race of a person is being invoked into the conversation by a non-Person of Color.[31]

Microaggressions: Societal Disparagement of People of Color

Colorblind racist expressions such as "what kind of plays do you like to direct" are often experienced by People of Color as microaggressions. Microaggressions are "brief, [unconscious or conscious] everyday exchanges that send denigrating messages to a target group, such as people of color."[32] The following four Workforce Diversity study respondents of Color describe the negative impact microaggressions have on their children, their professional accomplishments, and on their educational and work environments: First, an African American respondent remembers this "snubbing" incident that adversely affected her son:

Respondent #1: "I remember when he was ten years old. We were in Boston, and he's a very cute little all-American looking boy, big black eyes and long lashes. We're on a trolley in Boston, and not one White person would sit next to him. It was painfully obvious to me, that the folks treated the seat next to him like a hot seat. I was pissed, but I didn't want him to feel bad, and in that he was ten; perhaps he didn't notice it. So, I asked him, and he said, 'more room for me.' I let it be. But I saw it, and I see the societal disparagement of African American males."

Microaggressions can take also take the form of insulting questions that demean and devalue the accomplishments of People of Color:

Respondent #2: "I notice a 'difference' when I tell people I went to Howard Law School as opposed to maybe Harvard. It's like I must prove the quality of my legal education. They ask, 'Who were your professors? What did you learn? Did you really learn law?' Like excuse me honey. We're the ones that got integration into the schools. I think we know what we're doing, but there's an assumption if it's not Ivy League, it's less than. And if you went to a HBCU, Historical Black College or University, it's average, but not [thought of as] excellent."

The following two African American respondents experienced microaggressions in their educational and professional environments:

Respondent #3: "In college I had a professor that really respected my potential and cultivated my talents. He cast me in a show where I would be playing a nun. I was Mother Superior in *Agnes of God*. And everyone was like, 'Wow! How interesting that you got that role!' You don't know how many dang Whoopi Goldberg jokes I got for playing a nun in a show that had nothing to do with *Sister Act*."

Respondent #4: "I value audience members being respected and feeling comfortable. And I think there are ways that we can create a welcoming environment. There are micro-acts that are sometimes used to send a message to an audience member. I remember a group of people came in late, and they happened to be Black people. As they walked through the door, the house manager looked at her watch and went like this [taps watch with pointer finger]. I remember addressing her and saying, 'Number one, they know they're late. They're not children. Just say, "The show has started, I need you to do this, blah blah-blah," and look at them!' The house manager wasn't even aware that she did it, right? So, we had a conflict with that. You know, because of course she wanted to defend her position, and I responded, 'You did not make them feel welcome. That little [taps watch], that act, that gesture right there, made them feel like, 'This is not a place for me.' Or made them feel like they were being treated as children and not like a paying audience member who knew they were late. You don't know why they were late; you don't know what it took for them to get to there, and it doesn't matter. Just say, 'The show has started. I need you to stand here, and I'm going take you to your seat in five minutes.' That's all you needed to say. I believe that it's our job to make people feel comfortable in a new environment. And not make them feel less-than or self-conscious."

Though microaggressions are often viewed as unintentional by the White people who inflict them, a micro-assault or the "blatant verbal, nonverbal, or environmental attack [is] intended to convey discriminatory and biased sentiments."[33] Sociologists Leslie Houts Picca and Joe R. Feagin asked 626 White college students to keep a journal of "everyday events and conversations that deal with racial issues, images, and understandings." Among the 9,000 recordings of everyday accounts of racial events, "roughly three quarters of the total, [were] accounts of events involving clearly racist commentary."[34] Racist commentary, which takes the form of microaggressions and micro-assaults, are grounded in "ethnocentric values and beliefs [that] are manifested in the programs, policies, practices, structures, and institutions of society."[35] These institutionalized ethnocentric beliefs and values create career pathway access barriers for many People of Color in the performing arts workforce.

Career Pathway Access Barriers in the Performing Arts Workforce

Career pathways

describe the more fluid [informal] processes that influence one's ability to access an entry point and succeed after entry. . . . [In order to succeed], an individual must perceive that there are opportunities, and receive encouragement and mentorship from teachers, friends, and parents.[36]

The degree to which a child of Color will pursue the performing arts as a career begins early in childhood. A child of Color's socioeconomic background and access to early education and training opportunities play a large role in determining if a child will be exposed to and encouraged to pursue the arts as a profession. Even if he or she has the opportunity to be exposed and educated in the performing arts early in life, more obstacles potentially can restrict the career path of a Person of Color. These obstacles include racial and ethnic inequities found in the primarily White performing arts higher education and internship programs, as well as White-dominated performing arts homogeneous career networks that adversely influence inclusive recruitment practices in primarily White performing arts organizations; restrict opportunities for mobility and advancement in the historically White workforce; and limit contact with mentors to provide guidance throughout the career pathway. In addition, predominately White organizational controlled community partnerships that devalue the contributions of ALAANA-led performing arts organizations; and predominately White funding organizations that continue to perpetuate inequitable grantmaking practices, favoring predominately White performing arts organizations constitute a "cumulative disadvantage" for many People of Color seeking equitable career opportunities in the performing arts sector. One Workforce Diversity study respondent sized up the performing arts career path struggle in this way: "There is a Black tax, where we say we have to work twice as hard to get to the same place as many of our White counterparts, and they get there in half the time." In the next section the opportunity tax placed on People of Color within the historically White performing arts educational and training system is examined.

"There Is Inequality in Our Educational System"

The decline of childhood arts education programs as well as the inequities in access to early arts education in school is likely to affect the degree to which a child of Color will pursue the performing arts profession as an artist, employee, or manager. According to the National Endowment for the Arts,

> while the decline in the rate of childhood arts education among white children is relatively insignificant from 1982 to 2008, just five percent, the declines in the rate [in childhood education] among African American and Hispanic children are quite substantial—49 percent for African American and 40 percent for Hispanic children.[37]

More than 60% of Latino and African American children grow up in high poverty school districts, as opposed to 18% of White students.[38]

According to the U.S. Department of Education, the highest poverty schools have the least access to arts education.[39]

The following Workforce Diversity study respondent who identifies as Caucasian concurs with the findings of the U.S. Department of Education: "There is inequality in our educational system. In our organization, we see that schools that have less resources are in poor neighborhoods, and have less [access to] art. There are communities of Color, schools of Color that don't have these learning opportunities. They're not going to see performances; they're not getting connected to cultural institutions. They don't have parents that can afford the price of a ticket if the cost is too high."

In her *Music Educators Journal* article "Missing Faces from the Orchestra: An Issue of Social Justice?" author Lisa C. DeLorenzo explains that Black and Latino urban school students often have fewer financial resources for music programs, less adequate facilities, and fewer out-of-school opportunities (e.g., music camps, community orchestras) as compared to students in more affluent districts. Furthermore, the predominance of White teachers in the field often means that Black and Latino urban students have less access to teachers of Color who can serve as role models and mentors.[40] In assessing the success of 40 years of fellowships among musicians of Color in orchestras, the League of American Orchestras found that "'limited early exposure to classical music' and 'limited availability of out of school programs, private school instruction, and youth music ensembles' are barriers for young musicians of color entering the orchestra field."[41]

The following Workforce Diversity study respondent who identifies as Black concurs with the research:

> If you don't get exposed to playing musical instruments early, you probably aren't going to get into Curtis Institute of Music and if you don't get into Curtis then maybe you'll never play at the [New York] Philharmonic. We have so many people in this country who live under the poverty line: They can't buy an instrument or afford to go to dance class. You might naturally be a fairly proficient singer but if you can't afford voice lessons, or you don't have parents or guardians who understand that there's a benefit in that then you may not ever get to be competitive at the adult level.

Receiving arts training early in childhood is critical to pursuing careers as musicians, and ballet dancers as well. It can take ten years[42] of training to develop the necessary skills to be a ballet dancer as one African American respondent in the Workforce Diversity study noted:

> Training is hugely linked to employment in the professional performing art of ballet. Where you train, and how long you train, and how well you've trained are the make or break part of building a career in

ballet. It takes a tremendously long time to master this art form, so training is the deciding factor.

But having the proper dance training may not be enough, especially when your dance teacher does not encourage you to continue as the same African American respondent reported:

> I graduated from this special dance training school at eighteen and at that point my director said to me, "Well, you're not going to be a ballerina, because there aren't any Black ballerinas." That was the first time I'd heard that. I'd been at the school for five years.

"The Educational and Professional Opportunities Were Not Made Clear to Me"

The following three Workforce Diversity study respondents of Color talk about primary and secondary school experiences where they were not given the support and guidance needed to pursue future performing arts educational and professional opportunities:

Respondent #1: "I wanted to be a singer. And I sang in gospel choirs and talent shows. But the professional opportunities were not made clear to me in school. I wanted to go to LaGuardia High School, and I didn't know how. Growing up, performing was a hobby; my family thought it was a hobby. I thought it was my dream. My schools did not provide any sort of track for that."

Respondent #2: "The first obstacle I faced was in high school, when I went to my guidance counselor and said I wanted to pursue a career in the arts. And she just assumed because I was Asian American that I must be a violinist or pianist and that the whole realm of theater was just not even something on the radar for me."

Respondent #3: "I was valedictorian of my [high school] class. I was involved in every activity known to man and never once did somebody tell me what an Ivy League education meant. What did grad school look like? What college was for? So, few people went to college from my community. I didn't see the value in education. For me, school was very easy up to that point and I didn't really understand that having connections meant being connected to a larger world. And I think, 'Wow, that was really a missed opportunity.' And my parents knew about other possibilities, but my mom went to secretarial school, my dad was a forester. They were thrilled that I got a full ride to a local college. Going somewhere else was not part of the thinking of anyone there. I feel like there was just not a slate of options presented."

If the above respondent of Color had been presented with a "slate of college options," and had chosen to attend a performing arts degree program, where the majority of students and professors identified as White, to what extent would the respondent have felt welcomed as a Person of Color? To what degree is racial and ethnic ADEI considered a core value in predominately White institutions of higher education?

Is Racial and Ethnic ADEI a Core Value in Higher Education?

The American Council on Education's 2017 study on college presidents found that 83% are White, and 17% are People of Color.[43] According to the National Center for Education Statistics

of all [795,000] full-time faculty in degree-granting postsecondary institutions in fall 2016, 41 percent were White males; 35 percent were White females; 6 percent were Asian/Pacific Islander males; 4 percent were Asian/Pacific Islander females; 3 percent each were Black males, Black females, and Hispanic males; and 2 percent were Hispanic females. Those who were American Indian/Alaska Native and those who were Two or More Races each made up 1 percent or less of full-time faculty in these institutions.[44]

How does this largely White college leadership and professoriate pool affect the extent to which racial and ethnic diversity is a core value within predominately White institutions of higher learning? One Workforce Diversity study respondent who identifies as Caucasian answered this question:

I worked for a state university and the commitment to [diversity] at the organizational level, and at the department level, was lip service at best. There was no strategic thinking or action around making diversity into a reality and it wasn't a focus or a core value.

If racial and ethnic access, diversity, equity, and inclusion is not considered a core value in primarily White higher education institutions, then to what degree does the absence of this critical core value create economic access barriers for People of Color in college admissions and recruitment, limit the availability of a culturally responsive curriculum, and restrict contact with potential mentors in college and graduate school? Additionally, if a college student of Color does not have the opportunity to engage in a professional internship, what impact will that have on his or her career pathway?

Economic Access Barriers and Curriculum Restrictions

According to research conducted by the Urban Institute "White family wealth was seven times greater than Black family wealth and five times greater than Hispanic family wealth in 2016."[45] Additionally, in that same year, 33.8% of Native American children lived in poverty.[46] The Pell Institute's *2018 Indicators of Higher Education Equity in the United States: Historical Trend Report* recognizes that in colleges and universities "bachelor's degree attainment was five times greater for those from the highest family income quartile (58% vs. 11%)."[47] To what degree does the economic disparity between White families and Black, Latinx, and Native American families affect the extent to which Latinx students, students of the African Diaspora, and Native American students are receiving performing arts college four-year degrees and/or graduate degrees? While the specific correlation between race and ethnicity and socioeconomic status of those receiving performing arts college and graduate degrees has not been investigated as part of this study, it may be inferred from the data presented that White family wealth influences the higher education opportunity structure for those seeking a four-year college or graduate degree in the performing arts. In fact, the U.S. Department of Education reports that the majority of performing and visual arts undergraduate and graduate college degrees are awarded to White students. Of the 91,262 visual and performing arts bachelor's degrees awarded in 2017, there were 56,861 degrees (62%) conferred to White students as compared with 7,025 degrees (8%) awarded to Black students; 11,666 degrees (13%) awarded to Latinx students; 5,663 degrees (6%) awarded to Asian/Pacific Islander students; 395 degrees (0.4%) awarded to American Indian/Alaska Native students; and 4,059 degrees (4%) awarded to students who identify as Two or More Races.[48] Furthermore, of the 17,523 graduate students receiving degrees in performing and visual arts in 2017, 9,362 of the degrees, or more than half (53%), were awarded to White students, as compared with 1,155 degrees (7%) awarded to Black students; 1,296 degrees (7%) awarded to Latinx students; 870 degrees (5%) awarded to Asian/Pacific Islander students; 56 degrees (0.3%) awarded to American Indian/Alaska Native students, and 508 degrees (3%) awarded to students who identify as Two or More Races.[49] It should be noted that Black, Latinx, and Native American students earning bachelor's and/or graduate degrees in the performing and visual arts are not representative of the U.S. population.

The following Workforce Diversity study respondent who identifies as White agrees that there are economic barriers that prevent students of Color from receiving a performing arts college education:

> The college degree recruitment strategies are not yielding a lot of People of Color in all of the training programs, from acting to arts management. And then if they do, the economic barrier to so many of

those programs is prohibitive. There are economic barriers to being trained in our field. Also, if you get into a program, the curriculum can be focused on a more Western canon, so it's not as welcoming. What's actually in the curriculum? Are students learning about equity, access, and inclusion work in the curriculum?

That's a good question! Once a student of Color is admitted to college, to what extent is she or he comfortable in the White-majority environment? To what extent are there culturally responsive courses that employ a multiplicity of cultural perspectives? In his article, "A Survey of Arts Management Educators' Teaching on Diversity Issues," scholar Antonio C. Cuyler found that 69% of those arts management professors surveyed said that they don't have a specific course on diversity. Not having enough time to teach this course, lack of knowledge in teaching a diversity course, or the diversity course not being relevant were cited as barriers to teaching a course on diversity. It's interesting and not surprising to note that "one hundred percent of faculty who identified as of color, multiethnic, or LGBTQ+[50] in the survey, teach about diversity issues in their courses."[51]

The Lack of Mentors

A significant barrier for students of Color who attend predominately White colleges is the absence of a mentor to guide and prepare members of underrepresented communities for a career in the performing arts. In the next section, the first Workforce Diversity study respondent of Color who studied dance in college remembers how she was treated by her White professors and how the lack of support shook her confidence as a performer. The second Workforce Diversity study respondent of Color speaks about the critical need for mentors of musicians of Color during the conservatory or college years.

Respondent #1: "I remember some upper-classmen, who complained about the dearth of the number of students of Color who were accepted into the programs, and how the teachers, the technique teachers were White. And that can play a part in how you feel, in terms of your training, what you think that you are capable of. They always have their favorites, and it's rarely the Black girls. They assumed a lot of us had attitude. I was the one that they thought didn't have attitude because I was the quiet girl. And I made such a nice dancer. They had misconceptions and assumptions about Black women. Apparently, we all have attitudes.

"I never felt supported enough to feel confident enough, to know that I could have made it further in the professional realm. Yes, I danced with a small company, but I always thought I'd be an Ailey dancer, you know? No one supported us."

Respondent #2: "I've talked to musicians in orchestras that are from traditionally underrepresented communities and the ones who make it have had substantial mentorship. And [the mentorship] started when they were young. But on the college level it gets even more specific. It's not just mentorship, but it's having, at least on the orchestra side, a teacher that gives you the pathway to follow. And not only teaches you how to play but teaches you how to audition. That is huge. And it comes up again and again because especially in classical music, you can be the best musician in the world, but if you don't audition well, if you don't capture the right sound of the orchestra and match it, you won't be able to make the professional transition."

Low or Non-Paying Internships: Do They Really Pave the Way for Employment?

According to the National Association of Colleges and Employers (NACE) 2017 survey, almost 65% of employers want applicants with relevant industry experience and 56% prefer that the candidate has achieved the experience through an internship. NACE also reports that almost 40% of internships are unpaid.[52] What does this mean for People of Color? Does having an internship, which is often low- or non-paying, make a difference in gaining employment? In examining 40 years of orchestra fellowships for People of Color, the League of American Orchestras found that

there is no evidence that those orchestras who ran the fellowship programs are more diverse than those who didn't have people of color as fellows. . . . Fellowships don't change the fundamentals of the pipeline and by themselves are not a solution to persistent racial homogeneity of orchestras. . . . It's best to align the orchestra behind diversity goals prior to establishing fellowships across all functions and stakeholders: staff and management, board and governance, programming, repertoire, and audience and have shared values about inclusion. . . . Fellowships need to be welcoming and mentors need to be trained. . . . Meaningful relationships with communities of color are at the center of the process. . . . Building orchestra relationships with community music programs and conservatories can expand the pipeline.[53]

As the League of American Orchestras notes here, "Meaningful relationships with communities of color are at the center of the [fellowship] process." Since historically White colleges and predominately White performing arts organizations manage the internship process either together or alone, to what extent do they consider meaningful relationships with students and communities of Color central to internship process? It's apparent from the Workforce Diversity study respondents that once again communities of Color face obstacles within the White privileged internship process. The following two Workforce Diversity study respondents of Color comment on the problems with internships, including the lack of guidance they received in college about obtaining an internship and the lack of pay. The third respondent who identifies as White stresses the link between socioeconomic diversity and racial diversity when it comes to offering a decent internship educational experience that leads to employment.

> Respondent #1: "In college, I had work study. I worked in a psychology lab, I worked in a library, and I worked in a convenience store. I had jobs, but I didn't have internship opportunities. There was not, at the time, an office that helped me gain some experience in the arts. When I graduated, I didn't have the tools to know what to do next."

> Respondent #2: "If you've been accustomed to not having a lot of money in your life, why are you going to take an unpaid internship at an arts organization? Why are you going to work for fifty hours a week to make thirty thousand dollars a year when you may have a family to support or yourself to support?"

> Respondent #3: "The economic barrier is ridiculous. Nobody should work for free. We have a paid apprentice program. But it's not paying enough to really have the economic diversity that we need. And I think economic diversity directly links to racial diversity because of the systems and structures that White folks have created and benefit from. We're trying internally to build up our paid apprentice program so that it's enough money where people don't have to do their day job and can do the apprenticeship, get a great education here, and then go into the field or come onto our staff. We are trying to build a pipeline into staff to diversify the staff."

Low-paying internships, which often lead to initial access and possible employment in the historically White performing arts industry, remain inherent economic obstacles for individuals without power and privilege. While the White respondent here strives to disrupt socioeconomic barriers to racial diversity in his organization, People of Color face additional career pathway challenges because access to White privileged internships as well as other educational and job opportunities are found through and controlled by predominately White-member-homogeneous educational and career networks.

White-Member-Dominated Homogeneous Networks

In my 2002 published study on occupational transition from the profit to the nonprofit sector, I found that

> dominant members of a group control opportunities by recruiting members like themselves from homogeneous networks. The networks are comprised of people who have been trained, educated, or socialized together and thought to have the same values as well as shared class, race, and gender.[54]

This next Workforce Diversity study respondent is aware that he benefits from his networks:

> As a White male I am aware that not everyone has that same level of professional help [from their networks]. There are people who don't have someone to help them find a new job, serve as a reference for them; they are not part of the larger system of privilege.

Eighty percent of jobs are found through informal networks.[55] In his book, *Getting a Job*, sociologist Mark Granovetter found that "the structure and dynamics of the network . . . largely determine what information will reach a given person, and, to that extent, what possibilities will be open to him."[56] The Public Religion Research Institute, "a nonprofit, nonpartisan organization dedicated to conducting independent research at the intersection of religion, culture, and public policy," found that "among white Americans, 91% of people comprising their social networks are white."[57] People of Color are not likely to be part of a White employer's social network or circle of close friends. Within social networks, a close friend is someone you have to your home states this Workforce Diversity study respondent of Color:

> People might deal with their friends of Color at work or at different places where they actually socialize, but who is coming home for dinner? Most of these [White] people don't invite People of Color to their home. When you don't socialize in ways where you discuss your life and your family, then there's no way that you can integrate anything.

According to the Pew Research Center,

> few adults say they have a lot in common with those who don't
> share their own racial background. . . . Sixty-two percent of single-
> race white [Pew Research respondents] say they have a lot in com-
> mon with people in the U.S. who are white, while about one-in-ten
> or fewer said that they have a lot in common with people who are
> black, Asian or American Indian."[58]

Furthermore,

> 81% of single-race white adults said that all or most of their close
> friends are white; 70% of single-race black adults reported that all
> or most of their close friends are black; and 54% of single-race Asian
> American adults reported that all or most their close friends are
> Asian American.[59]

In *Two-Faced Racism*, Picca and Feagin report that "most whites claim-
ing black friends do not actually list them in their lists of good friends."[60]
Friendship circles are segregated by race and this "spatial separation of
racial interaction in U.S. society contributes to [the] lack of white understanding."[61] This lack of "White understanding" becomes obvious when
examining a predominately White performing arts organization's biased
recruitment and hiring practices.

Biased Recruitment and Hiring Practices

Although the dominant group controls career opportunities through
their homogeneous White-member networks, race-based hiring decisions
in U.S. employment are illegal:

> Under the laws enforced by the U.S. Equal Employment Opportu-
> nity Commission, it is illegal to discriminate against someone (appli-
> cant or employee) because of that person's race, color, religion,
> sex (including gender identity, sexual orientation, and pregnancy),
> national origin, age (40 or older), disability or genetic information.[62]

Despite this written law, over a 25-year period (1989–2015), White job
applicants were found to receive an average of 36% more [job] callbacks
than equally qualified African American respondents and 24% more
callbacks than Latino respondents.[63] Economists Marianne Bertrand and
Sendhil Mullainathan found that individuals with African American–
sounding names are less likely to be interviewed if they have names that
resonated with White employers as African American.[64] One reason for

favoring "White sounding names," during the recruitment process, can be explained by the lack-of-fit theory:

> The "lack-of-fit" theory suggests that the lack of congruence between attributes stereotypically ascribed to a poorly represented group and those stereotypically ascribed to a better represented group contributes to a belief that underrepresented group members are not a good "fit" for particular jobs.[65]

Jobs Aren't Publicly Advertised

Predominately White performing arts organizations often recruit and hire senior managers without a public job advertising announcement, thus restricting the numbers of applicants to individuals who are perceived to fit, meaning group members "[who are perceived to] curate from a White sensibility," as one Workforce Diversity study respondent of Color observed:

> The hiring system itself is entirely flawed. There's such a tight, tight secrecy around these positions until the very end of the search process, which is good because the candidates don't want to be exposed and they don't want to be vulnerable in their current jobs. The downside of that is that it has led to inequitable hiring practices. Because those job searches are not public, there's no pressure on those involved to ensure that the final candidates are diverse, meaning gender, culturally diverse, ethnically diverse. There's simply no pressure for it to be so. And at the very top leadership of our LORT theaters, we have hiring practices that are very simply not good enough. And again, I submit if they were transparent, we would see different outcomes.
>
> There are those in the field who and I don't agree, who think it's a pipeline question. That there just aren't people of Color who can do the math necessary to be the executive director of a LORT theater. And, of course, it's asinine. There are biases in the process. There are biases in who can be in one of these jobs. As a Person of Color, there's great suspicion that you will curate from one's ethnic or cultural background in a way that frightens White organizations. So, if you're a Person of Color who goes through these searches, you learn to step through the minefield that is in some of those questions. Nobody asks the White person if they're going to curate from a White sensibility. Everybody asks, or if they don't ask, are thinking, "Wow, is this person going to come in and just make plays around the Arab American experience?" These are powerful, powerful biases in the field.

In their work, *Managing Diversity: Human Resource Strategies for Transforming the Workplace*, Ellen E. Kossek and Sharon A. Lobel write that "human resource systems are based on models of homogeneity. . . . Selection practices stress choosing candidates similar to those who have been successful."[66]

Educational Credentialing is an Access Barrier

As was mentioned in the previous sections people are recruited from homogeneous networks who work and are trained or educated together. The following two Workforce Diversity study respondents, the first who identifies as Black and the second who identifies as White, agree that educational credentialing, which statistically favors White college graduates of performing arts degree programs, plays a role in keeping People of Color out of predominately White performing arts organizations.

> Respondent #1: "I think we live in a false meritocracy, where people think if you went to Harvard that means something other than you had good test scores. I'm a huge proponent of education, obviously, but just because you went to Princeton doesn't mean that you are good at your job, for instance. But I think that there's a belief [in credentialing] and it's an easy metric tool. I feel like I've learned as much with trial and error as I did in college. I don't necessarily see formal education as being the only type of education that's beneficial if you want to run an organization or be in a managerial capacity in an organization."

> Respondent #2: "And to the extent that educational attainment is used as a recruitment tool, I think it's widely done, and I believe it's a mistake. I think that we would do far better in addressing issues of diversity and equity if [educational attainment] wasn't so highly prioritized. It's code for 'I want a White person.' It's not that overt. It certainly is something that we should be very conscious of."

People of Color who break through and are hired by predominately White performing arts organizations may face additional biased attitudes and harmful decisions that ultimately result in their inability to lead, advance, or remain in the organization.

Advancement and Retention Barriers

In the 2017 *Race to Lead* study of more than 4,000 respondents, more than one-third of People of Color working in nonprofit organizations felt their race negatively impacted their career advancement. Seventy percent of those respondents gave write-in explanations, including the perceived inability to be selected for a leadership role, exclusion from social networks, and microaggressions.[67] In the Workforce Diversity study, one respondent of Color was overlooked for a leadership position in a Predominately White Organization because of perceived inability to lead:

> I remember the first time I went for an opportunity to step up; in my last three appraisal reviews my performance had been deemed as "outstanding." I had been encouraged by my line manager to apply for a senior manager role at a time when the organization was restructuring. I submitted my application, and I remember speaking to the recruiting director at the time. She called me in and explained to me that they had made a decision to not short-list me for an interview. The reason I was given was that I didn't have line management experience. I was left almost speechless. I remember my response to the director at the time, saying, "I've got a track record that's second to none in the organization. My performance record speaks for itself." I wasn't asking for the job, simply the opportunity to put my case forward on merit. As you look to develop your career there are going to be natural moments in a recruitment process where you may not be able to demonstrate your experience of doing particular tasks; you have to trust recruitment panels to also judge you on your potential to step up. If you're not given an opportunity to develop or do new things how can you be expected to develop the skills and experience to successfully apply for more senior roles? It was heartbreaking and my first but certainly not last experience of hitting a glass ceiling.
>
> Too often when people are looking to recruit, unconscious bias kicks in creating an aversion to appointing somebody that looks or thinks differently. I remember an interview experience where I was told I was a strong candidate for the role. I had all the skills and experience to do it. They gave the job to somebody who had covered the post previously. They wanted a safe pair of hands.

Respondents of Color interviewed for this study often reported having left a predominately White performing arts organization or the field because they don't feel connected to the mission or the public purpose of the organization. In addition, People of Color feel they are relegated to certain positions within their Predominately White Organizations and don't have the opportunity to lead. States one African American respondent:

> Some of my friends who have advanced degrees in nonprofit management, arts administration left the field because they couldn't find an organization where they felt deeply connected to the mission of the organization. You want to be connected to the art in a real way. And

the people I know who left, didn't feel connected to the mission of the organization. Most of us who came into the field, myself included were relegated to education and community outreach program positions. And that was it. We didn't see opportunities or didn't feel like we would have been supported to move into a track that would lead us to leadership positions within organizations. So, we left.

Explicit Racial Bias in the Workplace

Lack of leadership opportunities certainly contribute to the problem of retaining People of Color in performing arts organizations that choose to remain primarily White. In addition to the lack of leadership and advancement opportunities, what other factors contribute to a Person of Color's decision to leave the primarily White performing arts workforce? The 2017 *Unrealized Impact* study of educational organizations found that "38 percent of Latinx and 51 percent of Black staff members who are considering leaving their organizations agreed that the lack of diversity, equity, and inclusion is a factor when people of color leave the organization."[68] People of Color feel an emotional tax from exclusion and bias on a daily basis. In a report, conducted by Catalyst, called *Day-to-Day Experiences of Emotional Tax Among Women and Men of Color in the Workplace*, almost 60% of People of Color surveyed felt they "must be on guard to protect against racial and gender bias" at work. They were also more likely to want to leave their employers.[69]

The Lack of a Mentor Creates Self-Doubt

Without the support of a mentor or role model and particularly an ALAANA role model, it may be more difficult for a Person of Color to feel confident navigating the culture of a predominately White performing arts organization and assuming senior leadership. Here are two examples from the Workforce Diversity study:

Respondent #1: "I go back and forth with whether or not I want to hold an executive leadership position. Part of me wants to pursue it so that I can make a difference in the landscape and become a champion for change. Like many of us I struggle with self-doubt, questioning my worth and ability to be successful. I question my ability to relate to my colleagues at that level and struggle with acceptance: Will they welcome me, or will I be forced to not only fight to be successful but also fight for validation and respect? I don't know if that's a racial issue, as I believe many of us, from all ethnicities struggle with the same thing, however I believe if there were more women and men of Color in leadership positions, the idea of achieving such a goal wouldn't feel so unattainable. I suspect the path would still be challenging, but I would, at the very least, have individuals I could turn to for guidance."

Respondent #2: "I aspired to be in top management, but I didn't have the confidence, early in my career. Why didn't I have the confidence? I think because I didn't have a mentor, and I didn't see anyone who looked like me in top positions. I didn't think it was possible, so I didn't apply to be the managing director of a major theater. I aspired to be a managing director, but I didn't apply, because I didn't see a Black woman managing director and I didn't think I would be considered as a viable candidate. I placed limitations on myself. They weren't put on me. I didn't apply for those positions because I didn't feel comfortable. I didn't feel like I'd be accepted or taken seriously. If I had had someone who looked like me telling me, 'This is why you should apply, the work is no different than what you're already doing.' Someone who could have encouraged and advocated on my behalf, I would have made the effort. You have all these scenarios in your head, that are real or not real. Having a mentor would have helped me differentiate between what was real and wasn't real."

This Workforce Diversity study respondent of Color didn't have a mentor encouraging her and advocating on her behalf for senior leadership opportunities. The absence of a mentor and a role model of Color influenced the Workforce Diversity study respondent's decision not to apply for an executive leadership position. The respondent's self-inflicted leadership limitations are yet another consequence of a racialized performing arts opportunity structure.

As we have discussed, the racialized opportunity structure is found in early childhood education, higher education, and the primarily White-member-homogeneous networks that are used to control training, recruitment, and retention practices in historically White performing arts organizations. Without mentors or sponsors to guide ALAANA employees, opportunities may not be accessible for People of Color in White privileged performing arts organizations. Majority-White board members hold the power within these organizations and are loath to question and change these inequitable practices. So, they, together with the majority-White leadership continue to support these undemocratic practices both within the organization and outside through inequitable partnerships with ALAANA-led performing arts organizations and community members of Color.

Community Partnership Inequities:
Lack of Mutual Respect

The Wallace Foundation's Community Partnerships for Cultural Participation (CPCP) initiative funded a five-year cultural partnership project between large and small cultural organizations for building new audiences among the larger organizations and building greater capacity among the smaller organizations. "Seven of the ten large-small partnerships were cross-ethnic collaborations in which the larger partner had a predominately white staff, board, and audience, and the smaller partner had a predominately African-American or Latino staff, board, and audience."[70] The community partnerships between the large and small organizations were not equitable. The challenges included disparities between resources, as well as cultural and structural differences between the large and small organizations that were not addressed.[71] There were problems concerning mutual respect where the smaller organization didn't feel it was treated as a full partner.[72] An evaluation of the initiative suggested that agreements between larger and smaller organizations must outline the roles, responsibilities, leaders on board, assessment of costs, the accommodation of different organizational cultures, and schedules.[73]

Community Partnerships and Cultural Appropriation

To what extent have the Wallace Foundation's recommendations been followed by primarily White performing arts organizations today? To what degree are ALAANA-led performing arts organizations considered full partners in community partnerships with primarily White performing arts organizations? Two Workforce Diversity study respondents spoke about the ways in which cultural appropriation or the "wrongful taking of ideas, images, and designs without recognition, permission, or recognition"[74] fuels inequitable partnerships between primarily White performing arts organizations and ALAANA-led performing arts organizations.

> Respondent #1: "A large predominately White performing arts organization received funding to do a Caribbean festival. The small organization that had been doing it all along was not able to get their original grant because the funder said, 'We gave it to them [Primarily White Organization].' So now we have this issue of cultural appropriation, which we must be sensitive to. So, the small organization sat down with the large organization. The small organization was allowed to do the programming, so they would still get paid as producers and not be totally out of the loop.
> "White organizations must take responsibility and be sensitive to that [cultural appropriation]. And not be so greedy.
> "At the same time funders are telling the Primarily White Organization: 'We're not going to give you money unless you have diverse programming.' So, if you don't know where to do it, you're just going to go and grab what's in front of you and what's easy. 'I'm going to get money and I have to create something. So, do I do that on the fly? Is there any substance to it? Are there any partnerships? Have I thought this through?' Can these [Primarily White Organizations] do something

that's meaningful or is it just to check this box: 'We did a diversity program.' If that's the case the art suffers. If you keep the art as the center, then I think that allows us to be much more mindful."

Respondent #2: "Primarily White theaters will reach out to a Latinx theater, or people who run a Latinx program within another Primarily White Organization and say, 'Oh, we're doing this play by a Latina playwright. We want to get an audience. We want to really encourage the community. Could you help us, or could we partner with you?' And we say, 'Okay, Primarily White Organization: Have you been coming to our plays? Have you been supporting us before you needed us for your particular play? Have you been keeping up with the work of this Latinx theater, or becoming interested in these artists, or connecting with the community that goes to this Latinx theater? So, if you haven't, don't come to me then when you need something for the grant you want to get or the play you want to market. And then try to take our resources. Because it took a lot of time and energy and money to build up that community. To do the work we've been doing.'
"I don't mean to say that theaters shouldn't collaborate. Of course, we'd like to expand the audience that we reach. But I just feel like there's a bit of a colonial extraction: 'Let's go take the natural resources from South America and bring them to Spain.' There are people who are really not aware of their own colonialism, and their own colonial practices. And it's kind of shocking to me, but really, people are very clueless about it. Way too often.
"It's often so extractive, and yet it's the institution with more power that's extracting from the one that has been killing itself to survive for the last 25 years. But they want to come in and mine those relationships that took a long time to build. It's really an insult and disrespectful."

Funding Cultural Inequity Practices

Funding matters and contributes to the inequitable cultural partnerships described in this chapter and the racial and ethnic disparities within the entire performing arts workforce. According to the 2016 study conducted by DataArts of 701 cultural groups in ten U.S. cities, ALAANA-led cultural groups who explicitly serve ALAANA communities have less access to grants of substantial size and less capacity to develop reserves and generate investment income, which affects their ability to hire full-time dedicated staff, engage in professional development, and build capacity.[75] Holly Sidford and Alexis Frasz report in their *Not Just Money* study that "funding is more concentrated in the hands of institutions that already have resources. Two percent of all cultural institutions receive close to 60 percent of contributed revenue."[76] The majority of those organizations funded focus on "primarily Western European fine arts traditions."[77] Just 4% of foundation arts funding is allocated to groups with a primary mission of serving communities of Color.[78] The Greenlining Institute reports "it is estimated that communities of color receive less than 5% of all charitable donations from the more than 72,000 foundations in the country."[79]

This gross inequity in funding is confirmed by two Workforce Diversity study respondents of Color. One Workforce Diversity study respondent who identifies as Asian Pacific American stated:

> I just came from a conference where organizations of Color are struggling on the ground, and yet there was this initiative that gave a million each to the large Primarily White Organizations to do work around diversity. And people are angry about that; people are bitter about that. And you kind of understand why, right? It's such a slap in the face to organizations that are there 24/7 and who have the most primary and ongoing relationships in their communities.

Another Workforce Diversity study respondent of Color concurred:

> I know a Culturally Specific Organization[80] and they applied for a grant from a local funder and they didn't receive it. However, when a larger, Predominately White Organization applied to that same funder in order to connect with the Culturally Specific community, the Predominately White Organization received the grant. In the grant, the White organization said that they were going to be working with the Culturally Specific Organization [which didn't receive the grant]. The smaller organization wasn't aware of this. The main question is whether there's parity between the partners and if those organizations of Color have equal roles.

Implicit Bias in Foundations

Within the philanthropic sector, according to scholar john a. powell,

> power and efficacy of philanthropy work may be limited by the subconscious processes that work to reinforce structural barriers to equality. . . . Implicit bias in philanthropy affects not just which groups get funded, but also who sits on boards of philanthropic organizations (mostly white males), how grantmaking foundations set priorities, how decisions are made, who makes those decisions, and even who gets hired.[81]

One Workforce Diversity study respondent of Color shared insights about the ways in which implicit bias affects grantmaking for organizations of Color:

> There are a lot of funders that for a long time didn't even know that they were doing it [employing unconscious bias in grantmaking]. We

also have a [grantmaking] rigidity that has unintentionally excluded folks from Culturally Specific Organizations. We'd rather give it to the people that we trust, right? So, if we have a one-million-dollar grant to support a partnership between a historically White organization and a smaller Culturally Specific Organization, we would give the grant to the historically White institution. And we do that because we think that they can better manage the money. That is our unconscious bias. As funders, we look at things through a very rational viewpoint to ask ourselves, who is the most capable of doing this and who is the least risk? Because every single grant is a risk. You are taking on the risk, and the ultimate risk is that you lose all that money that you just invested in the communities, and it gets used inappropriately. And you don't get that back—that's the risk. That's the worst risk. The problem is, how do we determine what is "good?" And so, what we determine as good is what we know, and that is financial strength, right? And a certain level of responsibility. And we want to minimize that risk.

The other challenge is that if applications are so complicated and cumbersome and the organization doesn't even have one full time staff member, how are they going to complete the application process? Foundations are not flexible. Applications may not be written in multiple languages, and the application deadlines may only be issued quarterly. So, the application process, while not overtly racist, in and of itself precludes a certain type of organization from applying. And that is a huge issue and it is one that nobody wants to tackle. Because if we say, "How about if we have a different type of application for organizations with budgets under two-hundred and fifty thousand dollars?" Well, they become a higher risk. So that's the part that nobody wants to talk about. Yes, right now the conversation is, "We want more Culturally Specific Organizations applying to us. We're actively looking for them and want to support them." But are we providing the technical assistance to help them through those operations?

The difference between equity and equality is that equality is the process of giving everyone the exact same thing without acknowledging that they might be coming from very different viewpoints and advantages. Equity gives people the thing that they need to succeed at the same level but acknowledges that people are bringing in different life experiences. So, we are practicing equality as a field in some ways; we're practicing equality at the expense of equity, right? Give everyone the same application but we're not acknowledging that people are coming at it from entirely different levels of capacity. And that is completely unfair, and therein I think is the real challenge. I think it's about unconscious bias and not understanding how this rigidity is actually creating an inequitable space.

Foundations Are Driven by People Without Relevant Lived Experience

In her *Chronicle of Philanthropy* article "Elites at Work," author Nicole Wallace states that "the cultures of foundations and larger charities are geared toward people from prosperous economic backgrounds, with plenty of unspoken rules about how to communicate, debate issues, and make decisions."[82] Rodney Christopher, senior consultant at Fiscal Management Associates, reveals, "There's a lot of wanting to make other people's lives better. But the reality is that if no one in the [foundation] room understands what it's like to be one of those people, it's very easy to come up with solutions that are somewhat ignorant."[83] Furthermore, states Stephen Patrick, executive director of the Aspen Institute's Forum for Community Solutions, "People from the community need to be the [foundation] program designers. [Too often] foundations are driven by people without lived experience."[84] How do ALAANA members with lived experience get into this "invisible field?" A Workforce Diversity respondent of Color was dubious that foundations are intentionally recruiting People of Color:

> I think the philanthropic organizations are probably not doing much proactively to find People of Color to work there unless they're actually looking for someone in diversity and thinking critically and creatively about how to diversify themselves. A lot of these organizations probably don't really think they need to. It's unclear how to get into philanthropy if you're not already in it. And I think that there are a lot of people, probably larger percentages of whom are People of Color who either don't really have a clear sense of how one would go about getting a job in philanthropy, or because they have never encountered a Person of Color who works for a foundation, they probably don't even think about this line of work as being something that's available to them. I've met very few people who were college age or at the beginning of their careers who have been of Color and are interested in working in foundations. And when I've brought it up to people, they have had the same of reaction, "I've never thought of that," or "How do you get that kind of a job?" or even, "What do you do?" I think philanthropy really has to be intentional especially in a sector that is un-diverse as philanthropy is.

Conclusion

When asked why there are so few People of Color leading nonprofit organizations, less than half of the *Race to Lead* respondents of Color said it is because People of Color are reluctant to pursue executive positions in majority-White organizations. Instead most respondents of Color identified structural issues, such as biases from board members and executive recruiters.[85] As has been explored in this chapter, predominately White performing arts organizations fail in many cases to intentionally and authentically provide a welcoming and safe space for People of Color and ALAANA communities. Implicit or unconscious bias, which fuels White privilege and fragility, stereotyping, colorblind racist practices, and microaggressions, are found in many aspects of the racialized workforce ecosystem of intersecting predominately White educational, performing arts, and philanthropic organizations. Beginning in childhood, many People of Color report economic and social barriers that impede access to arts education and proper training that will lead to artistic careers in the field. Primarily White-member-homogeneous networks perpetuate inequities in access to training and recruitment opportunities, and the absence of mentors and ALAANA role models may also impact educational options and career opportunities for advancement and retention in primarily White performing arts organizations. Finally, the White privileged opportunity structure may further inhibit access through the overrepresentation of predominately White funders who continue to control the inequitable distribution of resources between historically White performing organizations and ALAANA-led performing arts organizations.

In combatting and dismantling these inequitable practices, there are leaders in historically White educational, performing arts, and philanthropic organizations that are working in unity with ALAANA-led performing arts organizations and communities of Color to create a transformative culturally plural performing arts workforce, where racial and ethnic access, diversity, equity, and inclusion is considered central to every decision made.

Notes

1. Max Weber, *Economy and Society*, Guenther Roth and Claus Wittich, eds. (Berkeley, CA: University of California Press, 1978), 953.
2. Tobie S. Stein, "Creating Opportunities for People of Color in Performing Arts Management," *Journal of Arts Management, Law and Society* 29, no. 4 (Winter 2000): 307.
3. Rosabeth Moss Kanter, *Men and Women of the Corporation* (New York, NY: Basic Books, 1977), 63.
4. Lee Anne Bell, "Theoretical Foundations for Social Justice Education," in *Teaching for Diversity and Social Justice*, 3rd ed., eds. Maurianne Adams and Lee Anne Bell, with Dianne J. Goodman and Khyati Y. Joshi (New York, NY: Routledge, 2016), 11–12.
5. Ibid., 11.
6. Rich Morin, *Exploring Racial Bias Among Biracial and Single-Race Adults: The IAT* (Washington, DC: Pew Research Center, August 19, 2015), www.

pewsocialtrends.org. "Pew Research Center bears no responsibility for the analyses or interpretations of the data presented here. The opinions expressed herein, including any implications for policy, are those of the author and not of Pew Research Center."

7. Ibid.
8. Ibid.
9. Project Implicit was founded in 1998 by Anthony Greenwald, Mahzarin Banaji, and Brian Nosek, https://implicit.harvard.edu.
10. Mahzarin Banaji and Anthony G. Greenwald, *Blindspot: Hidden Biases of Good People* (New York, NY: Bantam, 2013), 50, in Morin, *Exploring Racial Bias Among Biracial and Single-Race Adults*, www.pewsocial-trends.org. "Pew Research Center bears no responsibility for the analyses or interpretations of the data presented here. The opinions expressed herein, including any implications for policy, are those of the author and not of Pew Research Center."
11. Patricia Clark and Eva Zygmunt, "A Close Encounter With Personal Bias," *The Journal of Negro Education* 83, no. 2 (2014): 147–61.
12. Poonam Sharma and Denise Lucero-Miller, "Beyond Political Correctness," in *Teaching About Culture, Ethnicity, and Diversity*, ed. Theodore M. Singelis (Thousand Oaks, CA: Sage, 1998), 192.
13. Barbara Trepagnier, *Silent Racism*, 2nd ed. (Boulder, CO: Paradigm, 2010), 72.
14. Pierre Bourdieu, *Outline of a Theory of Practice* (Cambridge: Cambridge University Press, 1977), 95.
15. Daniel Goleman, *Social Intelligence* (New York, NY: Bantam, 2006), 300.
16. Ruth Frankenberg, *White Women, Race Matters: The Social Construction of Whiteness* (Minneapolis, MN: University of Minnesota, 1993), 1.
17. Nirmal Puwar, "The Racialised Somatic Norm and the Senior Civil Service," *Sociology* 35, no. 3 (August 2001): 656.
18. Allan G. Johnson, "The Social Construction of Difference," in *Readings for Diversity and Social Justice*, 3rd ed., eds. Maurianne Adams, Warren J. Blumenfeld, Carmelita Castañeda, Heather W. Hackman, Madeline L. Peters, and Ximena Zúñiga (New York, NY: Routledge, 2013), 20.
19. Peggy McIntosh, "White Privilege: Unpacking the Invisible Knapsack," *Peace and Freedom Magazine* (July/August, 1989): 10–12, https://national-seedproject.org.
20. Max Weber, *Economy and Society*, Roth and Wittich, eds., 953.
21. Ibid., 952.
22. Robin DiAngelo, "White Fragility," Journal of Critical Pedagogy 3, no. 3 (2011): 54. Tessa L. Dover, Brenda Major, and Cheryl R. Kaiser, "Members of High-Status Groups Are Threatened by Pro-Diversity Organizational Messages," *Journal of Experimental Social Psychology* 62 (January 2016): 59.
23. Michell Norris, "The Rising Anxiety of White America," *National Geographic* (April 2018): 88.
24. Brigitte Vittrup, "Color Blind or Color Conscious? White American Mothers' Approaches to Racial Socialization," *Journal of Family Issues* 39, no. 3 (2016): 688; Brigitte Vittrup, "How Silence Can Breed Prejudice: A Child Development Professor Explains How and Why to Talk to Kids About Race," *Washington Post* (July 6, 2015), www.washingtonpost.com.
25. Ibid.

26. Gordon W. Allport, *The Nature of Prejudice* (Reading, MA: Addison-Wesley, 1954), 191.
27. Galen W. Bodenhausen and Robert S. Wyer, "Effects of Stereotypes on Decision Making and Information-Processing Strategies," *Journal of Personality and Social Psychology* 48 (1985): 267, in Tobie S. Stein, *Workforce Transitions from the Profit to the Nonprofit Sector* (New York, NY: Kluwer Academic/Plenum Publishers, 2002), 85.
28. Puwar, "The Racialised Somatic Norm," 656.
29. Lee Anne Bell, *Storytelling for Social Justice* (New York, NY: Routledge, 2010), 31.
30. Evan P. Apfelbaum, Michael I. Norton, and Samuel R. Sommers, "Racial Color Blindness: Emergence, Practice, and Implications," *Current Directions in Psychological Science* 21, no. 3 (2012): 207.
31. Leslie Houts Picca and Joe R. Feagin, *Two-Faced Racism* (New York, NY: Routledge, 2007), 154; Lee Anne Bell, Michael S. Funk, Khyati Y. Joshi, and Marjorie Valdivia, "Racism and White Privilege," in *Teaching for Diversity and Social Justice*, 3rd ed., eds. Maurianne Adams and Lee Anne Bell, with Diane J. Goodman and Khyati Y. Joshi (New York, NY: Routledge, 2016), 136; Trepagnier, *Silent Racism*.
32. Christina M. Capodilupo and Derald Wing Sue, "Microaggressions in Counseling and Psychotherapy," in *Counseling the Culturally Diverse*, eds. Derald Wing Sue and David Sue (Hoboken, NJ: Wiley, 2013), 150.
33. Ibid., 154.
34. Picca and Feagin, *Two-Faced Racism*, 31.
35. Derald Wing Sue and David Sue, *Counseling the Culturally Diverse* (Hoboken, NJ: Wiley, 2013), 123.
36. Katherine L. Milkman, Modupe Akinola, and Dolly Chugh, "What Happens Before? A Field Experiment Exploring How Pay and Representation Differentially Shape Bias on the Pathway Into Organizations," *Journal of Applied Psychology* 100, no. 6 (2015): 1680.
37. Nick Rabkin and E. C. Hedberg, *Arts Education in America: What the Declines Mean for Arts Participation* (Washington, DC: National Endowment for the Arts, 2011), 47, www.arts.gov. The data is based on the 2008 Survey of Public Participation in the Arts.
38. Orfield and Lee, *Why Segregation Matters* (Cambridge, MA: Harvard University, 2005), 18, in Bell, Funk, Joshi, and Valdivia, "Racism and White Privilege," 150.
39. Prepared Remarks of U.S. Secretary of Education Arne Duncan on the Report, "Arts Education in Public Elementary and Secondary Schools: 2009–10," U.S. Department of Education (April 2, 2012), www.ed.gov.
40. Lisa C. DeLorenzo, "Missing Faces from the Orchestra," *Music Educators Journal* 98, no. 4 (June 2012): 39–46.
41. League of American Orchestras, *Forty Years of Fellowships: A Study of Orchestras' Efforts to Include African American and Latino Musicians.* A Report by the League of American Orchestras with Research and Analysis by Nick Rabkin and Monica Hairston O'Connell (New York, NY: League of American Orchestras, September 2016), 28.
42. Gia Kourlas, "Push for Diversity in Ballet Turns to Training the Next Generation," *New York Times* (October 30, 2015), www.nytimes.com.
43. "American College President Study 2017," *American Council on Education*, www.acenet.edu.

44. U.S. Department of Education, National Center for Education Statistics, *The Condition of Education 2018 (NCES 2018–144), Characteristics of Postsecondary Education* (2018), https://nces.ed.gov/fastfacts. Percentages do not sum to 100% due to unrounded numbers presented in the report.
45. Signe-Mary McKernan et al., *Nine Charts About Wealth Inequality in America (Updated)* (Washington, DC: Urban Institute, 2015). The chart title was updated on October 24, 2017, https://ggwash.org.
46. Valerie Wilson and Zane Mokhiber, "2016 ACS Shows Stubbornly High Native American Poverty and Different Degrees of Economic Well-Being for Asian Ethnic Groups," *Economic Policy Institute* (September 15, 2017), www.epi.org.
47. Perna M. Cahalan et al., *2018 Indicators of Higher Education Equity in the United States: Historical Trend Report* (Washington, DC: The Pell Institute for the Study of Opportunity in Higher Education, Council for Opportunity in Education, and Alliance for Higher Education and Democracy of the University of Pennsylvania, 2018), 96, www.pellinstitute.org.
48. U.S. Department of Education, National Center for Education Statistics, Table 322.30. *Bachelor's Degrees Conferred by Postsecondary Institutions, by Race/Ethnicity and Field of Study: 2015–16 and 2016–17* (Washington, DC: National Center for Education Statistics, October 2018), https://nces.ed.gov. The numbers do not sum to 100% due to rounding and because I did not include all categories presented in the analysis. There was no breakdown of visual vs. performing arts degrees awarded.
49. U.S. Department of Education, National Center for Education Statistics, Table 323.30. *Master's Degrees Conferred by Postsecondary Institutions, by Race/Ethnicity and Field of Study: 2015–16 and 2016–17* (Washington, DC: National Center for Education Statistics, October 2018), https://nces.ed.gov. The numbers do not sum to 100% due to rounding and because I did not include all categories presented in the analysis. There was no breakdown of visual vs. performing arts degrees awarded.
50. LGBTQ+ is an inclusive social identity term that stands for Lesbian, Gay, Bisexual, Transgender, Questioning or Queer. "The Plus Sign Represents Many Additional Identifications Within the [LGBTQ+] Community," *Horizon Blog* (January 12, 2019), www.horizon-health.org.
51. Antonio C. Cuyler, "A Survey of Arts Management Educators' Teaching on Diversity Issues," *Journal of Arts Management, Law & Society* 47, no. 3 (2017): 197–98, 200.
52. National Association of Colleges and Employers, "Employers Prefer Candidates With Work Experience," (April 5, 2017), www.naceweb.org; Andrew Crain, *Understanding the Impact of Unpaid Internships on College Student Career Development and Employment Outcomes* (Bethlehem: NACE Foundation, 2016), 11.
53. League of American Orchestras, *Forty Years of Fellowships*, 13, 28, 29, 30, 32, 33.
54. Stein, *Workforce Transitions*, 21.
55. Eduardo Bonilla-Silva, *Racism Without Racists*, 3rd ed. (New York, NY: Roman & Littlefield, 2010), 33.
56. Mark Granovetter, *Getting a Job*, 2nd ed. (Chicago, IL: University of Chicago Press, 1995), 17–18.
57. Daniel Cox, Juhem Navarro-Rivera, and Robert P. Jones, "Race, Religion, and Political Affiliation of Americans' Core Social Networks," *Public Religion Research Institute* (August 3, 2016), www.prri.org. The data was collected in 2013.

58. Kim Parker et al., "Chapter 5: Race and Social Connections-Friends, Family and Neighborhoods," in *Multiracial in America: Proud, Diverse and Growing in Numbers* (Washington, DC: Pew Research Center, June 2015). "Pew Research Center bears no responsibility for the analyses or interpretations of the data presented here. The opinions expressed herein, including any implications for policy, are those of the author and not of Pew Research Center."
59. Ibid.
60. Picca and Feagin, *Two-Faced Racism*, 116.
61. Ibid., 121.
62. U.S. Equal Employment Opportunity Commission, "Prohibited Employment Policies/Practices," www.eeoc.gov.
63. Lincoln Quillian et al., "Meta-Analysis of Field Experiments Shows No Change in Racial Discrimination in Hiring Over Time," *PNAS* 114, no. 41 (October 10, 2017): 1.
64. Marianne Bertrand and Sendhil Mullainathan, "Are Emily and Greg More Employable Than Lakisha and Jamal?" *The American Economic Review* 94, no. 4 (September 2004): 991–1013.
65. Heilman (1983, 1995, 2001), cited in Milkman, Akinola, and Chugh, "What Happens Before?" 1681–82.
66. Ellen Ernst Kossek and Sharon A. Lobel, eds., *Managing Diversity* (Malden, MA: Blackwell, 1996), 2–3.
67. Sean Thomas-Breitfeld and Frances Kunreuther, *Race to Lead: Confronting the Nonprofit Racial Leadership Gap* (New York, NY: Building Movement Project, 2017), 12, www.buildingmovement.org; The data was collected in 2016; Ofronama Biu, email to author, November 27 and 28, 2018.
68. Xiomara Padamsee and Becky Crowe, *Unrealized Impact* (Promise54, 2017), 30, http://promise54.org. The data was collected in 2016 and 2017.
69. Dnika J. Travis and Jennifer Thorpe-Moscon, *Day-to-Day Experiences of Emotional Tax Among Women and Men of Color in the Workplace* (New York, NY: Catalyst, 2018), 4, www.catalyst.org.
70. Francie Ostrower, *Partnerships Between Large and Small Cultural Organizations* (Washington, DC: The Urban Institute, 2004), 4, www.urban.org.
71. Ibid., 10.
72. Ibid.
73. Ibid., 12.
74. Tressa Berman, "Cultural Appropriation," in *A Companion to the Anthropology of American Indians*, ed. Thomas Biolsi (Malden, MA: Blackwell Publishing, 2004), 383.
75. Holly Sidford and Alexis Frasz, *Not Just Money: Equity Issues in Cultural Philanthropy*, (Oakland, CA; and Brooklyn, NY: Helicon Collaborative, July 2017), 14, 21, www.heliconcollab.net; Holly Sidford, email to author, February 28, 2019.
76. Sidford and Frasz, *Not Just Money*, 5, www.heliconcollab.net; Holly Sidford, email to author, February 28, 2019.
77. Ibid.
78. Ibid, 7.
79. Avis Atkins and Orson Aguilar, *A Promise to Diverse Communities: Summary of Foundation Coalition's Efforts* (Berkley, CA: Greenlining Institute, June 2012), www.greenlining.org.
80. Culturally Specific Organizations in this context are ALAANA-led organizations with missions that explicitly focus on ALAANA/POC populations.

81. john a. powell, "Implicit Bias and Its Role in Philanthropy and Grant-making," *Responsive Philanthropy* (Spring 2015): 12–13, www.ncrp.org/publication/responsive-philanthropy-spring-2015/implicit-bias-and-its-role-in-philanthropy-and-grantmaking.
82. Nicole Wallace, "Elites at Work," *The Chronicle of Philanthropy* (March 2017), 10.
83. Ibid. Rodney Christopher, email to author, May 9, 2019.
84. Ibid., 11. Stephen Patrick, email to author, May 8, 2019.
85. Thomas-Breitfeld and Kunreuther, *Race to Lead*, 16; The data was collected in 2016; Ofronama Biu, email to author, November 27 and 28, 2018.

5   The Racial and Ethnic ADEI-Centered Performing Arts Workforce

I spent a hundred days on a listening tour, and I articulated four core values for our organization. One of those four is equity, diversity, and inclusion, so it is imbedded within the very idea of ourselves. In addition to getting [multicultural competency] training as an organization, we have already instituted a policy that there's no longer such a thing as a non-diverse creative team. Every single creative team must be a diverse one. We have hiring practices in place that are new, which simply state that all searches are open until we have considered a diverse and qualified slate of candidates. The final group of candidates has to be inclusive, not just ethnically and racially, but by gender as well.

Palestinian American Workforce Diversity study respondent

Introduction

Racial and ethnic diversity in the historically White performing arts workforce can only be achieved when racial and ethnic ADEI is considered central to every organizational strategy and practice. This chapter focuses on pivotal strategies for developing a racial and ethnic ADEI-centered performing arts workforce. Respondents of all cultural backgrounds interviewed for this book lead the conversation in asking predominately White performing arts organizations to interrogate their core values and their motives for engaging specific communities of Color, demanding that leadership social justice practices be authentic and action oriented.

In a racial and ethnic ADEI-centered performing arts organization, the board and senior staff commitment to social justice or social action engagement is mandatory and communities of Color must be at the center of the social justice transformation. Transformative leadership, which disrupts the status quo,[1] must be focused on dismantling discriminatory practices in historically White performing arts organizations through a dedicated budget, hiring culturally diverse consultants and facilitators who will conduct antiracist training, as well as question, help reframe, and build new recruitment and retention strategies together with culturally plural staff and board leadership. Most importantly, in achieving a transformative racial and ethnic ADEI-centered performing arts workforce, antiracist White performing arts leaders recognize that genuine unity with ALAANA-led multi-party collaborations across intersecting sectors will produce social justice in the performing arts workforce.

Racial and Ethnic ADEI: Is There Alignment Between Words and Action?

A pivotal question for any Predominately White Organization to ask is whether there is an alignment between the rhetoric of diversity and the accessible, equitable, and inclusive activities of the organization.[2] Without racial and ethnic ADEI-centered core values and transformative social justice practices, both the PWO and the predominately White performing arts field will not become racially diverse. So, when determining the extent to which racial and ethnic ADEI is considered a core value, a Predominately White Organization must first question and analyze their motives for engaging communities of Color, as well as the degree to which the PWO's historical hiring and engagement processes may have harmed communities of Color.

"What Are Your Motives in Engaging Communities of Color?"

At the very center of the racial and ethnic ADEI core value are the ALAANA communities who must be viewed as the primary stakeholders. One Workforce Diversity study respondent who identifies as Nigerian American and from the African Caribbean Diaspora stated:

> Before you involve your community, it's important to interrogate what your motives are in actively seeking out People of Color. What do you think the benefits are to your organization, to the people who work there? What are the benefits to communities with which you're hoping to partner? What are the barriers you might face before even reaching out to other communities? It's important to poll people at your organization first and ask them what they think about diversity. If the poll results lack luster or it seems that people don't care, then maybe now's not the time to reach out to other communities for the sake of reaching out and then to check a box. Such results would indicate that probably there's some work you have to do first within your organization to make sure that when you do have those conversations with communities, that everybody's at least willing to work to be on the same page. It would be terrible to invite different communities to have a conversation and only twenty-five percent of your team is committed to doing the work.

"Is There Intentional ALAANA Community Engagement?"

The Annie E. Casey Foundation's *Race Equity and Inclusion Action Guide* emphasizes that in achieving race equity and inclusion, culturally diverse members of the community must be engaged and empowered to shape racial and ethnic ADEI-centered strategies through activities such as analyzing the historical root causes of race inequity, the solutions to achieving race equity, and the transformative impact those solutions will have on ALAANA communities.[3] For example one Black respondent interviewed for the Workforce Diversity study shared the way in which her organization intentionally engages with the community:

[The historically White performing arts organizations] that are successful are the ones that are intentional, and committed to doing the work all the time, and not just because it's timely. In St. Louis, we had the tragedy in Ferguson, the Michael Brown shooting. The city was divided, and it unearthed so many disparities in education, and access, and opportunity that went beyond this altercation between a White officer and a Black kid. The city is segregated in so many ways: Education and opportunities for different kinds of people are a problem. This situation unmasked all of that. Everyone needed to be in Ferguson at that moment; everyone needed to be working in Ferguson. Suddenly all these programs were created for kids in Ferguson; suddenly there were all these artists on the ground in Ferguson. There was all this attention to this neighborhood, and, mind you, it's just one neighborhood of many in this city that needs the support of the community, more access to opportunity, and quality education programs.

Something that I pride myself on, is that the organization that I work for, had been in that neighborhood for decades, working with schools and community centers, trying to effect change in education, and having a positive impact in the lives of students. If you want to really create a diverse performing arts organization, you have to be authentic in the way you're going about it, not just rushing into a situation because it's the topic of the day. Even in all this flurry, we were able to say, well we've always been in Ferguson, but we're not just in Ferguson, we are providing quality, free arts education programs in many neighborhoods that are grappling with some really, really tough issues, and through the arts, we believe we're making a difference. We believe that we are impacting the trajectory of these kids' lives.

The Racial and Ethnic ADEI Core Value and Stakeholder Buy-In

All organizational cultures consist of core values. If racial and ethnic ADEI is considered a core value then it must be central to every practice and policy within the organization. There must be stakeholder buy-in and accountability in which all stakeholders collectively define and agree to implement the actionable process of cultural and racial equity. In other words, there must be an alignment between cultural equity statements and the racial and ethnic ADEI-centered activities of the organization. In a racial and ethnic ADEI-centered organization, money and resources are allocated to the racial and ethnic ADEI assessment and implementation process. Racial and ethnic ADEI consultants are hired to objectively conduct the assessment and help develop and implement the plan. In transforming a Predominately White Organization into a Racial and Ethnic ADEI-Centered Organization, all stakeholders must collectively and continually question and build strategies around the extent to which they are using racial and ethnic ADEI as the dominant lens in organizational policies and practices.

Assessing the Racial and Ethnic ADEI Core Value

The next Workforce Diversity study respondent, who identifies as White, shared how racial and ethnic ADEI planning and implementation are strategic and central to transforming an organization that has been historically White:

> Equity, diversity, and inclusion is a core value. And it's a priority in our strategic plan, which is a board developed and approved document. It's more than a document; it's a road map for us. And we also have an internal equity, diversity, and inclusion Work Group that puts forth recommendations around how we can be as diverse, inclusive, and as equitable as possible. They've been working on how we operationalize that in terms of the staff. We do have a very diverse staff. When we hire for a position, we're pretty clear in the position description that we are an inclusive organization. We're conscious about interviewing a diverse pool of candidates, and we follow the hiring with a careful onboarding process. With the board, we analyze the composition every year and we put out a call for nominations and self-nominations. We make sure that there's balance in terms of gender, gender identity, race and ethnicity, geographic location, and budget size of the theater, because we have mostly a practitioner board. In our programming, it's the same thing. If you look at our convenings, you'll see how much programming we have that addresses how organizations and individuals can become more aware of equity issues in their lives as well as in their field. But we also have identity affinity spaces that run through our convenings. And that gives people the opportunity to meet and build allyship

around personal identity. There might be a queer and trans space. But there's also White allies against racism space. When everybody comes back together as a whole for various sessions, you really feel the power of the larger community as safe and welcoming. There are diverse voices and perspectives in the room at all times. Beyond that, all of our communications, our magazines, and our communications to the field are regularly addressing questions of equity, diversity, and inclusion.

If racial and ethnic ADEI is an intentional core value, there is a commitment to analysis and action. Within this Primarily White Organization that is working to transform itself, there is a task force dedicated to ADEI; the organization structures an accessible and equitable job search until it has identified a diverse applicant pool; the organization analyzes the diversity of the board of directors and develops an inclu--sive nomination process for recruiting new board members; within the programs of the organization, there are safe spaces for members to self-identify and meet around their social identities; and diverse perspectives are honored, respected, and empowered throughout the entire organization.

Do You Have Buy-in From Your Stakeholders?

Stating that racial and ethnic ADEI is a core value isn't good enough. In order to begin creating and implementing a racial and ethnic ADEI-centered plan, the historically White organization must first achieve buy-in from its stakeholders. One Workforce Diversity study respondent who identifies as White stated:

> In nonprofit organizations, there needs to be commitment and buy-in at three levels: The board, executive leadership, and staff. In my organization, we made it a priority through a strategic planning process, and I think it's important for people to really be able to discuss in an honest way what the state of the organization is, in terms of diversity and inclusion issues. I know in our case, when we started talking about it at the board level, which is diverse and includes many practitioners of Color, our organization thought we were doing a great job internally in terms of building more equity, diversity, and inclusion, so maybe we didn't have to focus on it as much in our plan. And some board members of Color, as well as White board members said, "Are you kidding? No! Look at the field. Look at the huge inequities that still exist in our field." We had a lot of passionate discussion about what those challenges were. And that's when EDI became a major strategic focus with board level approval. But

then the staff got very involved in figuring out what we were actually going to do. What our action plans would be. We wanted to model a new way forward for ourselves and others. And we knew we'd have to spend money to achieve our goals. Sometimes, when organizations start talking about equity, diversity, and inclusion, and it happens with other potential organizational priorities as well, the board and staff respond: "It's not in the budget. We don't have funding. We can't do it unless it's funded." But if you don't budget for something that's a priority, it won't ever happen. The important thing is to achieve agreement at those levels and develop some kind of plan to make it possible for everyone within your organization to participate. We worked with a consultant and did an internal assessment, and that assessment formed the basis of the initial work of our EDI Work Group. And so, it's establishing that sense of priority and then making sure that it's consistently carried out, and that there are financial resources and time available to really execute a plan.

Again, it comes down to the intentional and active commitment to make racial and ethnic ADEI a core value and priority. The stakeholders in the above primarily White performing arts organization were willing to face the fact that there was more transformative work to be done. The organization aligned its words with actionable steps: The organization dedicated the money to hiring an outside consultant to assess the state of the organization's commitment to diversity and then put together a plan where everyone could actively participate.

Cultural Equity Statement

The creation of an organizational cultural equity statement provides the roadmap and lens for implementing the cultural equity plan. "Cultural equity," according to Americans for the Arts,

> embodies the values, policies, and practices that ensure that all people—including but not limited to those who have been historically underrepresented based on race/ethnicity, age, disability, sexual orientation, gender, gender identity, socioeconomic status, geography, citizenship status, or religion—are represented in the development of arts policy; the support of artists; the nurturing of accessible, thriving venues for expression; and the fair distribution of programmatic, financial, and informational resources.[4]

One Workforce Diversity study respondent who identifies as White stated:

> Engaging the staff, or a subset of the staff, depending on how big you are, is vital in creating a commitment statement that is authentic and

represents the culture of the organization. Ask for volunteers from a cross-section of people in the organization who really want to come forward and be part of the process.

The Stage Directors and Choreographers Society (SDC) provides an example of a cultural equity statement that paves the way for a more accessible, diverse, equitable, and inclusive organization:

SDC believes that the American theatre must reflect the great diversity of our nation and affirms its commitment to equitable hiring practices in order to achieve that goal. As the Union that unites, empowers, and protects professional stage directors and choreographers whose work appears on stages across the country, we believe strongly that these values should manifest in the hiring of artists for projects and positions, as well as the representation of our Membership and our staff.

While SDC acknowledges the American theatre's longstanding dedication to diversity and inclusion, there remain inequities in hiring. We believe that despite good intentions there are biases in place that sometimes inhibit the hiring of qualified directors and choreographers from underrepresented groups. SDC further believes that this lack of opportunity contributes to the inability of these artists to create a sustainable career in the theatre.

In the creative enterprise of making theatre, SDC recognizes that the Union and its Membership have a great deal of influence, responsibility, and decision-making power in the industry. SDC acknowledges a need to cultivate a more diverse Membership within its own ranks as well as the need to examine hiring practices within the Union staff.

SDC challenges itself and the theatre community to ensure that qualified, diverse candidates are considered for each and every directing and/or choreography job on any given project or SDC staff position.

SDC is committed to taking the following actions:

Include, respect, and appreciate differences in ethnicity, gender, age, national origin, ability, sexual orientation, and identity, education, and religion in our goals and objectives.

Figure 5.1 SDC Diversity and Inclusion Statement of Commitment

Source: Stage Directors and Choreographers Society, *Diversity and Inclusion Statement of Commitment* (New York, NY: Stage Directors and Choreographers Society, December 7, 2015). This was published with permission from the Stage Directors and Choreographers Society.

Establish a Diversity and Inclusion Committee with a clear charter to oversee SDC's efforts and make recommendations to the Board through consistently integrated conversations.

Create structured opportunities for the Board and staff to increase awareness and understanding of the issues inherent in the work of inclusion and diversity.

Advocate for action on diversity, inclusion, and equity issues across all media platforms which are available to us; include current information on the Union's website detailing the efforts of the committee and the Union; maintain consistent, direct communication with our Membership about these issues on an ongoing basis.

Partner with SDC Foundation, ensuring that current and future programs align with SDC's inclusion and diversity goals of creating access and opportunities for underrepresented artists, and proactively support Artistic Directors.

Make available workshops and training opportunities regarding inclusion and diversity for our Membership.

Keep diversity, parity, and equity at the forefront of our considerations with regard to the nomination of candidates for our Board, and ensure our staff hiring practices fully reflect our commitment.

Collect, analyze, and share data with regard to hiring practices involving our Membership to better understand the issue in our field and work with employers to promote inclusion and diversity goals.

Support our Member Artistic Directors, opening communication and determining ways in which the Union can prompt more diversity in hiring.

Work with our fellow unions and service organizations to coordinate efforts and effect change in the field.

Recognize success and advocate for an American theatre that represents a robust body of work of both familiar and unfamiliar voices.

Figure 5.1 Continued

Putting Racial and Ethnic ADEI to Work: Implementing the Cultural Equity Action Plan

After it crafted its cultural equity statement, Americans for the Arts (AFTA) put it to work and created programs that intentionally address the organization's ADEI goals. President Robert L. Lynch states:

After conducting a staff retreat, the Americans for the Arts developed the AFTA Learning Lab, which is a year-round training program to help staff build diversity, equity, and inclusion skills and to foster a respective and appreciative work environment. Topics include: conflict management, understanding complex language, and recognizing implicit bias and privilege. In addition, the staff has expanded on board approved values for the organization to include staff agreements on behaviors that will support and advance our work together; designed strong staff orientation strategies; examined hiring practices; updated our employee handbook and are working to grow supervisor abilities.

Americans for the Arts continues to convene staff around the four external objectives in the Statement on Cultural Equity (cultural consciousness, leadership pipeline, research, and policy) with the objectives of mapping current work and articulating shifts towards cultural equity that they have made in the past year. Much of the cultural consciousness and systems change work, at least related to local-level impact, is coalescing around the EQUITY 360 project, an ambitious effort to transform the inequitable systems and structures inside local arts agencies that keep them from delivering equitable service in their communities. On a policy front, Americans for the Arts continues to push for Title 1 funding for the arts and the CREATE Act, both of which have strong equity focuses. We deployed a follow-up survey to the Local Arts Agency (LAA) Census specifically focused on the nature and depth of diversity/equity/inclusion statements and how they are driving programming at LAAs. We continue to develop both Arts U programming and a new multi-year fellowship specifically designed to tackle the arts leadership pipeline and the relationship of LAAs and others to the broader community.[5]

Americans for the Arts created a cultural equity plan that is action oriented and consciously focuses on dismantling and transforming its own inequitable systems, as well as the biased practices found in its member local arts agencies. Among those interviewed for this book both POC and White performing arts organizational members of historically White institutions agree that the transformative cultural equity process must stress an organizational commitment to race and cultural consciousness, which begins with immersion in multicultural competency or antiracist training.

Multicultural Competency Training

According to *Fortune* magazine, diversity training is an $8-billion-per-year business.[6] Why is there a need for multicultural competency training in historically White performing arts organizations? The underlying reason is that "our national narrative is in denial of the truth of who we are. We all need to know the truth about who we are and our histories."[7] Educational consultant and trainer Carmelita Castañeda states, "Achieving multicultural competency challenges the individual to know his or her own culture and the culture of others and to employ that knowledge by engaging people of other cultures in mutually gainful communication."[8] Scholars Aneeta Rattan and Nalini Ambady maintain that "a multicultural perspective argues that divisions between individuals must be acknowledged and valued as meaningful sources of identity and culture, and attempts to minimize such distinctions are viewed as a critical shortcoming of the colorblind perspective."[9] Being culturally competent, according to sociologist Estelle Disch is synonymous with having multicultural literacy or

> the ability to learn enough about another culture to begin to know the history of a particular cultural group; to understand some of the common and not-so-common experiences of people in that culture; to understand the widely shared values of the culture; and to understand the place of the group within the wider context of U.S. society.[10]

Achieving multicultural competence is not achieved overnight in historically White organizations and it must be conducted so that participants of Color feel safe and supported. One Workforce Diversity study respondent who identifies as White elaborated on this point:

> Cultural competency training can't be done in one session and training has to do no harm. Some diversity training can reignite some of the power imbalances that exist in the world and can generate microaggressions against the people who are "the other" in the room. That's why the training can't be done one time. There has to be a scaffolded way to have those conversations that is organic to the organization but acknowledges the organization's deficits in cultural competency. The danger of cultural competency is people ever feeling like they're an expert on someone else's culture, and then they begin to speak for that culture, that viewpoint. It's dangerous, and so for example, you have a White person who may say, "Black people don't x, y, and z." That has to be checked. We have to [question that assumption] and respond, "Where did you learn this? Why is that?"

One Workforce Diversity study respondent who identifies as non-White Hispanic mentions that in achieving multicultural literacy, it's vital to develop a lens of humility and a greater understanding of how much you don't know about someone else's culture. The respondent stated:

> I've just come to recognize over time that I cannot recognize if my reaction to someone in a job interview is culturally informed. I just

need somebody else to check me in this regard, and that's giving away power. It requires being open to considering that you might be wrong [about your assumptions]. It necessitates looking at a situation and evaluating your thought process. So, for example, "In this context, I might not know what I'm talking about and I simply might be wrong." Having to go through much of your life examining your decision-making processes is really humbling, exhausting, and very time consuming. I have to say whatever follows that learned [intentional] attitude is probably more helpful than anything you could do without acknowledging that attitude.

Multicultural competency among White employees and board members must not be conducted with the assumption that the People of Color in the organization have the responsibility to provide the education. One Workforce Diversity study respondent who identifies as Black stated:

My White colleague identified cultural competency as something to explore for our institution and for himself. He didn't put the burden necessarily on me to show him the way. He did his own investigation, he did his own inquiry, he did his own research. And then came to me and talked about it. It's not up to me to show you how to not be racist. You're figuring out what that means for you. And instead of doing the lazy thing and thinking: "I've got a Black manager on my staff: Help me understand privilege," he was committed to doing the research about his privilege and then asking me about the ways in which his privilege might relate to me. In that case I would want to explore his inquiry with him and figure it out together.

The Facilitator's Role

Within multicultural competency training, there is often a consultant or a team of consultants who share a multiplicity of racial and ethnic backgrounds, perspectives, and experiences. The consultants, trained in multicultural competency, lead the organizational participants in exploring cultural identity, cultural assets, racial consciousness, and the socialized origins of unconscious biased behaviors and attitudes, thereby promoting racial literacy, healing, and race equity.

Within a safe space, guidelines are set by both the facilitator and participants that allow respectful and meaningful dialogue to take place where everyone feels protected, heard, and that all voices and experiences matter. Participants of all racial and ethnic backgrounds focus on writing their cultural autobiographies and sharing their cultural identities and assets with all members of the group. In reflection papers and small groups, all participants may reflect and share the first time they were conscious of race, the racial composition of primary and secondary school teachers, fellow students, and friends, as well as the racial demographics of participant neighborhoods. Participants also may reflect, share, and compare with each other the impact that family, friends, movies, social media, and books have on the participant's understanding of race and racism.[11]

The multicultural competency facilitator may use films that underscore historical social injustice, resistance, and cultural empowerment and legacy. For example, "White Privilege 101: Getting in on the Conversation" and "Mirrors of Privilege: Making Whiteness Visible," document the ways in which the socially constructed notion of Whiteness is ingrained in every aspect of society as well as the antiracist actions of actively naming Whiteness, resisting, and actively combatting racialized socialization.[12] While some videos shown in multicultural competency training highlight structural racism and unconscious bias, additional videos reveal compelling histories of People of Color in the performing arts, disproving dominant racist narratives about White artistic and cultural superiority. One example of a cultural empowerment and legacy video series is Theresa Ruth Howard and Memoirs of Blacks in Ballet's "And Still They Rose: The Legacy of Black Philadelphians in Ballet."[13]

In other words, in multicultural competency training all participants learn how their own socialization has influenced their implicit bias and informed workplace decisions and practices. For example, one Workforce Diversity study respondent stated:

> I'm a Person of Color. I spend a lot of time in this space, obviously. If you said to me, "Name three directors for *Coriolanus*," I'm going to give you the name of three White guys. Because even as a Person of Color, even as somebody who is sensitized, unconsciously I've been given to understand that the best directors for these plays are White men. If, however, I slow it down, and I think about it broadly and objectively, I could indeed come to different conclusions about who might direct that play. We have put systems in place that insist that we pump the brakes and think intentionally about who we're inviting to the table.

Dealing With Discomfort in the Training Process

The multicultural competency facilitator helps the participants in a historically White organization develop critical consciousness and the self-awareness to work "with others in solidarity to question, analyze, and challenge oppressive conditions in their lives rather than blame each other or fate."[14] Oftentimes, the training may result in discomfort among its White member participants, which may result in a resistance to training. When White participants confront their own stereotypes, biases, and prejudices, it changes the self-image they may have of themselves. The anxiety and shame one may feel when confronting their own worldview may prevent some White participants from understanding the experiences of colleagues who feel devalued and marginalized.[15]

When defensive behavior occurs, the multicultural facilitator can intervene and steer the White participant to

> culturally responsive communication, where the participant would step back, depersonalize the emotional content of the interchange, [refrain] from being defensive, and [listen] to the message by allowing people to express their thoughts freely, when in a loud or soft voice, in anger or in frustration.[16]

This type of communication is called the FLEX Model (Foster interconnectedness; Listen and Communicate; Encourage Respect; and Explore Differences).[17] Through self-awareness of one's own beliefs, knowledge of the history of oppression experienced by groups who have been made to feel marginalized, and learning the skills to intervene, disrupt, and resolve conflict, all participants are better prepared to build bridges of empathy among cultures.[18]

Asset-Based Relationships

Building bonds between individual participants of different cultural backgrounds requires examining the ways in which verbal and nonverbal communication play a part. A participant's "gesture, tone, inflection, posture, or degree of eye contact may enhance or negate the content of the message."[19] In establishing trust, it's vital that the strengths and assets of the individual are respected and recognized.[20]

In establishing authentic bonds between multicultural participants, multicultural facilitators may use role-playing or simulation exercises where a member of one cultural group is asked to empathize or sense [a member of a different cultural group's] emotions, "sharing the inner state of the other person."[21] "Empathy," according to scholar Elizabeth A. Segal and her colleagues, "involves a balancing act between self-awareness and taking the perspective of someone else."[22] As Mead noted, "It is the ability of the person to put himself in other people's places that gives him his cues as to what to do in a specific situation."[23] One Workforce Diversity study respondent who identifies as Caucasian stated the belief that "[White managers] need to find opportunities to be the other: to place ourselves in circumstances where we are not part of the dominant culture or point of view." The respondent continued,

> I think if we experienced more of these situations, it would be invigorating. It's an effective tool that is not deployed very often. I seek out ways to put myself in these situations, where there's a level of

otherness for me personally. It inspires me, and I learn so much. I think there should be more of a focus on that, as opposed to asking, "How do we get People of Color in?" We need to find transformative moments, and that can happen when we open ourselves up to that exposure and place ourselves outside of our comfort zone.

Affinity Groups

Within multicultural competency training there is an opportunity for participants to form affinity groups based on specific cultural backgrounds and experiences. Each affinity group allows its participants to "honor their trauma" and to speak candidly to each other about the training. Antiracist White allies are counselled to support affinity groups of Color by "staying out of them." White antiracist allies are also encouraged to form their own affinity groups where they can deliberate about the ways in which they can support colleagues of Color in the training and in the workplace.[24]

Race Awareness in Primarily White Organizations

Facilitators encourage all participants to examine the historical factors that may have influenced discriminatory policies and practices through time.[25] In examining the history of the policies and practices of a primarily White performing arts organization, the participants can analyze the degree to which power relations have influenced the choices that are presently practiced and who those choices benefit.[26] Multicultural competency facilitators help those participants who don't benefit from organizational practices and policies to have a voice in a counter-narrative. By listening to the perspectives and experiences of underrepresented colleagues, the dominant members of the organization can develop greater race consciousness where they "become mindful of the impact of policies and practices on different racialized groups in our society."[27]

In *Silent Racism*, sociologist Barbara Trepagnier posits that "race awareness in well-meaning white people is instrumental in lessening institutional racism in the post-civil rights era."[28] Having high race awareness means that the White participant will be less likely to be "defensive, deny differences, and preserve the centrality of their own worldview by minimizing cultural differences."[29] With greater race awareness, the White participant will be more likely to ask, "Am I projecting my experiences onto individuals with different experiences?" or "Do I expect individuals from diverse cultures to take on my worldview?"[30] One Workforce Diversity study respondent who identifies as Caucasian explained the notion of having greater race awareness:

I am a White male and when I worked specifically with African American, Caribbean, Haitian, and other youth of Color, I just didn't have a clue. I wrote a scene for the students where one would play a hockey player. I had a mentor who was African American and she said to me, "Do you know, these kids don't play hockey? That might be what they do where you grew up but it's not what they play here." I was lucky to be in a space where I was able to ask a lot of questions and do a lot of listening. People of Color were willing to talk with me to challenge my ignorance, and I got to recognize my privileged worldview. I participated in antiracist training in which I was able to better understand racism, the systems of advantage, and how it was affecting my present-day attitudes and behaviors.

I remember a time where I was speaking to my African American colleague about the notion of the police having geo-tags—so that law enforcement would be able to use anyone's cellphone to pinpoint their specific locations. This was a decade before smartphones. And I remember saying to her, "I think that's a really great idea. Think of how quickly the police could get to you to help." And she responded, "I would never. . . ." We got in a big conversation about what it would mean for her as a female of Color to provide the police with that much information, right? And the powerlessness that she felt because her experiences had taught her the opposite when it came to the police: They weren't there to help her. I began seeing things through her lens, through the conversations that we had.

How often do individuals use culturally learned experiences to evaluate the experiences of those who may hold different perspectives? Alaska Native playwright Vera Starbard challenges the imposed dominant worldview and offers a culturally empowering alternative: "It's not about how [Native artists] can help our people adapt to Western theater, but how we can help Western theater to be a more dynamic and beautiful thing."[31] The multicultural competency facilitator helps White participants ask these essential questions of themselves: Have I incorporated racist notions into my perspective? Am I open to learning about my own racism?[32] In increasing greater race awareness in programming and audience development practices, for example, it's important to question everything, shining the light on all cultural perspectives.

"Question Everything"

In her article "Some Notes for Facilitators on Presenting My White Privilege Papers," author Peggy McIntosh recommends that White participants [in antiracist training] talk about their experiences, such as autobiographical lists of the ways in which unearned privilege has impacted their lives and the ways in which unearned assets such as power, money, time, and connections can be shared with those who have been oppressed and marginalized.[33] A Workforce Diversity study respondent who identifies as African American also challenges White arts professionals to become conscious of the power they have in changing exclusionary programming and audience development practices:

> Question everything. "How come we only have one dance company here that's diverse? How come we only have seniors coming to the orchestra? Who's cultivating the younger audiences?" Ask the questions. And keep asking for answers. I don't think we have to wait on one person to do it. I think everyone should be involved in examining, asking questions, and then taking action. This is where I think the White staff could be more persuasive because you're going to be heard. You're going to be heard more than me. So, for a White person to say, "This is unacceptable. We should have this, this, and this." That's going to have more weight than me saying it. I'm expected to say it. In fact, it's like, "Oh there she goes again." So that's where I think the difference can be. Just an awareness and a consciousness that you have power. And each of you can change this dynamic. But you have to own it, and claim it, and use it. Today. We need it now.

One Workforce Diversity study respondent of Mixed Race also believes that primarily White performing arts organizations must question programming and marketing practices that adversely affect and exclude communities of Color. The respondent challenges Primarily White Organizations to ask these questions:

> Is this work for these communities? Does this work speak to all in these communities? Is this the right ticket price? Are we marketing in any of these communities or are we marketing in our same publications? Are we reaching outside of the networks we already have? Or is it an echo chamber? To what degree do we spend time listening to our communities? I think that it goes back to listening and meeting with organizational leaders in each of these communities. What would be useful to them?

"Shine the Light on All Cultural Perspectives"

One Black respondent in the Workforce Diversity study shared how racial and ethnic ADEI-centered programming in the organization can provide opportunities for conversations aligned around increased race awareness, cultural pride, and empowerment:

> We had an annual show that traces African American history through dance, and we did that for nine years. It was sold out and had a diverse audience. After the show, we would open up the conversation to talk about race, and the current state of race, and it was a

really safe space for audiences to dialogue with the kids on stage who ranged from eleven to eighteen years of age, and came from all different types of socioeconomic, geographic, and ethnic backgrounds. And in being part of that show the kids had to do a lot of homework and research, and they were finding that they were learning through that show things they weren't learning in school. Because the cast was diverse, they had opportunities to have conversations they otherwise might not have had. We try to make sure that in our performance season we are creating opportunities for performers of all types; and providing safe spaces for people to have conversations about race and diversity, shining a light on some cultures that are not necessarily embraced as part of the mainstream.

Racial and Ethnic ADEI-Centered Recruitment and Hiring Strategies

In creating a racial and ethnic ADEI-centered workforce, primarily White performing arts organizations must restructure recruitment and hiring strategies. For example, in becoming a transformative culturally plural organization, the PWO must examine and actively transform the racial and ethnic diversity of its board and senior leadership, build an expansive multiracial network, select executive recruiters with a track record in hiring leaders of Color, interrogate current recruitment advertising methods and language, intentionally hire ALAANA creative teams, and design training programs to specifically welcome future employees of Color.

Changing the Racial and Ethnic Composition of the Board and Executive Staff

Actionable steps in transforming a historically White organization's discriminatory structure challenge the racial and ethnic composition of its homogeneous White staff and board. An authentic commitment to racial and ethnic ADEI-based leadership must have the PWO's board and the board chair's public involvement. For example, as part of the strategy to increase the racial and ethnic diversity of the board, The Public Theater's board chair led a recruitment effort, resulting in four new board members of Color.[34] The African American Board Leadership Institute, which is committed to "recruiting, preparing, and assisting with the placement of African Americans on a broad range of governing boards,"[35] is just one organization dedicated to supporting an ADEI-centered leadership transformative process.

In changing the racial and ethnic composition of the board, the primarily White performing arts organization must examine and dismantle discriminatory practices that prevent board members of Color from serving. As a first step, PWO leadership must be willing to examine potential discriminatory practices by asking specific questions: Does the board represent the racial and ethnic demographic profile of the entire community? Are racial and ethnic ADEI core values and policies written in the by-laws and strategic plan of the primarily White organization? What is the minimum monetary give or get policy and how might the policy prevent some community members of Color from serving on the board? To what degree is the PWO willing to change give or get policies and expand the give or get definition? To what extent are ALAANA community members not recruited as board members based on racial and ethnic socioeconomic stereotypes? Does the organization share board vacancies with its communities of Color? To what degree are members of ALAANA-led performing arts organizations and community members of Color invited to sit on the board? What are the ways in which new board members of Color are oriented and welcomed into the organization? To what degree are board members of Color viewed as assets and empowered to lead the transformative ADEI-centered board and staff recruitment process? To what extent do board members of Color feel comfortable sharing expertise? To what degree are racial and ethnic ADEI outcomes shared with the board so that progress can be measured? To what degree are racial and ethnic ADEI-centered programs and statistics publicly shared on the organization's website? To what degree is the board willing to participate in long-term antiracist training, as well as support antiracist training for staff members throughout the Primarily White Organization?[36]

When historically White boards intentionally make racial and ethnic ADEI an organizational priority, they share leadership power with communities of Color through board recruitment and hiring executive leaders of Color, as one Workforce Diversity study respondent who identifies as African American personally experienced:

> It has to be a priority to hire a Person of Color in a leadership position. In my experience, pursuing non-traditional routes is valuable; you can't only post the job listing in Arts Reach. They went to colleges, universities, and individuals. They kept the process open longer than they had anticipated until they found qualified individuals for that position. And then ultimately, they were able to hire a Person of Color in a leadership position and that person was me. I was hired as the managing director of a theater company that was not a Black theater company. But it was intentional; it was deliberate. It was established from the person in the top position. It was something that the board supported. And they were open to non-traditional approaches and ways to find those individuals. I was recruited by a board member who knew that I was looking for something different, who knew me, and she came to me and said, "You should apply for this job." I told her, "No, I'm not interested, I don't want to do it." But she convinced me, and it worked out.

Building an Expansive Multiracial Network

In the case described above the historically White performing arts organization took "non-traditional routes" in the search for a leader of Color. But to what degree do primarily White board members have a multiracial network that can support the organization's transformative executive search goals? In his book *Racial Paranoia*, scholar John L. Jackson, Jr. maintains that "most people don't inherit a multiracial social network."[37] Homogeneous social networks largely consist of members of the same social identity group.[38] Primarily White Organizational members who are creating transformative equitable cultures must intentionally examine their everyday professional personal networks and question the degree to which the networks are authentically inclusive of culturally plural relationships. Cross-group intimacy only occurs when there is an effort to respect and accept each other's differences and perspectives.[39] In this next example, one Workforce Diversity study respondent who identifies as White speaks about the ways in which he developed a Native cultural network and how it now informs his work with Native and non-Native people:

> I spent eight years in a tribal organization and inside that environment I learned that it's culturally different [from my own culture]. In order to be successful in the Tlingit culture, I had to understand that it's an exogamous culture: There's two moieties of Eagle and Raven: Exogamous means that if you're an Eagle then you marry a Raven. It's matrilineal: Your traditions and your crest are inherited from your mother's line. There are two moieties and then clans underneath those moieties. So, there's a set of clans underneath the Eagles and a set of clans underneath the Ravens.
>
> In order to be working in that tribal organization, I had to have an understanding of all the clans. I needed to know the relationships between the clans, as well as the hierarchy. Understanding and knowing people and elders within these various tribes, or rather various clans was really important to whether I succeeded in and navigated within that tradition. That's not unlike the outside, the White world, where there are people from different institutions, and different cities, and different communities. And so, your connection to these various points will help you navigate and succeed in advancing this work.
>
> We have a couple of programs here [in my present organization] which are for emerging artists to help them build networks with our member organizations. We give them a little stipend, we help them get to the conference, and we connect them to the advanced people within the performing arts field. We bring in consultants to help them develop a work plan to advance their work.

But a large part of it is simply connecting them to the appropriate people within our network. We're in conversation right now with Native Arts and Cultures Foundation and a few others to do a Native American version of this program. It will help Native Americans build a network so that they can be successful in the touring market.

In our interview with this Workforce Diversity study respondent, we found that the respondent's early childhood socialization helped him identify and empathize with another culture, different from his own. While not a member of the Tlingit culture, the respondent found acceptance through his willingness to "learn, understand, and respect" the Tlingit Nation, people, and culture.[40] He has spent many years living among and working with Indigenous people and has developed empathy by being socially involved and committed to actively honoring Native communities through supporting Indigenous-led and -designed cultural practices and work. Furthermore, he has devoted his professional life to intentionally and authentically continuing his relationships and alliances with Indigenous people and is vigorously dedicated to establishing genuine relationships between Native artists and his own networks.

Many historically White organizational members have not invested or immersed themselves in building authentic relationships within a multiracial network, which will ultimately lead to a dearth of candidates of Color in the recruitment process. In addition to intentionally building authentic and lasting relationships within a multiracial network, it's essential for White leaders to focus recruitment efforts on selecting an executive recruiter with a track record of placing ALAANA candidates. In addition, White leaders must interrogate the extent to which recruitment advertising channels are both accessible and inclusive. Furthermore, within each job description advertisement, there must be deliberate language that invites the participation of individuals from multiplicity of cultural backgrounds and perspectives.

Creating an Inclusive Applicant Pool: The Role of the Executive Recruiter

In selecting an executive recruiter for a senior leadership position, it is vital that the recruiter has a track record in recruiting and placing ALAANA candidates as this Workforce Diversity study respondent, who identifies as White, stressed:

> Interviewing is the last step of hiring. We are working with an executive search firm to replace me and we told the firm that if they

wanted to bid on this job, we would need to see their records in placing ALAANA candidates. The three top candidates that we had because of where we posted and how our job description read were all ALAANA members. Then we had to decide from among the three finalists, whom we wanted to hire as the next director.

Where Are You Advertising?

Selecting the right publications and social media sites are critical to being seen by a racially and ethnically diverse pool of applicants. In addition, the type of publication or social media site selected signifies that the reader is welcome to apply. One Workforce Diversity study respondent who identifies as African American told a poignant story that influenced the decision to go to a particular graduate school:

> The only reason I applied to Yale was that while flipping through *Black Enterprise* magazine, I saw an advertisement for the Yale School of Drama. I thought: "They're advertising in a Black magazine; they're looking for Black students." And I applied. Had I not seen that; I would not have applied. But that's an example also of being intentional and deliberate. You know, because, why else would you advertise in a Black magazine? It wasn't a theater magazine; it was a business magazine. And that's how I applied, and that's how I got there. From that one ad, on a Saturday morning.

Language and Access Matter

In the report *Reaching and Engaging with Hispanic Communities: A Research-Informed Communication Guide for Nonprofits, Policymakers, and Funders*, the authors note that

> messages that align with the values and beliefs of the audience and its culture tend to be received and interpreted as intended. . . . Since Latino communities can be very diverse regionally, culturally, and linguistically, it is critical that service providers create messages that are community-specific.[41]

When visiting American Ballet Theatre's website, the community-specific language introducing the Project Plié administrative internship is clear and intentional: "ABT is committed to identifying, training, and supporting emerging arts administrators from underrepresented communities."[42] Furthermore, the internship uses welcoming language, stressing that barriers, which might prevent some from applying, are considered and addressed:

Selected Project Plié interns will be eligible to receive a scholarship so that they may travel to and live in New York City for the duration of the internship with limited financial constraint. The scholarship may include: round trip transportation, housing assistance, a monthly MetroCard for travel.

In order to apply, students must submit the ABT intern Application form, a resume, a cover letter indicating which administrative areas of interest, a letter of recommendation, and the Project Plié Scholarship Application form, and an essay no more than one page answering the following question: As a person of color, why do you believe diversity is important in arts administration and why are you drawn to this field?

Figure 5.2 ABT Project Plié Administrative Internship

Source: American Ballet Theatre, "Project Plié: Administrative Internships," www.abt.org, Courtesy of American Ballet Theatre.

Language in recruitment strategies matters. Having easy access to job opportunities communicates that the organization is inclusive and isn't reserving its job opportunities for industry insiders. When creating an inclusive job description, the organization might ask for "fluency in another language, experience working with [underrepresented] communities, and accepting work or life experience instead of a college degree."[43] In terms of establishing recruitment practices that are ADEI-centered, one Workforce Diversity study respondent of Color noted that his organization has, in some cases, eliminated the need for a degree:

We've actually removed educational degrees from all of our job postings and job descriptions, because we think it unfairly limits, and sometimes minimizes what could be outstanding professional experience, because somebody doesn't have a terminal degree. We have historically asked for an M.F.A., a master's degree, or the terminal degree in their field from middle management up in the organization. For some jobs here, we need a real wealth of experience. But we understand that experience can come in a lot of forms, and education can come in a lot of forms, and there are places where you've got people who've been working professionals for a dozen years who we were not allowing into the candidate pool by virtue of not having that terminal degree. So, we've taken it away from our job postings, because we feel it's more equitable to move it aside. That said, in some of these positions, you need absolute and measurable experience and skills, and we look for those things, but we're also inviting one another to think cross-disciplinary. Once again, why are people building our sets all White, and people who build our houses are way more plural? Certainly, there's some transferable skills involved there, so we are looking outside of the field to find people who have the same or similar attendant skills, who can bring those to bear in our organization.

At the time of this writing, the Oregon Shakespeare Festival (OSF), "one of the nation's oldest rotating repertory theatres" was seeking a new artistic director. The job description, placed prominently on OSF's "Work With Us" website page noted,

> The Artistic Director will lead an artistic vision for OSF that builds on its world-class reputation and furthers its commitment to equity, diversity, inclusion, and social justice through a sophisticated understanding and lived commitment to these values. . . . The ideal candidate will be an artist who is known for, and a keen judge of, artistic excellence, great theatricality, inventive use of language, broad cultural representation, and expansive aesthetics. The next artistic leader will demonstrate a commitment to Shakespeare, to new works, to the unique power of repertory theatre, and to OSF's four core values (Excellence, Inclusion, Company, Stewardship).[44]

Furthermore, OSF described its search process below the artistic director job description. It states,

> OSF is an equal opportunity employer, dedicated to the goal of creating a diverse and inclusive working environment. We strongly encourage applications from women, persons of color and LGBTQ individuals. All qualified applications will receive consideration for employment with regard to age, race, ethnicity, color, religion, gender, gender identity, gender expression, national origin, ancestry, citizenship status, disability status, protected veteran status, marital status, sexual orientation or any other characteristic protected by law. This position will remain open until a diverse pool of candidates has been identified.[45]

Casting and Hiring Artists of Color

Racial and ethnic diversity hiring extends to the entire creative team of the performing arts organization. One Workforce Diversity study respondent who identifies as Palestinian American shared his strategy for hiring diverse artists of Color:

> Artistic leadership has to want it. You need an artistic director who understands that diverse voices make for more exciting and more

interesting programming. Inviting diverse artists into the building is huge, and not just during those diverse plays. So, in other words, to have an Asian American director on a David Henry Hwang play of course makes great sense, and having an African American director on an August Wilson play of course makes great sense. But we spend half the time at our theater on classical work, meaning, work out of the Western European and American canon of plays, not exclusively, but largely, canons that are dominated by dead White men. So, then the question is: "Who gets to tell those stories?" If you grow up in this country, and I ask you to tell me the story of *Romeo and Juliet*, you can tell me that story in rough terms, whether you're White, or Black, or Asian, or Latinx. If we agree that those classic plays are commonly held, then who gets to tell those stories? Through whose eyes do we get to see those plays? Through whose lens? So then, who's the director, who's the scenic designer, costume designer, lighting designer, sound designer, choreographer, composer, et cetera, et cetera. What does that creative team look like? So, even in those received classics out of the Western European and American canon, having a diversity of voices in the telling of that, changes opportunities for artists really, really meaningfully. We've simply institutionalized it here. There is no such thing as a non-plural creative team here anymore. You're not going to see all-White all-male creative teams.

Recruiting Employees of Color: Training and Internship Programs

Performing arts organizations often use internships as a method of recruitment and training the future workforce. Two notable examples of historically White performing arts organizations who are providing employment opportunities for ALAANA members through organizational training programs are the Roundabout Theatre Company and the American Ballet Theatre. In partnership with the theatrical union IATSE (International Alliance of Theatrical Stage Employees), the Roundabout Theatre Company has created a three-year technical theater program called the Theatrical Workforce Development Program, which seeks to "diversify a branch of the industry that has been heavily white and male."[46] Through the program, participants aged 18–24 with high school diplomas or the equivalent receive a living wage, hands-on training, networking opportunities, and job placement in organizations such as The Public Theater, Abrons Arts Center, Atlantic Theater Company, Playwrights Horizons, and the Roundabout Theatre Company. The program is funded through a consortium of public and private institutional and individual funders, including the Andrew W. Mellon Foundation, The Ford Foundation, and the Mayor's Office of Media and Entertainment.[47]

In 2013, the American Ballet Theatre

> launched the Project Plié initiative to further expand its diversity and inclusion efforts and bring greater awareness to the lack of racial and ethnic diversity in the classical ballet community. Through concerted outreach efforts, ABT has identified promising young dancers, dance teachers, and emerging arts administrators of color to participate in high-quality training programs.[48]

Retaining People of Color in the Workforce

Again, it's not enough to simply recruit racially and ethnically diverse board members, leaders, employees, and artists. An authentic effort to retain leaders and employees of Color is vital to sustaining a transformative culturally plural ADEI-centered workforce. In the Catalyst study, *Day-to-Day Experiences of Emotional Tax Among Women and Men of Color in the Workplace,* authors Dnika J. Travis and Jennifer Thorpe-Moscon report that "when employees feel included, there is a lower intent to quit, more creativity, and a greater likelihood that they will speak up."[49] Retention solutions include educating and training managers to identify their own biases and the impact the bias may have on their decisions. Observing, for example, the extent to which employees of Color are "heard, validated, or dismissed" must be a conscious and intentional practice among all employees in the organization.[50]

"Live Your Commitment: Value What I Have to Say"

One Workforce Diversity study respondent who identifies as Black shared her retention strategy:

> Organizations that outwardly say that they are invested in diversity and inclusion need to show it; there needs to be buy-in from the top down. I don't need a welcome wagon, saying, "Hey, welcome Black girl!" Not necessary. At the end of the day, what all people want is to feel like they are an equal in the workplace. When I speak, listen to me. Give me the opportunity, by listening to everything I say, then you can respond, or react. Value what I have to say. You don't have to agree with it, and perhaps you'll take bits and pieces of my ideas and merge them with someone else's to make a bigger and better one: I do believe that two heads are better than one.
>
> African American people, often feel marginalized in the workforce, because they don't feel like they're being heard, and that their thoughts and opinions are valued. We often feel judged before we even walk into the room. Some of this may be our own insecurities,

but even if that is the case, those insecurities manifested from previous experiences where we've been talked over, dismissed, ignored, or simply made to feel invisible. Having us physically sit at the decision-making table without making efforts to include us in the conversation means nothing. That's the difference between diversity and inclusion. When you see me, say hello, as opposed to walking into a room, looking at me, and thinking: "What are you going to bring to the table?" That's happened to me. I'm coming from a good place and may have a knowledge base that's valuable. I might be bringing something to the table and you have no idea what it is, you know? And if that is the case, be open to that, don't question what I'm saying.

A Workforce Diversity study respondent who identifies as both Puerto Rican and Black advised:

Those in charge set the tone by their actions. Talk up the commitment and live it. Let the employees see that every once in a while, you have lunch with [your colleagues of Color]. If you're walking out the door at the same time as your colleague, say, "Hey Jim, let's grab a coffee." That's what I mean by living it. Also, let it be known that actions that are hurtful and disrespectful of others will not be tolerated in the organization and that promotions are based on merit.

Professional Development Opportunities for Colleagues of Color Matter

Employees of Color must have the ability to pursue professional and self-development opportunities and be encouraged to share newfound knowledge and expertise with the organization. One exceptional professional development program, Rising Leaders of Color, was created by the Theatre Communications Group, a membership organization of over 700 member theaters and affiliate organizations, for early-career leaders of Color, including journalists of Color. Participants first gather in connection with TCG's National Conference, then engage in a year-long program that includes

professional development workshops and networking opportunities, job search training, access to veteran leaders in the field, access to a national network of peers, one-on-one career counseling with TCG staff, and for journalists—participation in the Eugene O'Neill Theater Center's National Critics Institute.[51]

In transformative ADEI-centered organizations, White performing arts organizational leaders are consciously aware that when they make a deliberate effort to share professional opportunities with colleagues of Color, everyone in the organization benefits. Furthermore, when employees of Color who have professional lives outside of the workplace are encouraged to continue professional and self-development, employees of Color are more likely to bring their entire selves to work. In the following paragraphs, two colleagues, the first who identifies as Caucasian and of Scottish heritage, and the second who identifies as Black and of African descent, discuss the importance of developing and nurturing employees of Color:

Respondent #1: "There's a national conference within my field that I've attended for many years, and it really lacks in diversity. My organization has a budget for two people to go, and this is the first year that I chose not to attend and to recommend that two of my colleagues of Color attend. I intentionally took myself out of the equation to give them the opportunity. Sending my two colleagues was both an investment in them, but also in the field of which I am part. I spoke to the president of the organization and said, 'I need you to meet with these individuals, and you know as well as I do, they represent a very small minority of what the landscape should be, and so we also need to do more to make sure that they're connecting with people and having these conversations.' And he gets it. My colleagues came back from the conference and now they are developing their own relationships in the field and diversifying the conversation. And I benefit from what they bring back from their experience, I get to see what's happening in our field through their eyes, because I have my own biases."

Respondent #2: "I have not had to in any way, shape, or form, or fashion change the trajectory of how I see myself as a professional administrator, educator, and artist. And I've been able to maintain those things and thrive in those things. I've been fully supported. I've been in positions where anything outside of the walls of that institution is looked at as a threat. They don't realize that maybe the things I'm doing outside of the organization are feeding and fueling what I'm doing inside the organization. Everything that I'm doing directly is a result of what my portfolio looks like, what my programming looks like. And my present organization recognizes me."

A racial and ethnic ADEI-centered transformative organization and its leadership intentionally recognize that ALAANA leaders, employees, and creative teams are institutional assets, as are equitable community partnerships with ALAANA-led organizations and communities of Color.

Equitable Community Partnerships With ALAANA-Led Organizations and Communities

Equitable partnerships between historically White performing arts organizations and ALAANA-led organizations and communities of Color must be viewed as essential to a racial and ethnic ADEI-centered strategic plan. In an equitable partnership, members of ALAANA communities with "lived experience" must be empowered to lead the racial and ethnic ADEI-centered organizational transformative strategy, serving on the ADEI planning task force, the board, and hired as leaders and staff members in the ADEI-centered organization. An equitable partnership with a community of Color engages members of the community in every ADEI-centered organizational practice.[52] In the next section, Workforce Diversity study respondents speak about successful equitable partnerships between majority-White performing arts organizations and ALAANA-led organizations and communities of Color, including the importance of honoring ALAANA community-defined roles in the partnership; creating organizational programs that disrupt barriers to ALAANA community member engagement; producing programming for, with, and by ALAANA communities, and sharing equitable power with ALAANA-led performing arts organizations and community members of Color.

ALAANA Community-Defined Roles in the Partnership

In order for an equitable partnership to occur, ALAANA-led performing arts organizations and communities of Color must articulate their own specific needs and priorities—their own role in the partnership and be supported by a transformative organization that is willing to relinquish its traditional controlling role. For example, one Workforce Diversity study respondent reported that,

> a predominately White performing arts organization wanted to engage a certain population in their community. They said [to the community], "We have some great programs and we'd like you to come." Through their artists they started building relationships with those [community] organizations and realized, "The programming that we're trying to do for these young teens of Color is not necessarily to their taste: They are already engaged and are making art, but they need a venue to do this and they need those resources." So, they worked together to make that happen. It drew in the community, the teens felt like they had a place where they could do their artistic work and then the presenting organization learned, "Oh, this is what it's all about: Making ourselves available to the community and serving the community." That was a good example of how they

built a partnership within the community and came to a realization that it's about resources on both sides, and the level of trust that they needed to establish.

Disrupting Barriers to ALAANA Community Engagement

One Workforce Diversity study respondent who identifies as Black spoke about her organization's role in disrupting barriers to ALAANA community engagement. By actively living transformative values and participating in antiracist training, the organization is better equipped to support the financial, educational, and the cross-cultural needs of the community. The Workforce Diversity study respondent elaborated:

> The mission of my organization is to enrich lives and build community through the arts. We are committed to being an inclusive organization, which is reflected in our values. The staff and the board spend a lot of time revisiting these values every few years, to make sure we are aligned as an organization. These values are listed publicly, including on our website. Being the type of organization we are, we authentically attract a diverse clientele, and serve as a safe space for people from all backgrounds to learn together through the arts. We are also committed to accessibility and removing barriers to participation; this value is executed by our commitment to providing financial assistance, free transportation, dancewear, healthy snacks, tutoring, physical therapy, and ACT prep for our high school students. And then for the students we serve in the community, we provide arts education programming at no cost for under resourced schools. We believe that arts education can positively transform lives and that it should be available for all students, and so we are committed to ensuring that our school partners are getting the arts programming they need to meet their objectives. It is also an institutional priority for our organization to advance as an Anti-Bias/Anti-Racist (ABAR) organization. A number of staff and board members have participated in ABAR workshops and my organization hosted a day-long workshop on-site for faculty, staff, and board (facilitated by an expert consultant). Since this work has begun, the staff have drafted an Equity and Inclusion statement, and an internal committee has been created to focus on this work, and to set benchmarks to continue advancing the organization forward.
>
> We are located at the crossroads between very affluent neighborhoods and very poor ones, and also right in the crossroads of very White communities and People of Color communities, ethnic communities. People from all over are coming to work together, and it's one of the few places in a segregated city, where people can have

cross-cultural experiences. Students who are rich are taking class with someone who might be living below or at poverty level, but the two of them may not know that. But they're working together, they're learning through the arts, and they're being creative. The interaction between cultures and classes happens organically in our organization.

Producing Work For, With, and By ALAANA Communities

Transformative performing arts organizations are committed to working with ALAANA communities in producing work for, with, and by the specific community of Color. One Workforce Diversity study respondent who identifies as African American shared this story of working with a primarily White opera company in developing a Black audience:

> You have to want People of Color to come. You have to actually want it. Because again it's in the environment; it's in the DNA; you have to want it. So that's the first step. And two, you have to have programs that People of Color would want to see. Shakespeare is great, but that's not all. Ballet is great. But that's not all. I worked with a well-known opera company in New York. They did a piece called *Margaret Garner* that was an amazing three-hour opera based on Toni Morrison's book *Beloved*, which was grounded in this true story about a slave woman who murdered her child rather than her being brought up as a slave. The case went to court. It was the first case adjudicated on whether or not a slave murdered their child versus destroyed property because the result would be different. So, it was ruled that she had destroyed property. And so, she died.
>
> The opera company hired my company to help cultivate a Black audience. Now, the worst thing you could talk to a Black mother about is killing her child. And you want to use that to bring people in? Okay. But we did it. They sincerely wanted to cultivate a Black audience. The director of marketing gave us a budget. At that time, I rarely received a budget for anything. People expect me to snap my fingers and it will happen. But he gave us a substantial budget. He called us six months in advance. We had time to build promotions and engage in discussions on the topic of a mother protecting her child. They hired a Black catering company for opening night. We were physically in the community throughout the summer months. He gave us time to think about our plan and how to execute it.

One Workforce Diversity study respondent who identifies as Korean described his organization's efforts to bring people of different cultural backgrounds together through cross-cultural innovative programming created by the ALAANA communities themselves:

> We present two different music groups with different ethnic backgrounds at the same time in our organization. We began by offering a Spanish dance lesson and Garifuna dance lesson, followed by the concert by the Spanish group and the Garifuna group. And at the end, the artists jam together, and dancers dance together too. The program connects people from both communities within this building.
>
> One of the reasons we started this programming is that we found that Korean folks come to only Korean programming, Chinese folks more than likely come to the Chinese programming; they don't come to our jazz programming, which is primarily attended by an African American and Caucasian audience. It's unfortunate that we have a huge Asian population around this building, and then when we have the jazz programming, very, very few, almost no Asian folks attend these performances. We posed this question: "Why don't we have a program where different cultures meet each other through cross-cultural programming?" For example, programming where Japan meets Puerto Rico. Puerto Rican community members will come to see this, because they know a Puerto Rican group is performing, but now they have been exposed to the Japanese culture that they may not have been exposed to before. And they found it's very inspirational, and it's really entertaining. So then maybe they will be interested in coming to our Japanese programming in the future. In the past, we had a program called Brazil Meets India. And the day before the collaborative performance, we had an Indian exhibition opening, and a couple came who were really excited about this programming. They were not aware of that programming before they came to the Indian exhibition opening, but they found it, they purchased tickets, and they came to Brazil Meets India. The husband was Indian, and the wife was Brazilian, and they had never actually had that experience before, where the programming encompassed both of their cultural heritages. We even changed our mission statement to include our values: Global arts for a global community.

Sharing Power With ALAANA Communities

Tim Wilson, who identifies as White, is the executive director of the Western Arts Alliance (WAA). During our interview, he discussed his strategy for building an equitable partnership with Indigenous leaders from around the world:

> We built this program with a group of Indigenous arts leaders from Australia, Canada, the United States, and New Zealand: They were directors, producers, agents, and performers. Most of them had never been to WAA and had no experience or knowledge of WAA. We turned over design of this program to them. It became the Indigenous Performance Symposium, which was hugely successful for us. For example, as a result of this program, we almost tripled the participation among our members in the pre-conference program. We had a hundred people. Almost half, 45% of the participants were from Native communities, representing Indigenous communities. Our success was based on creating a space and empowering the right people in order to tell their story.[53]

Sharing power begins with humility—an acknowledgement of and respect for the multiplicity of cultures that thrive in ALAANA communities combined with an authentic and intentional commitment to honoring and participating in equitable community partnerships with ALAANA-led organizations and communities of Color.

Land Acknowledgement and Actively Honoring Indigenous People

Adam Horowitz, founder of the non-governmental agency the U.S. Department of Arts and Culture, published *Honor Native Land: A Guide and Call to Acknowledgement*. According to Horowitz,

> The publication, which has been downloaded 11,000 times, calls on cultural organizations to acknowledge the traditional Indigenous inhabitants of the land on which their events take place. Since the guide was published over 400 organizations have taken the pledge to acknowledge the Indigenous people and land and to move beyond words into programs and actions that embody a commitment to Indigenous rights and cultural equity.[54]

The U.S. Department of Arts and Culture shares this statement on its website:

> Acknowledgement by itself is a small gesture. It becomes meaningful when coupled with authentic relationship and informed action. But this beginning can be an opening to greater public consciousness of Native sovereignty and cultural rights, a step toward equitable relationship and reconciliation.[55]

The #HonorNativeLand Pledge states:

> As a step toward honoring the truth and achieving healing and reconciliation, our organization commits to open all public events and gatherings with a statement acknowledging the traditional Native lands on which we stand. Such statements become truly meaningful when coupled with authentic relationships and sustained commitment to Indigenous rights and cultural equity.[56]

With guidance from The Lenape Center and resident artist Emily Johnson, The Abrons Arts Center in New York city has placed an Indigenous Land Acknowledgement in its lobby that reads:

> Abrons Arts Center is situated on the Lenape island of Manhahtaan (Mannahatta) in Lenapehoking, the Lenape homeland. We pay respect to Lenape peoples, past, present, and future and their continuing presence in the homeland and throughout the Lenape diaspora. We offer our care and gratitude to the land, water and air of Lenapehoking, and are committed to resisting colonialism and imbalance with Mother Earth through the support of Indigenous-led programming and Indigenous artistic practices.[57]

True to their word, the Abrons Arts Center has partnered with the Lenape Center to cosponsor programming that recognizes and respects Lenape arts and culture.[58]

ALAANA Transformative Leadership in the Performing Arts: Multi-Party Collaborations

Ali Michael writes that "racial justice requires a consciousness of the inequities on which the entire society has been built and a willingness to restructure the foundation."[59] Two ALAANA-led organizations, The International Association of Blacks in Dance (IABD) and the Sphinx Organization, are leading efforts to restructure racial inequities found in the predominately White fields of ballet and music through multiparty collaboration. Harvard Business School faculty member and noted author Mark R. Kramer stated that, "in multi-party collaboration, multiple parties come together to achieve shared expectations."[60]

The International Association of Blacks in Dance "preserves and promotes dance by African ancestry or origin, and assists and increases opportunities for artists in advocacy, audience development, education, funding, networking, performance, philosophical dialogue, and touring."[61] Founded almost 30 years ago, by Joan Myers Brown, IABD has created collaborative partnerships with primarily White ballet companies to provide auditions, training, and employment opportunities for ballerinas of Color. In addition, IABD has instituted training programs to support the next generation of Black-led dance company leaders. In our interview, Joan Myers Brown stated:

> Most of the ballet companies in the country do not have Black dancers or if they do, they're usually male. To provide opportunities for girls of Color, we had a major national audition for ballerinas and we had 81 girls show up.[62] IABD does multi-company auditions, where one person can audition for ten companies at once. We brought in fifteen artistic directors of major ballet companies, including New York City Ballet, American Ballet Theatre, Oregon Ballet, and the National Ballet, among others. We brought all those leaders in together to see that there were girls capable if given the opportunity—not only for a job, but also to be trained.
>
> We also started what we call the second-generation leaders, where we're training young Black leaders to step up and take our place. So, every organization that's a [Black-led] member [company] of The International Association of Blacks in Dance is looking within their own organization to develop someone to be a leader, to help them.[63]

In addition to its work on creating opportunities for dancers of Color in traditionally White ballet companies and supporting the next generation of Black dance leaders, the IABD regrants funds from the Andrew W. Mellon Foundation to Black-led member companies throughout the United States. The second round of Managing Organizational Vitality and Endurance (MOVE) grants were distributed to 25 dance companies in 12 states, including the African American Dance Ensemble, Atlanta Dance Connection, Deeply Rooted Dance Theater, Forces of Nature, Urban Bush Women, and Washington Reflections Dance Company, as well as others throughout the United States. In addition to receiving a $10,000 general operating grant, each company participates "in a peer-to-peer online learning community that includes technical assistance, financial planning, organizational development strategies and training with the Nonprofit Finance Fund and IABD."[64]

Additionally, IABD in partnership with the Dance Theatre of Harlem and Dance/USA are leading The Equity Project: Increasing the Presence of Blacks in Ballet. Within this initiative 20 ballet companies and one school have "come together to support the advancement of racial equity in professional ballet . . . including American Ballet Theatre, Atlanta Ballet, Boston Ballet, New York City Ballet, San Francisco Ballet, and the Joffrey Ballet."[65] The Equity Project, which is funded by the Andrew W. Mellon Foundation, has "established a unique consulting team to coach and educate ballet companies about topics like undoing racism, the intersection of history and ballet, discussing systems of power and privilege, and determining concrete ways companies can change."[66]

The Sphinx Organization, "launched in 1997 by Aaron P. Dworkin and now led by Afa S. Dworkin, addresses the underrepresentation of people of color in classical music."[67] In 2018, with the support of a four-year $1.8 million grant from the Andrew W. Mellon Foundation, the Sphinx Organization became the lead program administrator and fiscal agent of the National Alliance for Audition Support in partnership with the New World Symphony, America's Orchestral Academy, and the League of American Orchestras.[68] The National Alliance for Audition Support offers Black and Latinx musicians "a customized combination of mentoring, audition preparation, financial support, and audition previews."[69] The more than 40 partner orchestras include the Cincinnati Symphony Orchestra, the Houston Symphony, Los Angeles Philharmonic, and the New York Philharmonic, among others.[70] The multi-party collaborative efforts led by the Sphinx Organization and IABD incorporate elements found in Mark R. Kramer and John Kania's collective impact model.

Systemic Change in the Performing Arts: Collective Impact and Catalytic Philanthropy

Throughout this book, we have examined societal systems and structures that collectively produce racial injustice in the performing arts. Kramer and Kania's collective impact work focuses on social change through cross-sector collaboration.[71] Cross-sector collaboration includes organizations from the nonprofit, educational, corporate, government, and philanthropic sectors, which are collectively working in partnership to achieve social change. In their model, there is "a centralized infrastructure, a dedicated staff, and a structured process that leads to a common agenda, shared measurement, continuous communication, and mutually reinforcing activities among all participants."[72] There must be a "systemic approach to social impact that focuses on the relationships between organizations and the progress toward shared objectives."[73]

Catalytic Philanthropy

Collective impact is also one of the ways that donors can leverage catalytic philanthropy. Kramer maintains that when philanthropy is catalytic, it "stimulates cross-sector collaborations, mobilizing stakeholders to create shared solutions."[74] "Catalytic donors work across other sectors, reaching out to business and government. . . . They engage directly with individuals at neighborhood and community levels, listening to them and mobilizing them in the campaign to advance their cause."[75]

Both the National Endowment for the Arts and The W.K. Kellogg Foundation (WKKF) incorporate elements of collective impact and catalytic philanthropy in achieving systemic change and social justice, utilizing cross-sector collaborations. The National Endowment for the Arts collective impact grants "increase student access to arts education through collective, systemic approaches. Projects ensure that all students across entire neighborhoods, schools, school districts, and or states—in communities of all sizes participate in the arts over time."[76] In this model of funding, "cross-sector partners work to determine a common vision, define goals, develop strategies, and identify measurable objectives for arts education. Priority is given to projects that include a managing partner or group of partners that acts as the coordinating entity, and involve at least three cross-sector organizations, one of which is an arts/cultural organization. Partners may include arts councils, units of state or local government, school systems, funders, businesses, community service organizations, economic development organizations, trade associations, parent/student networks, social service organizations, or institutions of higher learning."[77]

The W.K. Kellogg Foundation (WKKF) created Truth, Racial Healing & Transformation (TRHT), a "comprehensive national and community-based process to plan for and bring about transformational and sustainable change to address the historic and contemporary effects of racism."[78] Granting $24 million to 14 multi-sector community collaborations across the United States, "a broad array of participants—including elected officials, faith leaders, philanthropists, grass roots activists, and business leaders can pave the way to deeper understanding and empathy among people on different sides of an issue."[79] Following the *Truth, Racial Healing & Transformation Implementation Guidebook*, communities conduct an assessment of their racial history, create a vision that is inclusive of a multiplicity of community voices, set clear objectives for achieving racial equity, diversity, and inclusion that culminate in a "commitment to some form of reparative or restorative justice and to policies that can effectively foster systemic change."[80] When the Truth, Racial Healing & Transformation Framework was used in New Orleans, the community collectively decided to eliminate Confederate Monuments.[81]

Conclusion

Racial and cultural access, diversity, equity, and inclusion in the performing arts workforce can only be achieved when ALAANA community members with lived experience drive transformative change in unity with White antiracist allies who are also committed to championing social justice in the performing arts sector, and in collaboration and coordination with other sectors as well. Primarily White Organizations, across sectors, who genuinely value systemic change through social action engagement, must have organized and collective stakeholder buy-in and a monetary commitment from leadership to measure and evaluate the extent to which there are intentional and active efforts to realize transformative cultural and racial ADEI in the performing arts workforce. When racial and ethnic ADEI is a workforce core value in the performing arts and across sectors, historically White organizations mutually recognize the need to dismantle and transform their organizational cultures by working together with ALAANA-led organizations and communities of Color to produce racial and ethnic ADEI-centered solutions that are systemic and catalytic in scope. In the final chapter, two social change agents of Color, Brea M. Heidelberg, a culturally responsive and restorative educator in higher education, and Abid Hussain, a socially just philanthropist, share transformative leadership stories.

Notes

1. Kimberly Kappler Hewitt, Ann W. Davis, and Carl Lashley, "Transformational and Transformative Leadership in a Research-Informed Leadership Preparation Program," *Journal of Research on Leadership Education* 9, no. 3 (September 29, 2014), 229.
2. Daryl G. Smith, *Diversity's Promise for Higher Education* (Baltimore, MD: Johns Hopkins University Press, 2015), 79.
3. Terry Keleher, *Race Equity and Inclusion Action Guide* (Baltimore, MD: The Annie E. Casey Foundation, 2014), 6, 8, www.aecf.org.
4. Americans for the Arts, "Statement on Cultural Equity," (October 16, 2016), www.americansforthearts.org.
5. Robert L. Lynch, interview with author, May 11, 2017. This quotation was published with permission from Robert L. Lynch, President and CEO, Americans for the Arts.
6. Ellen McGirt, "Leading While Black," *Fortune* (February 1, 2016), 79.
7. W.K. Kellogg Foundation, Truth, Racial Healing & Transformation Implementation *Guidebook* (Battle Creek, MI: W.K. Kellogg Foundation, December 2016), 17.
8. Carmelita Castañeda, "FLEXing Cross-cultural Communication," in *Readings for Diversity and Social Justice*, 3rd ed., eds. Maurianne Adams, Warren J. Blumenfeld, Carmelita Castañeda, Heather W. Hackman, Madeline L. Peters, and Ximena Zúñiga (New York, NY: Routledge, 2013), 135.
9. Aneeta Rattan and Nalini Ambady, "Diversity Ideologies and Intergroup Relations: An Examination of Colorblindness and Multiculturalism," *European Journal of Social Psychology* 43, no. 1 (2013): 13.
10. Estelle Disch, "Multicultural Literacy Assignment," in *Teaching About Culture, Ethnicity, and Diversity*, ed. Theodore M. Singelis (Thousand Oaks, CA: Sage, 1998), 47.
11. Julie Kailin, *Antiracist Education* (New York, NY: Rowman & Littlefield, 2002), 76–77.
12. Debby Irving, *Waking Up White* (Cambridge, MA: Elephant Room Press, 2014), 87; Valerie Garr, "White Privilege 101," (2004), www.whiteprivilegeconference.com; Shakti Butler, "Mirrors of Privilege," (2006), https://world-trust.org.
13. Jennifer Stahl, "Why Philadelphia Was an Early Hub for Black Ballerinas," *Dance Magazine* (October 23, 2017), www.dancemagazine.com; Theresa Ruth Howard and Memoirs of Blacks in Ballet, "And Still They Rose," (2017), http://mobballet.org.

14. Lee Anne Bell, "Theoretical Foundations for Social Justice Education," in *Teaching for Diversity and Social Justice*, 3rd ed., eds. Maurianne Adams and Lee Anne Bell, with Diane J. Goodman and Khyati Y. Joshi (New York, NY: Routledge, 2016), 16.
15. Derald Wing Sue and David Sue, *Counseling the Culturally Diverse* (Hoboken, NJ: Wiley, 2013), 333.
16. Castañeda, "FLEXing Cross-cultural Communication," 134–35. "The FLEX Model was adapted from the training program developed by M. Arsenault, R. Castañeda, and T. Williams (2001) that was used in the Office of Training and Development at the University of Massachusetts, Amherst." (134).
17. Ibid.
18. Derald Wing Sue and David Sue, *Counseling the Culturally Diverse* (Hoboken, NJ: Wiley, 2016), 59–60.
19. Derald Wing Sue and David Sue, *Counseling the Culturally Diverse* (Hoboken, NJ: Wiley, 2013), 213.
20. Ibid., 250.
21. Daniel Goleman, *Social Intelligence* (New York, NY: Bantam, 2006), 25; Margery B. Ginsberg and Raymond J. Wlodkowski, *Diversity & Motivation: Culturally Responsive Teaching in College* (San Francisco, CA: Jossey-Bass, 2009), 238–43.
22. Elizabeth A. Segal et al., *Assessing Empathy* (New York, NY: Columbia University Press, 2017), 44.
23. George H. Mead, *Mind, Self, and Society*. Charles W. Morris, ed. (Chicago, IL: University of Chicago Press, 1934), 270.
24. Ali Michael, *Raising Race Questions* (New York, NY: Teachers College, 2015), 115–16.
25. Bell, "Theoretical Foundations," 11.
26. Ibid., 18.
27. Lee Anne Bell, Michael S. Funk, Khyati Y. Joshi, and Marjorie Valdivia, "Racism and White Privilege," in *Teaching for Diversity and Social Justice*, 3rd ed., eds. Maurianne Adams et al. (New York, NY: Routledge, 2016), 138.
28. Barbara Trepagnier, *Silent Racism*, 2nd ed. (Boulder, CO: Paradigm, 2010), 85.
29. Pamela M. Norwood and Deborah Carr Saldaña, "Who Should Be Hired," in *Teaching About Culture, Ethnicity, and Diversity*, ed. Theodore M. Singelis (Thousand Oaks, CA: Sage: 1998), 73.
30. Trepagnier, *Silent Racism*, 116–17.
31. Frances Madeson, "Indigenous States," *American Theatre* (March 20, 2018), www.americantheatre.org.
32. Trepagnier, *Silent Racism*, 117.
33. Peggy McIntosh, *Some Notes for Facilitators on Presenting My White Privilege Papers*, (Wellesley, MA: Wellesley Centers for Women, 2010), https://nationalseedproject.org.
34. Jacob Bernstein, "The Disrupters: Making New York's Cultural Boards More Diverse," *New York Times* (July 30, 2016), www.nytimes.com.
35. "About," *African American Board Leadership Institute*, www.aabli.org.
36. Rebecca Koenig, "Why and How to Build a Diverse Nonprofit Board," *Chronicle of Philanthropy* (August 11, 2016), www.philanthropy.com.
37. John L. Jackson, Jr., *Racial Paranoia* (New York, NY: Basic Civitas Books, 2008), 203.
38. Daniel Cox, Juhem Navarro-Rivera, and Robert P. Jones, *Race, Religion, and Political Affiliation of Americans' Core Social Networks* (Washington, DC: Public Religion Research Institute, 2016), www.prri.org.

39. Rachel D. Godsil et al., *The Science of Equality, Volume 1: Addressing Implicit Bias, Racial Anxiety, and Stereotype Threat in Education and Healthcare* (Perception Institute, November 2014), 50, https://perception.org.

40. Rosalie H. Wax, "The Ambiguities of Field Work," in *Contemporary Field Research*, ed. Robert M. Emerson (Prospect Heights, IL: Waveland Press, 1983), 194.

41. Alicia Torres et al., *Reaching and Engaging With Hispanic Communities: A Research-Informed Communication Guide for Nonprofits, Policymakers, and Funders* (Bethesda: Child Trends and the Crimsonbridge Foundation, 2016), 19, www.childtrends.org.

42. American Ballet Theatre, "Project Plié: Administrative Internships," www.abt.org, Courtesy of American Ballet Theatre.

43. Rebecca Koenig, "How-and Why-to Hire a Diverse Nonprofit Staff," *Chronicle of Philanthropy* (March 3, 2016).

44. Oregon Shakespeare Festival, "Work With Us," www.osfashland.org. Used by Permission OSF HR Department, Oregon Shakespeare Festival, Ashland, OR.

45. Ibid., Used by Permission OSF HR Department, Oregon Shakespeare Festival, Ashland, OR; States Bill Rauch, "Nataki's [Garrett] historic appointment, as an African American woman running one of the largest-budget theaters in the United States, is a direct expression of OSF's decades-long commitment to helping create a more equitable field." "OSF Announces Sixth Artistic Director: Nataki Garrett to Take the Helm August 2019," www.osfashland.org. Used by Permission OSF.

46. Laura Collins-Hughes, "Falling for the Lure of the Stage: The Backstage," *New York Times* (June 18, 2018), www.nytimes.com.

47. Collins-Hughes, "Falling for the Lure of the Stage," www.nytimes.com; Roundabout Theatre Company, www.roundabouttheatre.org; Miriam Kreinin Souccar, "Roundabout Theatre Company Aims to Increase Diversity Backstage," *Crain's New York Business* (March 5, 2017), www.crainsnewyork.com; BWW News Desk, "Roundabout's Entire Theatrical Workforce Development Program Cohort Lands Jobs," *Broadwayworld.com* (December 13, 2017), www.broadwayworld.com.

48. American Ballet Theatre, "Project Plié," www.abt.org, courtesy of American Ballet Theatre.

49. Dnika J. Travis and Jennifer Thorpe-Moscon, *Day-to-Day Experiences of Emotional Tax Among Women and Men of Color in the Workplace* (New York, NY: Catalyst, 2018), 22, www.catalyst.org.

50. Ibid., 24.

51. Theatre Communications Group, "Equity, Diversity, & Inclusion Initiative," www.tcg.org.

52. Equity in the Center, *Awake to Woke to Work: Building a Race Equity Culture* (ProInspire, 2018), 16, https://equityinthecenter.org.

53. Tim Wilson, interview with author, November 8, 2018.

54. Adam Horowitz, email to author, November 19, 2018.

55. U.S. Department of Arts and Culture, *Honor Native Land: A Guide and Call to Acknowledgement* (U.S. Department of Arts and Culture, 2017), 3, https://usdac.us/nativeland.

56. Ibid.

57. Craig T. Peterson, email to author, November 14, 2018. The author was granted permission by the Abrons Arts Center to publish the Abrons Arts Center's Indigenous Land Acknowledgement.

58. Ibid.

59. Michael, *Raising Race Questions*, 56.
60. Mark R. Kramer, phone call with author, April 26, 2019. I wish to thank Mark R. Kramer, Joan Myers Brown, Denise Saunders Thompson, Johnnia Stigall, and Rebecca L. Noricks for their support and guidance on this section.
61. The International Association of Blacks in Dance, https://iabdassociation.org.
62. The audition was conducted in Denver, 2016.
63. Joan Myers Brown, interview with the author, December 7, 2018.
64. The International Association of Blacks in Dance, Facebook announcement, September 25, 2018.
65. Madeline Schrock, "These 21 Organizations Are Banding Together to Increase the Presence of Black Dancers in Ballet," *Dancemagazine.com* (October 5, 2018), www.dancemagazine.com; Denise Saunders Thompson, email to author, February 28, 2019.
66. Ibid.
67. Sphinx Organization, "About the Sphinx Organization," www.sphinxmusic.org; Johnnia Stigall, email to author, February 28, 2019.
68. Sphinx Organization, "National Alliance for Audition Support," www.sphinxmusic.org.
69. Ibid.
70. Ibid.
71. John Kania and Mark Kramer, "Collective Impact," *Stanford Social Innovation Review* 9, no. 1 (Winter 2011): 36–41, https://ssir.org.
72. Ibid., 38.
73. Ibid., 39.
74. Mark R. Kramer, "Catalytic Philanthropy," *Stanford Social Innovation Review* 7, no. 4 (Fall 2009), 34.
75. Leslie R. Crutchfield, John V. Kania, and Mark R. Kramer, *Do More Than Give* (San Francisco, CA: Jossey-Bass, 2011), 9.
76. National Endowment for the Arts, Grants, "Art Works: Arts Education Collective Impact Grants," www.arts.gov. For a listing of NEA Arts Education Collective Impact Grants, please see arts.gov.
77. Ibid.
78. W.K. Kellogg Foundation, "Taking Collective Action for Racial Healing," https://healourcommunities.org.
79. Alex Daniels, "Kellogg's Racial-Healing Effort Draws Attention from Mayors and Governors," *Chronicle of Philanthropy* (August 21, 2017), www.philanthropy.com.
80. W.K. Kellogg Foundation, *Truth, Racial Healing & Transformation*, 21.
81. Daniels, "Kellogg's Racial-Healing Effort," www.philanthropy.com.

6 Social Change Champions in the Performing Arts

Tobie S. Stein, Ph.D.

> Change movements are filled with people who made decisions to interrupt the cycle of socialization and the system of oppression.
>
> Bobbie Harro, "The Cycle of Socialization"[1]

Introduction

Transformative leaders in the intersecting performing arts, educational, and philanthropic sectors must collectively produce a performing arts culturally plural workforce that is racially and ethnically accessible, diverse, equitable, and inclusive. Transformative leadership "involves the critique and disruption of the status quo."[2] Transformative leaders believe that "deep and equitable change [requires] a deconstruction and reconstruction of the knowledge frameworks that generate inequity [and] evidence of moral courage and activism."[3]

This chapter shares the wisdom and insights of two transformative social-change champions: Brea M. Heidelberg, program director of the Entertainment & Arts Management program at Drexel University, and Abid Hussain, director of diversity at Arts Council England. Heidelberg's "Teaching Culturally Responsive Performing Arts Management in Higher Education" discusses the critical role culturally responsive and restorative college education plays in students becoming racial and ethnic ADEI change agents. In "The Public Funder's Impact on Racial and Ethnic Diversity in the Arts," Hussain reveals his contributions in designing a public sector cultural equity philanthropic model that can be replicated throughout the world.

Notes

1. Bobbie Harro, "The Cycle of Socialization," in *Readings for Diversity and Social Justice*, 3rd ed., eds. Maurianne Adams et al. (New York, NY: Routledge, 2013), 52.
2. Kimberly Kappler Hewitt, Ann W. Davis, and Carl Lashley, "Transformational and Transformative Leadership in a Research-Informed Leadership Preparation Program," *Journal of Research on Leadership Education* 9, no. 3 (September 29, 2014), 229.
3. Ibid.

Teaching Culturally Responsive Performing Arts Management in Higher Education

Brea M. Heidelberg, Ph.D.

Introduction

Demographic changes in the United States have seen a significant increase in racial and ethnic diversity that is expected to continue.[1] These shifts present opportunities to reach a more diverse student population in our arts management college classrooms, and train future arts managers of all backgrounds how to reach increasingly diverse audiences. These opportunities coincide with field-wide calls to diversify the arts management workforce in order to reflect the populations already served by many arts organizations.[2]

Calls to diversify arts management have also emerged within the field of arts management higher education.[3] It is increasingly acknowledged that arts management higher education curricula in the U.S. is largely based on Eurocentric models. White privilege shapes the curriculum not only in what is presented, from the ways organizational structures are taught to the artwork, but also in the ways in which it is presented through choices for guest speaker, organizational partnerships that often accompany classroom work, and in the fact that majority of arts management educators identify as White.[4]

In order to best serve the next generation of arts management leaders, educators must be prepared to provide a culturally responsive educational experience to not only serve an increasingly diverse student population, but also to equip all arts management college students in higher education with the skills necessary to engage audiences from a variety of backgrounds and lived experiences. This article provides an overview of culturally responsive teaching in arts management.

Culturally Responsive Teaching

The pressing need to have more organizations that fully embrace and embody equity, diversity, and inclusion (EDI) exists for a variety of reasons, ranging from the purely transactional need to replace the dwindling support of the silent and baby boomer generations to the more altruistic desire to see all people have equal access to the benefits of engaging in and with the arts.[5]

Culturally responsive teaching is the practice of "using the cultural characteristics, experiences, and perspectives of ethnically diverse college students as conduits for teaching them more effectively."[6] Within the learning environment context "cultural characteristics" include values, communication and learning styles, traditions, language and language in use, and relationship norms.[7] An important part of culturally responsive teaching is the practice of acknowledging the sociopolitical context of underrepresented college students and the "explicit acknowledgment to students that you are aware of the iniquities that impact their lives."[8] The main focus of culturally responsive teaching is to provide agency and cultural relevance to underrepresented students, who often have to "culturally translate" concepts and examples into their own culturally relevant context. However, placing college students who operate largely within hegemonic norms and rarely, if ever, have had to do this type of work into a context where they must adapt and learn that skill is a positive externality of culturally responsive pedagogy. In the higher education setting, which is still largely White and heteronormative, I argue that culturally responsive teaching requires consideration of the voices that are not represented in the room, until such time that the sociopolitical factors preventing them from being there are addressed. This consideration will create a space for individuals not currently represented in college classrooms and programs. It will also train current college students to create and maintain that space, regardless of who is currently in the room.

Laying the Foundation

In order for culturally responsive education to be fully operationalized within the arts management context, EDI strategies must be infused throughout the higher educational setting and experience. This includes EDI considerations in individual courses, overall curricula, and program administration. In my work as an educator and consultant helping arts organizations with EDI, my approach to culturally responsive work is a combination of considerations from culturally responsive teaching resources[9] as well as cultural competency.[10] The work from both areas can be distilled down to three categories for everyday practical use: Self-awareness, knowledge-seeking and sharing, and exposure.

Awareness is mostly internal work on the part of the educators and program administrators. This area focuses on the individual's knowledge of and critical reflection on their own preferences, biases, lived experiences, sensitivities, and areas where they need to educate themselves, especially with regard to the sociopolitical context around race and the impact it has had in their own lives as well as those of others with a different lived experience.[11] This is in addition to educating themselves about the academic program's and institution's history with underrepresented populations, as culturally responsive teaching requires educators to "critique both personal and discipline-based knowledge systems."[12]

Knowledge-seeking requires college and university educators to interrogate the underlying systems and power structures that have shaped the field of arts management. Consider the following questions when looking at field norms and structures: Who holds the power? How did they come to hold the power? How do they maintain the power they have? Whose voices are silenced by the current structure? Are there ways to increase the number of voices that are heard? Picking apart organizational structures, funding policies, and longstanding "best practices" will strengthen educators' capacity to not only share information with students, but also model the kind of critical reflection and lifelong learning we want to instill in them.

As a woman of Color who has experienced arts management education at the Master's and Ph.D. degree levels as a student and later as both a college educator and administrator, my primary concern is to avoid recreating the problematic experiences I faced as a student and faculty member. This first required me to delve deeply into the organizational structures and practices that created and nurtured environments where micro- and macro-aggressions[13] as well as symbolic, modern, and ambivalent biases[14] could be perpetrated by White college educators and administrators without consequence. Additionally, many People of Color (POC) have internalized the racist practices so ubiquitous throughout society in ways that reify White supremacist structures. This often manifests itself in "model minority" biases and politics of respectability barriers for underrepresented college students, with POC acting as the perpetrators and gatekeepers.[15] The work of interrogating my own biases in this context focused mainly on dissecting norms within the field of arts management and determining which aspects of those norms were relevant and important for the field to function and grow and which aspects were simply reflections of White, male, heteronormative dominance. Of particular note for me were notions of "professionalism" a term often used to imply a benign preference for White aesthetics, but in practice can be coded language that signals a rejection of the cultural and communication norms of POC that can impact college admissions, hiring, and program administration decisions.

Exposure is about becoming more intimately familiar and comfortable with the cultural practices and norms of underrepresented populations. This category encourages partnership building and collaborative exploration throughout the arts ecosystem in your university's geographic area. This area is an excuse to go experience different arts offerings from a variety of arts organizations in order to surround yourself with people that come from a different cultural background. This is often a very uncomfortable experience that many White educators have rarely, if ever, experienced. However, most underrepresented students experience this on a regular basis. It is an important element of the double-consciousness required of underrepresented students that is hard to demonstrate care and empathy for if you have not experienced it firsthand.[16]

I treat the exposure category like donor cultivation. If there is an organization that represents a population I would like to collaborate with and expose my students to I first attend a few performances or events. I then reach out to individuals within the organization and begin having conversations about the ways in which we can collaborate, ranging from a guest speaker experience to field trips and internship opportunities. These partnerships are important as they provide me with a diverse cadre to help with the work of revising classes, curricula, and programs. It is important to note that underrepresented populations are not a monolith, so it is necessary to build relationships with an array of Culturally Specific[17] Organizations in order to avoid the trap of tokenism.

Doing the Work

The work of transitioning to a culturally responsive educational experience is best done as a tiered process. Starting with classes and coursework allows the opportunity to get faculty buy-in to the process, to start the process with the college students that the program currently serves, and to build knowledge and strategies that will be useful when it is time to tackle curricula and program administration.

Some arts management programs in higher education create a standalone course that is designed to address all elements of EDI. While this may seem like a more streamlined way of incorporating EDI into an arts management curriculum that previously had no explicit consideration of the topic, I argue that it is not the most theoretically sound way of addressing the need for culturally responsive and restorative educational experiences. Having EDI and social justice show up in only one or two courses reifies the "othering" that is often associated with these topics, implying to students that they may consider these topics when they feel like it, when it is convenient, or only when it is comfortable for them. This is a surefire way to train predominately White arts managers to engage in the practice of only having "diverse" programming once a year (e.g., Black History Month) or other problematic tokenism-based tactics that often do more harm to marginalized communities.[18]

Each individual course within an arts management program should be infused with EDI in order remedy the fact that a Eurocentric bias has been infused into all of these courses. This is often difficult for people to conceptualize because Eurocentric biases are often simply considered "the default" way information is presented. These biases manifest themselves in required readings, examples, cases, and guest speakers that highlight and amplify White, heteronormative, male perspectives at the expense of all other voices and lived experiences.[19] The restorative practice of acknowledging that this has largely been the case throughout arts management in higher education is a necessary first step toward creating a safe space for underrepresented college students and faculty members.[20] This space is necessary in order to encourage the further diversification of arts management programs. Empowered voices of Color are an important aspect of successful EDI work within arts management programs.

In collaboration with current students and alumni, faculty can use the culturally responsive and restorative framework as a guide to assess the following course elements:

- Learning objectives
- Course assessment tools (e.g., group assignments, quizzes, tests, writing assignments)
- Evaluation methods (e.g., grading rubrics and feedback mechanisms)
- Course materials (e.g., in-class activities, artistic and organizational cases or examples, presentations)
- Guest speakers
- Practitioner and organizational collaborators

While the exact ways in which culturally responsive and restorative practices are incorporated into each course will vary depending on the available faculty and their respective knowledge and comfort levels with anti-bias work, EDI, and culturally responsive teaching, there are some tactics that can act as a starting point while faculty receive additional education and training to do this work. At a minimum are the culturally responsive practices of including women and POC authors on required reading lists, providing examples and cases from Culturally Specific arts organizations, and inviting a wide array of diverse guest speakers to address a variety of topics throughout the curriculum. Experiential learning opportunities should include organizations with ethnically diverse leadership.

Curricular choices are another place where a Eurocentric bias has manifested itself in educational settings. Arts management educators must first investigate their curricula, identifying elements of Eurocentric bias and openly acknowledging them among full-time and adjunct faculty, students, and alumni. The following are some questions to consider when investigating curricula:

- Are the voices and experiences of current students reflected in the curricular choices?
- Would students taking this curriculum be equally equipped to run a Culturally Specific Organization and a Predominantly White Organization?
- Does the current curriculum expose students to more than one art form? More than one tradition within each art form discussed?
- Does the current curriculum encourage students to interrogate the history of the field and its problematic relationships with race/ethnicity?
- Are the opportunities to explore diverse voices only included in the elective options? Or are diverse artists and perspectives a part of the core curriculum?

If, in the process of addressing the above questions, specific ways that problematic practices have become ingrained in the curriculum become clear, it is necessary to name the practice when informing faculty, administrators, and students about changes that will be made to remedy the practice. The ownership of past practices is an integral part of culturally responsive teaching. Naming is important, as it signifies to all stakeholders that this work is important and offers the space for feedback about the named practice and the proposed remedy, encouraging agency among previously silenced voices. Furthermore, the acknowledgement of problematic past practices would model desired behavior for students who will become EDI change agents within the organizations they enter upon graduation.

After acknowledging problematic past practices, educators should then interrogate those practices to determine the best ways to dismantle and replace them. At the curricular level this can be a heavy administrative burden as it may be necessary to change courses that are considered "core" and "electives," course titles and sequencing, and create new courses. It is very likely that the systems of inequity are so ingrained in the curriculum and the institution that it may be hard to discern the problematic practices. In these instances, it is best to bring in an outside consultant who can help guide faculty and administrators through an inclusive process of discovery and idea generation for remedies.

As educators work to identify and change problematic practices White college students will also have to adjust to a new learning environment, one that is increasingly welcoming and inclusive of diverse voices. While many students will welcome this, there will be some students that perceive this process as a threat. It will be necessary for educators to be equipped with classroom management techniques in case those students seek to derail efforts to establish and maintain a culturally responsive and restorative learning environment. This kind of diversity resistance may be demonstrated by combative behavior during lectures and class discussions, the emergence of problematic language in written assignments, and in interpersonal communication during group work.[21] Working through diversity resistance starts with setting the ground rules for interaction between peer learning and managing expectations of the student and teacher relationship. This work is started in the syllabus, which should include clear guidelines for online and in-person class discussions, policies for language in use, preferred terminology, and a statement about the inclusive intent of the instructor, course, and program. In addition to explicitly articulating behavioral expectations, there should be class documents that explicitly define consequences that accompany actions that are outside the scope of acceptable behavior. This will help create an environment that is socially safe and hopefully reduce social-emotional stress among underrepresented students. It is imperative that all students be held accountable for maintaining an inclusive and welcoming environment. Harmful behavior, whether it is implicit (e.g., a microaggression) or an explicit macroaggression, should not be tolerated. Mixed messages about harmful practices are especially harmful to underrepresented students, who are more likely to experience social-emotional stress in the classroom setting. Should harmful behavior occur it should be stopped immediately and the offending parties should be held accountable.

Preparing Students to Become EDI Change Agents

I have heard many administrators and educators say that younger generations are naturally more inclusive and welcoming of diverse backgrounds. This is a bit of wishful thinking that attempts to absolve educators and administrators from acknowledging that bias is nurtured, often in the institutions and programs run by individuals using this assumption to avoid critical self-reflection. I have experienced a wide variety of diversity tolerance among college students at both the undergraduate and graduate levels, and among the faculty and administrators responsible for their education. Some actively and purposefully work to increase consideration of and care for underrepresented individuals, while others use benign methods of discrimination like modern bias[22] to reify problematic power structures. Most of the people I have come into contact with within higher education are simply apathetic to the plight of those that are not like themselves. It is important to help guide students through their apathy and past the tendency to blame the victims of systemic oppression for their own plight.[23] This is done by incorporating multiple education points throughout the curriculum that articulate and demonstrate both historical and contemporary forms of systemic oppression that negatively impacts marginalized communities while increasing and maintaining privilege for others. Some students come to higher education with either a complete lack of or only passing familiarity with these issues. We cannot hold students responsible for knowledge we actively avoid providing.

One way to incorporate critical consciousness of systemic issues into arts management education is by fully explaining underlying assumptions that helped shape the field as it currently stands. It does not require deep digging to uncover systemic inequality that is built into public funding for the arts, board and executive-level recruitment and selection, or access to the arts. Instead of simply acknowledging the current manifestation of these issues, explaining how the field got to this point is a relatively seamless way to infuse EDI considerations throughout the curriculum. This practice has the added benefit of connecting arts and culture to other fields such as city and regional planning, economics, education, and public administration.

Once students understand the sociopolitical history of the field they are inheriting, it becomes easier to try and work past or through victim-blaming and increase students' capacity for empathy because they will have real-life, field-specific examples of how decision-makers can positively or negatively impact peoples' lives. The ability to understand lived experiences other than their own is a strong foundation upon which more specific social justice training can take hold.[24] Exposing students to Culturally Specific arts organizations is a strategic way to look at a cultural institution, discuss systemic issues, and increase empathy. Founder's syndrome at a Black dance company that has been routinely underfunded for systemic reasons is going to look different than founder's syndrome at a major predominately White cultural institution that has historically received a disproportionate amount of public funding. Purposefully pulling back those layers for students will make them better arts managers.

Making the Case for Change

Administrative pushback to the practices involved with culturally responsive teaching and program administration, if not the actual concepts, is common within higher education settings.[25] It should be expected that the kind of changes called for by this work may cause discomfort, especially among those who have long held power.[26] Connecting to institutional offices of EDI within the university can help build your program's supply of partners and resources to help make the case when working through college administrative pushback. While I am willing to extend the psychological energy convincing college students that this work is important for the sake of the work and the people impacted, I find that I am increasingly unwilling to expend that energy with higher education administrators. In these instances, it is far easier to build career-related cases for the work, bringing in organizational partners from arts and cultural organizations that can help articulate the importance of building these knowledge bases and skill sets among graduates. Earlier in my career, I spent a lot of time frustrated by efforts to try and get higher education educators and administrators to buy into EDI work for the "right reasons." For self-care purposes, I have transitioned to a mindset that focuses more on getting the work done and getting people to the table, and less on interrogating the reasons why people are coming to the table.

Conclusion

This article was designed to provide an overview of culturally responsive teaching in order to equip arts management educators and administrators with a foundation upon which they can begin to build more diverse and equitable programs. As arts management educators begin doing this work, it will be important to provide formative evaluation information to other educators to inform field-wide learning about what works and in which programmatic contexts. Information about unsuccessful attempts to do this work and the process of rebounding and trying again are essential for field learning and field building in this area. Cases that focus solely on successes are less helpful as this is hard work and many people and programs make a number of missteps along the way. Guidance on what to do in order to work through those missteps is a vital part of the conversation that is often missing. Establishing and maintaining equitable and inclusive classrooms and arts management education programs is essential to ensure that future arts administrators are equipped with the knowledge and skills to sustain an equitable, diverse, and inclusive field.

Notes

1. Sandra Colby and Jennifer Ortman, *Projections on the Size and Composition of the U.S. Population: 2014 to 2060* (Washington, DC: U.S. Census Bureau, 2015), www.census.gov//content/dam/Census/library/publications/2015/demo/p25-1143.pdf.
2. Antonio C. Cuyler, "Diversity, Equity, & Inclusion (DEI) in the Cultural Sector: What's Next?" *CultureWork* 21, no. 3 (2017): 2–3.

3. Roxy Hornbeck, "Decolonizing Arts Administration Instruction," (Presentation, Association of Arts Administration Educators Conference, Houston, TX, 2018).

4. Ibid.

5. Richard Peterson, *Changing Arts Audiences: Capitalizing on Omnivorousness* (Chicago, IL: Cultural Policy Center at the University of Chicago, 2005), 1; Americans for the Arts, "Americans Speak out About the Arts in 2018," (Washington, DC: Americans for the Arts, 2018), www.americansforthearts.org/sites/default/files/Public%20Opinion%20National%20 2018%20Report.pdf.

6. Geneva Gay, "Preparing for Culturally Responsive Teaching," *Journal of Teacher Education* 53 (2002): 106–16.

7. Ibid.

8. Zaretta Hammond, *Culturally Responsive Teaching and the Brain* (Thousand Oaks, CA: Corwin, 2015), 77.

9. Ibid.

10. Brea M. Heidelberg, "Initial Considerations for Seeking Cultural Competence in Arts Management Education," *American Journal of Arts Management* 4, no. 3 (2016): 2–11.

11. William Howe and Penelope Lisi, *Becoming a Multicultural Educator: Developing Awareness, Gaining Skills, and Taking Action* (Thousand Oaks, CA: Sage, 2013), 10.

12. Juliana McLaughlin, "'Crack in the Pavement': Pedagogy as Political and Moral Practice for Educating Culturally Competent Professionals," *The International Education Journal: Comparative Perspectives* 12, no. 1 (2013): 249.

13. Microaggressions are everyday verbal, behavioral, or environmental slights that demonstrate a hostile environment to underrepresented individuals. These actions may be intentional, but are largely unintentional demonstrations of bias or bigotry. Macroaggressions are overt, intentional displays of bigotry, including verbal attack and physical violence.

14. Christine A. Wiggings-Romesburg and Rod P. Githens, "The Psychology of Diversity Resistance and Integration," *Human Resource Development Review* 17, no. 2 (2018): 183.

15. Fredrick C. Harris, "The Rise of Respectability Politics," *Dissent* 61, no. 1 (2014): 34.

16. W. E. B. Du Bois, "Double-Consciousness and the Veil," in *Social Class and Stratification: Classic Statements and Theoretical Debates*, ed. Rhonda Levine (Lanham, MD: Rowman & Littlefield Publishing Group, 2006), 203–10.

17. This term was chosen because it reflects the language used in the sources reviewed for this article.

18. Yolanda Flores Niemann, "The Social Ecology of Tokenism in Higher Education," *Peace Review* 28, no. 4 (2016): 451–58.

19. This list is not exhaustive.

20. While the term "safe space" has largely been co-opted in order to diminish its value, I use the term here to describe a space that is designed and curated with the intent of making traditionally underrepresented and marginalized individuals comfortable so that they may be empowered.

21. Ilene C. Wasserman, Plácida V. Gallegos, and Bernardo M. Ferdman, "Dancing With Resistance: Leadership Challenges in Fostering a Culture of Inclusion," in *Diversity Resistance in Organizations*, ed. Kecia Thomas (New York, NY: Taylor and Francis, 2008), 175–200.

22. Wiggings-Romesburg and Githens, "The Psychology of Diversity," 183.
23. James Kluegel and Eliot Smith, *Beliefs About Inequality: Americans' Views of What Is and What Ought to Be* (New York, NY: Routledge, 2017), 63.
24. Elizabeth Segal, "Social Empathy: A Model Built on Empathy, Contextual Understanding, and Social Responsibility That Promotes Social Justice," *Journal of Social Service Research* 37, no. 3 (2011): 266–77.
25. Christine E. Sleeter, "Confronting the Marginalization of Culturally Responsive Pedagogy," *Urban Education* 47, no. 3 (2012): 562–84.
26. Kris D. Gutiérrez et al., "Backlash Pedagogy: Language and Culture and the Politics of Reform," *Review of Education, Pedagogy, and Cultural Studies* 24 (2002): 335–51.

The Public Funder's Impact on Racial and Ethnic Diversity in the Arts

Abid Hussain

Introduction

My route into the arts did not follow a traditional trajectory. While working at a gas utility company in the risk management department, I started volunteering for a disability arts organisation which led to a job opportunity at Arts Council England for a junior position in their policy and development team, supporting the equality and diversity unit. I had no hesitation in putting in an application, even though I'd never formally worked in the arts sector before. My purpose as an aspiring policy maker back then is the same as it is now as Director of Diversity at Arts Council England, which is simply to create the conditions to ensure that the arts and cultural sector in England is inclusive and reflective of the diversity we see in society across the workforce, boards, programmes, and audiences.

The Arts Britain Ignores

In 1976, Naseem Khan published a ground-breaking report *The Arts Britain Ignores*.[1] The report presented the case for arts and culture in England to better reflect the talent, contribution, and stories of ethnically diverse and migrant artists to the creative life of Britain. Khan's report was a milestone moment for arts and culture in England. It called out the inequity of recognition given to work produced and presented by artists of colour. It challenged arts and cultural institutions to respond to the exclusion and invisibility of work by artists of Black and Minority Ethnic backgrounds across our major theatres, galleries, and concert halls. The *Arts Britain Ignores* would serve as a catalyst for the development of equality and diversity policies and initiatives by public funding agencies and challenge the notions of who defines excellence.

Making the Creative Case for Diversity

Historically in England we've talked primarily about the business or legal case for diversity. The legal case for diversity has been influenced by various iterations of historic legislation relating to disability, gender, and race that were brought together under the Equality Act in 2010 to protect people from direct or indirect discrimination in the workplace and wider society as well as harassment or victimization.[2]

In 2011 Arts Council England, our national arts funding agency, developed the Creative Case for Diversity with a view to advocate the artistic value of diversity in addition to the legal case. At the heart of the Creative Case is a simple commitment to recognizing and celebrating the talent and stories of people of all backgrounds in the work that is commissioned, produced, and presented by arts and cultural organisations in England.

The Creative Case is underpinned by the principles of equity, recognition, and opportunity. It was developed as a response to the historic inequity in arts and cultural programming and commissioning, making the case for the talent and stories of all communities to be equally recognized. It is not just about having a Black actor play the lead role in a Shakespeare play: The Creative Case advocates for presenting authentic Black stories on our stages and in our arts centres that are presented and produced from a diverse perspective. Rather than seeing diversity as a barrier to producing work of quality, the Creative Case advocates and recognises the importance of diversity as a driver for excellence and innovation.

Reaching a Tipping Point

In the summer of 2014 Arts Council England announced our National Portfolio Organisations for 2015–2018 (arts organisations and museums that receive regular funding over that period). Within the National Portfolio, we had seen a decrease in the number of Black and Minority Ethnic (BME) and Disability-led organisations. We also received very few applications from BME and Disability-led organisations from outside of the Portfolio applying for regular funding for the first time. Our equality analysis also highlighted ongoing challenges around the lack of diversity in the publically funded arts and cultural workforce and in board of director membership. Change was needed.

The tipping point for developing a radical new approach towards our equality and diversity work at Arts Council England came on December 9, 2014, at a landmark speech at the Sadler's Wells theatre in London delivered by the then Chair of Arts Council England Sir Peter Bazalgette who remarked: "This is one of the most important speeches I'll make as Chair of Arts Council England. Today I'm committing the organisation, which belongs to all of us, to a fundamental shift in its approach to diversity."[3]

At the centre of this new approach to diversity was a requirement that responsibility for advancing equality and diversity in the arts and cultural sector was the responsibility of all publically funded organisations and not just those run by BME or Disabled leaders.

The new strategy made five clear commitments that were published under our Equality and Diversity action plan:

a) Promote the Creative Case for Diversity
b) Invest to encourage more diverse audiences across Arts and Culture
c) Support diverse leaders and promote a more diverse workforce, fairer entry, and progression routes
d) Improve the quality of data available to inform our decision-making on equality and diversity
e) Continue to develop the Arts Council's capacity to respond to the equality and diversity agenda[4]

Critically the action was also supported by a commitment of investment with £6,000,000 earmarked specifically for equality and diversity initiatives.

Transparent Reporting: Introducing the Equality, Diversity and the Creative Case Report

Our second pivotal moment came in December 2015 when we published our first ever *Equality, Diversity and the Creative Case* report.[5] The publication of the report was a turning point. It was the first time that the Arts Council had openly published equality and diversity data on our investment and the arts and cultural workforce. The report served two primary functions, first it was published to increase transparency and accountability and second it also provided the quantitative data to inform the continued development of our equality and diversity policy work.

The report provided an analysis of our equality and diversity data in relation to Age, Disability, Ethnicity, Gender and in later editions of the reports, Sexual Orientation. In more recent editions[6] we have also published additional data on the diversity of key leadership roles, including Artistic Directors, Chief Executives, and [Board] Chairs, and also published aggregated analysis of how National Portfolio organisations are responding to the Creative Case for Diversity.

Our equality analysis and data reporting provided both the strategic imperative and evidence base I needed to radically rethink how we could strategically respond to the challenge of diversifying our future National Portfolio and its leadership, paving the way for the launch of two new ambitious strategic funding programmes: Elevate and Change Makers.

Elevate

Elevate[7] was developed in response to our National Portfolio equality analysis decision-making process in 2014, which highlighted a decrease in the number of BME and Disability-led organisations in our National Portfolio, coupled with a lack of new applications emerging from diverse-led organisations. In developing the Elevate programme's goals, I was determined to focus on strengthening the resilience of BME and Disability-led organisations with the aim of increasing both the number and quality of applications to future National Portfolio investment rounds. I wanted Elevate to be the first strategic step in addressing some of the barriers that had built up over the years that resulted in greater inequity in the distribution of public funding.

I found that for many diverse-led organizations, the challenge was not in relation to delivering high quality arts and cultural programming, it was developing sustainable and resilient business models where arts and cultural organisations could afford to retain staff, develop their fundraising capacity, and invest in strengthening their boards and governance. Organisations that are able to cover their core running costs and retain salaried positions have a competitive advantage over those who primarily receive project funding solely to support artistic activity.

In designing the eligibility criteria for the programme I went a step further. Elevate was the first strategic funding programme developed at the Arts Council where National Portfolio organisations in receipt of regular funding were not eligible to apply. This was essential to ensure that applicants were competing against other similarly resourced (or otherwise) organisations and to create a more equitable funding platform. With a budget of £2,200,000 committed I was all set to go.

Within weeks of launching, the programme had captured the imagination of the sector. The Arts Council received over two hundred expressions of interest and invited ninety arts organisations to submit full applications. The level of demand was beyond all expectations; the programme had struck a chord with applicants and provided a glimpse of what the future could look like. It also posed a challenge. Was £2,200,000 sufficient to make an impact? The answer was, "No." As the director of diversity at the Arts Council, I approached our executive board for additional resources. They, in turn, provided unequivocal backing and recommended awards totalling £5,300,000, representing an additional £3,100,000 to invest in a total of forty organisations.

The additional investment paid significant dividends in 2017 as thirty of the forty successful Elevate applicants also applied for regular funding for the 2018–2022 National Portfolio. In 2018 the Arts Council welcomed twenty of those organisations into our most diverse National Portfolio to date.

Change Makers

Through developing the Elevate programme my focus was on developing a pipeline of diverse-led organisations. Change Makers[8] was developed in many ways as a sister initiative in response to our arts and cultural workforce data analysis to develop a pipeline of individual BME and Disabled leaders. My starting point was to not reinvent the wheel; I didn't want another off-the-shelf leadership programme or to duplicate existing initiatives such as the Clore fellowships, a tailored professional and personal development leadership programme for creative and cultural leaders in the UK. Change Makers was developed as a bespoke initiative that would respond to the individual requirements of diverse leaders, recognizing that the path to leadership is influenced by both art form and place. It is no surprise that in England the majority of BME leaders running buildings within the performing arts sector are based primarily within the theatre sector in London at venues including the Kiln Theatre, Bush Theatre, the Young Vic, Theatre Royal Stratford East, and more recently at the Southbank Centre, a large scale multi art form centre. This diversity of BME leadership is less apparent and visible across the rest of the country particularly across the building-based arts and cultural infrastructure.

In designing the Change Makers programme I had two aims. The first was to identify a cohort of talented BME and Disabled leaders who would receive the opportunity to participate in a transformative leadership journey, working in partnership with a significant arts organisation or museum in England. The second was to identify arts organisations and museums in England who were open to hosting a BME or Disabled leader while also committing to a programme that would challenge them institutionally to address some of the cultural barriers that may have excluded previous BME and Disabled talent from working within their organisations.

As with Elevate it was critical to not follow traditional design convention, with the Change Makers programme I made it a requirement for applicants to submit joint applications involving both the potential Change Maker (individual) and the host organisation. This allowed us to articulate clearly the importance of the named individual and their influence in the application process as much as the host organisation.

The ultimate aim of the Change Makers programme was to develop a cohort of BME and Disabled leaders that would have the experience of working in major arts and cultural organisations so that they could compete on merit for future leadership positions and opportunities. Equally it was extremely important that the Arts Council was encouraging host organisations that were part of our National portfolio to develop a more inclusive work culture that was more receptive to recognizing, recruiting, and retaining diverse talent.

In total the Arts Council invested in twenty Change Makers across different artistic disciplines nationally based at organisations, including Battersea Arts Centre, Sheffield Theatres, Manchester Museum, Hull Truck Theatre, and Birmingham Museum and Art Gallery. Already a number of our Change Makers have transitioned into permanent senior leadership roles across organisations including the Museum of London, the Wellcome Trust, and the Creative Diversity Network.

The programme has also highlighted some uncomfortable challenges including the pressure facing BME and Disabled leaders when they are the only BME or Disabled person in the boardroom. How can arts and cultural institutions develop a more open and inclusive culture that welcomes difference of perspective? How do we get beyond the point of having a solitary Black or Disabled leader in a large cultural institution?

Today the Change Makers brand is recognized internationally: I've had approaches from Europe, Asia, and Australia to explore how a similar scheme might work internationally. While seeing encouraging early signs of impact from the programme, the longer-term success of the programme will require a more longitudinal evaluation of the career trajectory of the twenty participants over an extended period of time.

Agency

Change is not possible without agency. Since the Bazalgette speech in 2014, our investment in equality and diversity initiatives increased from a planned £6,000,000 to just under £12,000,000. Equality and diversity have also become an increasingly integrated requirement and priority across a suite of strategic and National Portfolio funding programmes. National Portfolio funding now requires arts and cultural organisations to demonstrate how they will contribute to the Creative Case for Diversity through their programming offer, how they will engage diverse audiences, and demonstrate how they plan to diversify their workforce and boards.

Diversity is no longer a priority at the margins: It is a requirement at the centre. Annual conferences and reports have focused a spotlight on progress, accountability, and the case for change. There is now an expectation that diversity should be the norm and not the exception. How much longer can we continue to celebrate every single appointment of a new BME leader to an arts and cultural institution? At what point will it become the norm and no longer a cause to celebrate and rally around? We haven't quite reached that tipping point, much of the progress in diversifying the arts and cultural leadership has taken place in London, more is needed across the country in super diverse cities such as Birmingham and Manchester too.

Conclusion

Five years on from accepting responsibility for leading the Equality and Diversity agenda at the Arts Council there is much to reflect upon. Change does not come easily, making the case for greater equality, diversity, and inclusion in the arts requires uncomfortable conversations. Without strategic interventions and policy directives progress will remain painfully slow, resulting in incremental change most frequently at the periphery and rarely at the centre.

As director of diversity at a public funder with a policy making remit, I'm determined to create the conditions for greater inclusivity and change through my role as an advocate for equality, inclusion, and equity at England's national development agency for arts and culture. The challenge for any funder is to achieve balance in the distribution of investment and resources. There needs to be a recognition and a strategic response to addressing the historic inequity that has developed over an extended period of time. This has resulted in resources becoming more concentrated into an ever-decreasing pool of institutions. Subsequently, they are better equipped to navigate the funding maze as a result of having access to funding over a sustained period, while remaining less reflective of the diversity of the communities they serve in their workforce, programming, and audiences.

Diversity as an all-encompassing term is becoming increasingly problematic, its breadth of interpretation risks dilution. As a policy maker I'm interested in greater cultural and resource equity, fairness, and systematic institutional change that creates the conditions for women, people of colour, and disabled people to be fully represented, engaged, and empowered to lead our arts and cultural organisations. If market forces are failing to create those conditions then public funders must have the confidence and support of legislators and government to be given the mandate to intervene and disrupt practices and processes that create inequity in the distribution of power and influence within the arts and cultural sector that result in monocultural power structures.

As we embark on developing a new ten-year strategy at Arts Council England, there is an opportunity to create the conditions for the changes Naseem Khan first advocated for back in 1976. There has been progress over the past forty-three years but also moments of regression. In that timespan BME representation in the arts and cultural workforce (12%[9]) remains below the national BME working age population (16%); the underrepresentation of disabled and D/deaf[10] people in the arts and cultural sector is an even more acute challenge. This should not be the case today. If larger arts and cultural institutions that receive more public funding are less representative of the communities they serve, should more funding be redistributed to those organisations that are?

Looking forward, Arts Council England is publishing a new ten-year strategy that will seek to address many of the questions posed here. I envision a future where aspiration is replaced by action, when priorities are outpaced by progress, and equity, inclusion, and fairness become the norm rather than the exception. By 2030 we should no longer be talking about the art Britain ignores but celebrating the art that is vital to our creative renewal as a nation.

Notes

1. Naseem Khan, *The Arts Britain Ignores: The Arts of Ethnic Minorities in Britain* (London: Community Relations Commission Press, May 1976).
2. UK Government, "Chapter 15," in *Equality Act 2010*, www.legislation.gov. uk/ukpga/2010/15/contents.
3. Peter Bazalgette, "Arts Council and the Creative Case for Diversity," (Presentation, Creative Case for Diversity Conference, Sadlers Wells, London, December 2014), www.artscouncil.org.uk/sites/default/files/download-file/ Sir_Peter_Bazalgette_Creative_Case_speech_8_Dec_2014.pdf.
4. Arts Council England, *Arts Council England Corporate Plan 2015–18* (Manchester: Arts Council England, 2015), www.artscouncil.org.uk/arts-council-england-corporate-plan-2015-18.
5. Arts Council England, *Equality, Diversity and the Creative Case: A Data Report, 2012–2015* (Manchester: Arts Council England, 2016), www.arts-council.org.uk/sites/default/files/download-file/Equality_Diversity_and_the_ Creative_Case_A_data_report_2012-2015.pdf.
6. Arts Council England, *Equality, Diversity and the Creative Case: A Data Report, 2016–2017* (Manchester: Arts Council England, 2018), www. artscouncil.org.uk/publication/equality-diversity-and-creative-case-data-report-2016-17.
7. *Arts Council England*, "Elevate," (2016), www.artscouncil.org.uk/funding-finder/elevate.
8. *Arts Council England*, "Change Makers," (2016), www.artscouncil.org.uk/ funding/change-makers.
9. Arts Council England, *Equality, Diversity and the Creative Case: A Data Report, 2017–2018* (Manchester: Arts Council England, 2019), www.arts-council.org.uk/sites/default/files/download-file/Diversity_report_1718.pdf.
10. When used as a cultural label especially within the culture, the word **deaf** is often written with a **capital D** and referred to as "big **D** Deaf" in speech and sign. When used as a label for the audiological condition, it is written with a lowercase **d**.

Author and Contributor Biographies

Antonio C. Cuyler, Ph.D. (Foreword), is Associate Professor of Arts Administration & Coordinator of the M.A. program at Florida State University (F.S.U.) where he teaches Doctoral and Master's students.

Emma Halpern (contributor) is a dramaturg and arts journalist. She served six years as co-artistic director of New York City Children's Theater, and is a regular contributor to *American Theatre Magazine*. She has an M.F.A. in Dramaturgy from Brooklyn College, where she has taught as an adjunct lecturer.

Brea M. Heidelberg, Ph.D. (contributor) is an arts management educator, consultant, and researcher. She is currently Program Director of the Entertainment & Arts Management program at Drexel University. She is also Founder and Principal of ISO Arts Consulting, a firm focused on promoting equity within the cultural workforce.

Abid Hussain (contributor) is Director of Diversity at Arts Council England, the national development agency for arts and culture in England. He is an alumnus of the U.S. International Visitor Leadership Program and the Salzburg Global Seminar.

Tobie S. Stein, Ph.D. (author), is a sociologist and Professor Emerita in the Department of Theater at Brooklyn College, The City University of New York. A two-time Fulbright Specialist in Taiwan and Israel, she has written four other books on nonprofit leadership and management, including *Leadership in the Performing Arts* (Allworth Press, 2016). She is a member of the Diversity Scholars Network at the University of Michigan and the American Sociological Association.

Index

Printed in the United States
by Baker & Taylor Publisher Services